THE CAPTIVE STAGE

THEATER: THEORY/TEXT/PERFORMANCE

Series Editors: David Krasner and Rebecca Schneider

Founding Editor: Enoch Brater

**Recent Titles:**

*Looking Into the Abyss: Essays on Scenography* by Arnold Aronson

*Avant-Garde Performance and the Limits of Criticism: Approaching the Living Theatre, Happenings/Fluxus, and the Black Arts Movement* by Mike Sell

*Not the Other Avant-Garde: The Transnational Foundations of Avant-Garde Performance* edited by James M. Harding and John Rouse

*The Purpose of Playing: Modern Acting Theories in Perspective* by Robert Gordon

*Staging Philosophy: Intersections of Theater, Performance, and Philosophy* edited by David Krasner and David Z. Saltz

*Critical Theory and Performance: Revised and Enlarged Edition* edited by Janelle G. Reinelt and Joseph R. Roach

*Reflections on Beckett: A Centenary Celebration* edited by Anna McMullan and S. E. Wilmer

*Performing Conquest: Five Centuries of Theater, History, and Identity in Tlaxcala, Mexico* by Patricia A. Ybarra

*The President Electric: Ronald Reagan and the Politics of Performance* by Timothy Raphael

*Cutting Performances: Collage Events, Feminist Artists, and the American Avant-Garde* by James M. Harding

*Illusive Utopia: Theater, Film, and Everyday Performance in North Korea* by Suk-Young Kim

*Embodying Black Experience: Stillness, Critical Memory, and the Black Body* by Harvey Young

*No Safe Spaces: Re-casting Race, Ethnicity, and Nationality in American Theater* by Angela C. Pao

*Artaud and His Doubles* by Kimberly Jannarone

*The Problem of the Color[blind]: Racial Transgression and the Politics of Black Performance* by Brandi Wilkins Catanese

*The Sarah Siddons Audio Files: Romanticism and the Lost Voice* by Judith Pascoe

*Paul Robeson and the Cold War Performance Complex: Race, Madness, Activism* by Tony Perucci

*Passionate Amateurs: Theatre, Communism, and Love* by Nicholas Ridout

*Dark Matter: Invisibility in Drama, Theater, and Performance* by Andrew Sofer

*Simming: Participatory Performance and the Making of Meaning* by Scott Magelssen

*Acts: Theater, Philosophy, and the Performing Self* by Tzachi Zamir

*The Captive Stage: Performance and the Proslavery Imagination of the Antebellum North* by Douglas A. Jones, Jr.

# The Captive Stage

**PERFORMANCE** AND THE

**PROSLAVERY IMAGINATION** OF THE

**ANTEBELLUM NORTH**

*Douglas A. Jones, Jr.*

**THE UNIVERSITY OF MICHIGAN PRESS**

*Ann Arbor*

Published in the United States of America by
The University of Michigan Press
Printed and bound by CPI Group (UK) Ltd, Croydon, CR0 4YY


2017   2016   2015   2014      4   3   2   1

A CIP catalog record for this book is available from the British Library.

ISBN 978-0-472-07226-2 (cloth : alk. paper)
ISBN 978-0-472-05226-4 (paper : alk. paper)
ISBN 978-0-472-12043-7 (e-book)

Cover illustration: E. W. Clay, *Life in Philadelphia*, "Dat is bery fine Mr. Mortimer . . .". Philadelphia: S. Hart & Son. Courtesy of The Library Company of Philadelphia.

To the loving memory of my grandfather,
Robert C. Jones (1931–2009),
who taught me the beauty of books and baseball.
*Et tu, Brute?*

# Acknowledgments

*The Captive Stage* emerged out of my dissertation for the Department of Drama at Stanford University. For that project, I could not have asked for a more supportive and stimulating set of pedagogues than that I enjoyed at Stanford. In class and in conversation, Alice Rayner, Jisha Menon, Branislav Jakovljevic, Shelley Fisher Fishkin, Allyson Hobbs, Gavin Jones, and Michele Elam were and continue to be my teachers. I owe Michele a special debt of gratitude for providing intellectual avenues and teaching opportunities in the Department of English; I hope my interloping there was not too much trouble. The members of my dissertation committee—James Campbell, Peggy Phelan, and Harry J. Elam, Jr.—were nothing but nurturing and bracing, and their excitement for the project continued to sustain me away from The Farm as I worked on pulling some sort of manuscript out of the dissertation. The peripatetic, one-on-one "seminars" I shared with Jim were terrifically generative and delightful; I will always cherish the hours we spent walking around campus, drinking coffee, and talking about everything from the economic history of guano to the relationship between critical theory and the historiography of American slavery. Although Jim had just arrived at Stanford when it was time for me to form my committee, he embraced my work and me from the beginning. I still recall my first meeting with Peggy, when I interviewed for admission to the department, and even in that brief conversation she inspired me to become the best scholar I could be, to always pursue the "fire in the bones." My work is all the better because of her warmth and generosity, and I will always consider her a kindred spirit, not least because of our mutual love of Beckett and basketball. There are not enough laudatory adjectives to describe the intellectual, professional, and personal support I received from Harry. A recurring scene will suffice, I suppose: after someone learns that Harry was my advisor and dissertation chair, he or she pauses, then utters something along the lines of, "Whoa. Lucky." Lucky, indeed. Thank for you everything, Harry.

For necessary diversions and stimulating conversations I thank fellow

Stanford graduate students Eric Shed, Daniel Stringer, Jakeya Caruthers, Virginia Preston, Imeh Williams, Isaiah Wooden, Derek Miller, Jessica Nakamura, Sebastián Calderón Bentin, Lindsey Mantoan, Angela Farr-Schiller, Nigel Hatton, Jennifer Harford Vargas, Lupe Carrillo, Elda Maria Roman, James Estrella, James Hairston, Jamillah Bowman, Robyn Beavers, and Jason Mercer; my Bay Area crew: Tristan and Amoy Walker, Tyler and Faith Scriven, Nic and Lindsey Barnes, Marlon and Sharifa Nichols, Matt Hunter, Erin Teague, Damon Jones, Erica Campbell, and Kelsey Moss; friends in the field, especially Kyla Tompkins, Nicole Fleetwood, Soyica Colbert, Uri McMillan, La Marr Bruce, Harvey Young, Heather Nathans, Julia Fawcett, John Muse, Christopher Grobe, Brandi Catanese, Faedra Carpenter, Shane Vogel, Gerry Cadava, Aaron Tobiason, and Michelle Granshaw; and, of course, my boys from Baltimore: Brent Englar and Ryan Hollis.

After Stanford, I was fortunate enough to begin my career at Princeton University, where colleagues in the Department of English and the Center for African American Studies (CAAS) always offered encouragement, guidance, and models of excellence. For this, I am especially grateful to Bill Gleason, Diana Fuss, Anne Cheng, Daphne Brooks, Tera Hunter, Wallace Best, Caroline Rouse, Noliwe Rooks (now at Cornell), Imani Perry, and Eddie Glaude. I also thank Keith Wailoo from Princeton's Department of History and Woodrow Wilson School of Public and International Affairs for his kindness and mentorship. Both Keith and Eddie took me under their respective wings, and I wish for all those who are beginning their careers in academia the kind of care and encouragement these senior colleagues continue to give me. Although I held faculty positions in English and in CAAS, my primary home at Princeton was the Society of Fellows. My time at the Society was invaluable: our Friday seminars, Tuesday lunches, and informal exchanges have made me a more venturesome critic and historian. I thank Carol Rigolet, former director of Princeton's Council of the Humanities, and her incredible staff—Cass Garner, Susan Coburn, Penny Stone, Jay Barnes, and Lin DeTitta—for their generous administrative support. Mary Harper, Executive Director of the Society of Fellows, is nothing less than a marvel, and the ways in which she ushers young scholars into the profession is exemplary. Susan Stewart, Director of the Society of Fellows and my colleague from the Department of English, leads with dignity and magnanimity, and the grace that she brings to the professoriate is unmatched. I am forever indebted to Susan and Mary for welcoming me into the Society. The beauty of being dedicated to the life of the mind shined forth from the senior and junior fellows at the Society, and I am especially appreciative of the laughs, camaraderie, and cognac I shared with the fellow fellows of my cohort: Hannah Freed-Thall, Ellen Lockhart, Tey Meadow, and Joel Lande. I miss you all.

I thank my colleagues in my new institutional home, the Department of English at Rutgers University, New Brunswick, who have wholly embraced me and my work from the time of our first meetings, especially Carolyn Williams, Cheryl Wall, Elin Diamond, Michael McKeon, Emily Bartels, Meredith McGill, Evie Shockley, Brad Evans, Michelle Stephens, Abena Busia, Chris Iannini, Ryan Kernan, Nick Gaskill, Andrew Goldstone, Margaret Ronda, Carter Mathes, Stepháne Robolin, and Bode Ibironke. My undergraduate students at Princeton and at Rutgers always kept me grounded and tolerated my tangents, and the graduate students I worked with at both institutions—especially Kameron Collins, Brittney Edmonds, Eric Glover, Joshua Bennett, and Francisco Robles of Princeton as well as Alex Mazzaferro at Rutgers—have shown me that the futures of the fields of (African) American cultural studies and literary history shine brightly.

My editor, LeAnn Fields, has remained a stalwart supporter of this project since our first conversation over our first gin and tonic while I was still a graduate student. I am honored to be part of her esteemed list, and the impact that she has made on our field is inestimable. It has been a pleasure getting this book through production, and for that I am grateful to LeAnn, the anonymous readers, Alexa Ducsay, Marcia LaBrenz, and the entire staff at University of Michigan Press for their efforts and expertise. An excerpt version of chapter 2 appeared as "Black Politics but Not Black People: Rethinking the Social and 'Racial' History of Early Minstrelsy," *TDR: The Drama Review*, 57.2 (2013): 21-37. I thank my editors, Catherine Cole and Tracy C. Davis, for their wise counsel on the piece, and MIT Press Journals for permission to reprint parts of the article.

Several archivists, curators, and collections supervisors have assisted me during all phases of my research and writing. I thank the librarians at Stanford University Libraries, Princeton University's Firestone Library, National Archives, Library of Congress, John Hay Library at Brown University (especially Rosemarie L. Cullen and Kathleen Brown), New-York Historical Society (especially Rob Delap), Somers Historical Society (especially Grace Zimmerman), Harvard Theatre Collection, National Gallery of Art, and Metropolitan Museum of Art. I also thank the kindly baristas and staffs at the many coffee shops where I wrote, read, or edited parts of this book, especially those of Philz Coffee (Palo Alto, Middlefield), Small World Coffee (Princeton), and Lenox Coffee (Harlem).

Three friends deserve special recognition. Aida Mbowa became my best friend during graduate school. Her infectious smile and *joie de vivre* allayed the strains of seminars, exams, the dissertation process, and the job market. Robin Bernstein, an exemplary scholar and selfless teacher, read parts of the manuscript at a late stage in the process, and provided invaluable feedback; she rescued this book in many ways. And Radiclani Clytus is always at the ready when I need help with a problem or want to grab some steak-frites. That all our discussions somehow make their way to questions of nineteenth-century cultural production and literary history makes our friendship all the more productive and, probably, a bit wacky.

My family's unconditional support of my work propels me forward. The Enumahs—Festus, Lois, Lisette, Sam, and Zach—have made me feel nothing but welcome in their learned clan, and I cherish the quiet and not-so-quiet times we share in southwestern Georgia. My father, stepmother, siblings, aunts, uncles, and cousins always know how to get me away from work when I need to get away from work, and my mother has always affirmed, and helped me to achieve, my dreams. I didn't make it to the major leagues, Ma, but I was always too slow, anyway—and I don't have to take steroids to write books! Finally, no one has done more for me during this process than Tirzah Enumah. Our life together has made me a better teacher, scholar, and, most important, man.

# Contents

# Introduction

*The "Common Sense" of Slavery in the
Free Antebellum North*

In his keynote speech at the 1848 National Negro Convention in Cleveland, Ohio, Frederick Douglass offered perhaps the most incisive description of free black subjectivity in the antebellum north: "In the Northern states, we are not slaves to individuals, not personal slaves, yet in many respects we are the slaves of the community."[1] Although they were not human chattel "entirely subject to the will of . . . masters," to use the words of the 1847 Louisiana slave code, African Americans in the north were denied the basic individual rights and equitable social relations that defined freedom in the American polity.[2] The official policies and everyday customs that exacted these denials derived in large part from the institution of slavery itself. That is, legislative bodies and common (white) Americans relied on the underlying premises and institutional practices of slavery to create a world of race-based inequities, proscriptions, and violence that legitimated Douglass' characterization. To be a "slave of the community" that was the antebellum north was to live a decidedly captive life, one beset by daily repudiations of both positive liberty ("freedom to") and negative liberty ("freedom from").[3] Of course, the "typical" life of a slave and the "typical" life of a free African American were hardly one and the same; Douglass himself resisted that equivalence, as his qualified rhetoric suggests. Nonetheless, the ever-growing numbers of free black people in the north from the beginnings of gradual emancipation in the late eighteenth century found themselves bound by a society that believed their very freedom was a hindrance to its progress and must be curbed as much as legally and socially possible.[4]

The irony, of course, is that white northerners believed slavery, too, was an economic, moral, and social blight. Thus, the anomalous or "peculiar" existence they imposed upon African Americans, the "slaves of the community," might solve the ills of chattel slavery *and* the "problem" of black freedom.[5] Animating this solution was a complex of assumptions, ideals, and logics that, *in toto*, deemed African Americans were, on the one hand, unfit for equal participation in the polity, while on the other, ideally suited to serve the personal and collective interests of their white counterparts. In other words, northerners cultivated a proslavery imagination with which to maintain and, over time, widen the gulf between black freedom and full black inclusion. On the whole, this public mind did not amount to a defense of the propriety of chattel slavery as an institution or a call for the re-enslavement of African Americans therein.[6] Rather, it conditioned the development of a new set of social and political relations built on the simultaneity of universal freedom and an indissolubly hierarchical racial dichotomy.

Benjamin Martin, a delegate to the 1837–38 Pennsylvania Constitutional Convention, deftly captured this ideological balancing act: "No person would go further to protect [African Americans] in all their natural rights [than I] . . . but to hold out to them social rights, or to incorporate them with ourselves in the exercise of the right of franchise, is a violation of the law of nature and would lead to . . . the resentment of the white population."[7] Though white northerners frequently infringed African Americans' natural rights—most notably during the 1830s with the spate of mob attacks against black people and their property—Martin's distinction is a useful one. Whereas southerners rejected the doctrine of universal natural rights outright, black freedom compelled invested publics and thinkers in the north to concern themselves primarily with the question of race and social rights. They strove to accommodate the belief in fundamental racial difference (e.g., inherent black inferiority) and satisfy the demand for race-based distinctions (e.g., black disenfranchisement) in a polity that no longer had slavery to perform that resolution. The proslavery forms and figures they relied on and further developed offered the most compelling affective and conceptual terms with which to justify and project new forms of black captivity within a free society.

It was the proslavery imaginative work that northerners undertook in their cultural and social practices that allowed for the juridical, legal, and statutory rejections of black inclusion, such as Pennsylvanians' decision to heed Martin's entreaty and vote to disenfranchise all African Americans in the state. Indeed, the law and other systematized formations of social thought very often emerge from, and respond to, the unofficial, disorganized, and contradictory complex of knowledge we enact in cultural formations. Antonio Gramsci termed this knowledge "common sense," and in order to trace the (ongoing) formation of economic, legal, and political structures, he argues, "the starting point must always be that common sense which is the spontaneous philosophy of the multitude and which has to be made ideologically coherent."[8] While social and cultural historians have thoroughly charted the specifics of those structures that coalesced into new frameworks of socio-racial life in the antebellum north, there has been too little emphasis on the ways in which the popular attitudes that produced those structures were fundamentally proslavery.[9] *The Captive Stage* centers on the formation of this proslavery imagination because, as common sense, it constituted the "terrain of conceptions and categories on which the practical consciousness" of antebellum northerners was "actually formed."[10]

Put another way, the frightful conditions African Americans endured were not the products of an abstract racism or generalized racial aversion; rather, they emerged as the effects of northern constituencies with specific desires that renderings of black bondage as a positive good articulated and legitimated. Because of the "metaphorical aptitude" of blackness in the dominant imagination, which Saidiya Hartman defines as either the "fungibility of the commodity" or "the imaginative surface upon which the master and the nation came to understand themselves," they crafted multiple proslavery figurations with distinct and even contradictory aims in mind.[11] The wide array of means and ends that made up this intellectual work underlines its functionality as common sense because, as Gramsci conceptualizes it, common sense is not "a single unique conception, identical in time and space" but "takes countless different forms."[12]

The diverse constituencies who fashioned the proslavery imagination of the antebellum north ranged from paternalistic patricians to the white working class of urban centers, from nostalgists of the Revolutionary era to perfectionist social reformers. As I consider throughout this book, they did so in an array of theatrical practices, performative texts, representational modes, discursive regimes, and literary genres. Despite their respective ideological and representational differences, however, they all found African Americans somehow useful to the polity. This conceptual affinity differentiated them from other white northerners who also rejected full black inclusion, such as the legislatures and invested publics who hoped emancipation would lead to the end of black people in the region or those who created and contributed to the colonization movement.[13] American proslavery thought and culture always valued black people, economically or otherwise, and affirmed they belonged in the U.S., however coerced and circumscribed their place therein might be.

James Gilbert Burnett's drama *Blanche of Brandywine*, which premiered in New York City in 1858, provides an instructive illustration of how northerners imagined this socio-racial arrangement. Burnett adapted the play from dime novelist George Lippard's book of the same title. He and his partner, Joseph Jefferson, decided to mount a production of *Blanche of Bran-dywine* because they were looking for a strong "military drama" with "marches, and counter-marches, murders, abductions, hairbreadth es-capes, militia trainings, and extravagant Yankee comicalities boiled over in every chapter."[14] Performed at the height of sectionalist tension and only two years before southern secession and Civil War, Burnett and Jefferson's production offered audiences a grand re-staging of a historical event that all Americans cherished: the American War of Independence. At the center of the narrative is the slave character Sampson, whose acts of heroism and self-sacrifice signify the importance of black people to the founding of the American republic and, somewhat more obliquely, suggest that their per-petual subordination to their white counterparts is necessary for the repub-lic's ongoing welfare.

In its representations of the import of a subjected black presence to the U.S., the play imagines a world of romanticized interracial reciprocity. For example, when British and Hessian soldiers attempt to capture American colonists whose hideout Sampson guards, he stands firm and pledges him-self to his master and future nation.

> Look heah, you may tear dis niggar limb from limb, but you no pass
> this door; had been watching you tis ten minutes. Dam scouldrels all
> ob you. My moder was sick, hab no friend in de world, war dyin;
> massa Frazier gib her wittals, missa Blanche gib her medicin; spose
> I let you pass dis door, see you to debil fust! Stan' off—stan' off.[15]

Sampson's position recasts proslavery claims of the supposed benignity of the institution as a saving grace for himself, his race, and society. In this view, slavery facilitates a necessary quid pro quo between black and white. But the institution no longer existed in the north, and its resurrection was far beyond the realm of possibility in 1858. For this reason, *Blanche of Bran-dywine* suggests that the most productive forms of racial complementarity in a free society require African Americans to maintain roles as similar to those of slaves as the law will allow.

That Burnett and Jefferson did not use Sampson's actions to question slavery in any way evidences northerners' confidence in, or at the very least toleration of, proslavery thought in terms of the socio-racial possibilities it allowed them to imagine. Indeed, despite conflicts with the south over the expansion of, and political power accorded to, slavery, the play was ex-tremely popular, and two of the era's most celebrated actresses, Laura Keen and Sara Stevens, starred in its initial run.[16] *Blanche of Brandywine* did not become a kind of rallying cry for northerners to declare a moral superiority over slaveholders and their apologists. The action of the play would have allowed Burnett, Jefferson, and their audiences to do just that, but they refused. In the final scene, for example, Sampson fights alongside George Washington in the Americans' victory in the Battle of Trenton (1776), which, historically, boosted the morale of the Continental Army and revitalized American resolve. Burnett and Jefferson describe it this way: "Bus[iness] of fight ad. lib., and then Washington appears on a bridge with offices and Standard Bearer. [Etc.] Sampson has a Hessian. R[ight]."[17] Rather than promote his valiant and selfless acts to press for freedom and citizenship, as those slaves and free people of color who aided in the Revolutionary effort actually did, Sampson champions his place in the national family as a slave.[18] The refusal to re-stage those demands was normative in dominant cultural production; it reflected not only northerners' rejection of black citizenship but also their acceptance of black captivity in its many forms.

Such refusals also help explain the seeming inconsistency that characterized the north throughout the antebellum period: namely, the simultaneous elimination of chattel slavery within its borders but its continued protection of the institution elsewhere. In his first Inaugural Address on March 4, 1861, Abraham Lincoln gave this sentiment its most memorable articulation: "I have no purpose, directly or indirectly, to interfere with the institution of slavery in the States where it exists."[19] Rather than categorize northerners' moral aversion to slavery and their acceptance of it elsewhere as paradoxical, I argue they maintained an essentially proslavery stance because to protect and perpetuate an institution, wherever it might exist, is to defend it. Thus the proslavery imagination that northerners cultivated not only served their own (imagined) social ends, it also aligned them with slaveholders and their apologists, and helped preserve the nation in the first half of the nineteenth century.

In works such as *Blanche of Brandywine* and in words such as Lincoln's, we also find, however implicitly, a position that further accorded with slaveholding interests: the rejection of black colonization.[20] Like the texts and practices I consider in this book, colonization emerged as a solution to the "problem" of free blackness. Although late eighteenth-century thinkers, most notably Thomas Jefferson, sometimes considered the merits of black re-settlement outside the U.S., colonization did not become a concerted national movement until the formation of the American Colonization Society (ACS) in 1816. The ACS began primarily through the efforts of clergymen who envisioned it as an organ of benevolent reform. Its members argued that African Americans would be better off in their "natural" environment, Western Africa, and could serve as permanent Christian missionaries there. Furthermore, they believed the removal of African Americans would remedy the strain the black presence caused intra-white relations. The organization's founder, Robert Finley, lamented how slavery and white racism exacerbated geographical, ideological, and political differences. A Presbyterian minister from New Jersey who served as president of Franklin College (which became the University of Georgia), Finley even castigated northerners for their negative views of the south: "No people are more alive to the claims of justice, humanity and generosity" than southern planters.[21] This view did not mean Finley approved of slavery; on the contrary, he believed the institution

> has an injurious effect on the morals and habits of a country where it exists. It insensibly induces a habit of indolence. Idleness seldom fails to be attended with dissipation. Should the time ever come when slavery shall not exist in these States, yet if the people of color remain among us, the effect of their presence will be unfavorable to our industry and morals. The recollection of their former servitude will keep alive the feeling that they were formed for labor, and that the descendants of their former masters ought to be exempt, at least, from the more humble and toilsome pursuits of life.[22]

In Finley's view, only total colonization, which included abolishing chattel slavery throughout the U.S., would restore social harmony and position the nation on course toward its most productive constitution: an all-white polity of highly industrious citizens.[23]

Thus, colonizationists like Finley conflicted with proslavery-minded northerners because the latter did not want to rid the U.S. of all black people. This ideological difference is indicative of these groups' demographic makeup: relatively, colonization was most popular in areas with the smallest proportions of black residents, whereas the proslavery imagination I trace was cultivated in locales with the largest free black populations. In the colonial and early national north, most slaves lived in cities, and after emancipation they stayed there and were joined by ex-slaves from rural areas.[24] As social historians have documented, cities such as Boston, Philadelphia, Providence, and especially New York City offered African Americans greater autonomy and more economic opportunities than did the country and smaller towns.[25] Thus, the concentration of free black people gripped the legislative bodies and ordinary white citizens of those cities, prompting them to undergo a sweeping reconsideration of the meaning and possibilities of racial difference. I argue that proslavery ideology was constitutive of these efforts, as those northerners who rejected black citizenship and racial equality in general molded and re-molded defenses of chattel slavery to fit their particular socio-historical contexts. To call the proslavery imagination of the antebellum north an exclusively urban phenomenon would be too absolute, however, because of its non-urban influences and its wider reaches. Nonetheless, because the majority of African Americans lived in cities, where they crafted their most conspicuous forms of resistance and most lasting political identities, nearly all of the texts and practices I explore in this book were produced in those locales.

In its effort to detail the proslavery mind that antebellum northerners fashioned as means to regulate the course of black freedom and counter the aims of black activism, *The Captive Stage* turns most centrally to cultural performance. This approach attends to historical and historiographical demands as well as theoretical ones. For one, it was the performative sphere (e.g., oratory, marches and parades, protests such as the Boston Tea Party) that affirmed colonists' revolutionary mettle against the British before the onset of extended armed conflicts. Americans not only conceived self-rule in these acts, they also *embodied* it, which is why literary historian Jay Fliegelman has defined their "independence as a rhetorical problem as much as a political one."[26] Consequently, the young nation established performance as its favored mode of expressivity with which to project collective possibility and social prescription. Furthermore, performance seemed to inscribe the democratic ideal within its very ontology: the form invited all Americans, as either actors or spectators, to participate and make (literal) sense of themselves and their relation to each other. And, indeed, all segments of the population—rich and poor, white and black, free and enslaved—relied on practices such as theatre, dance, oratory, and civic display to grapple with, and shape the direction of, their respective worlds. Most important for this book, they very often used the stage to come to terms with an untested and unfolding social reality in their midst—widespread black freedom—and to guide its trajectory going forward. Thus, an examination of northerners' culture of performance yields perhaps the most comprehensive and operative scope of their proslavery imagination.

The collective affective and intellectual work that *The Captive Stage* explores was part and parcel of the "rich shared public culture" that, according to Lawrence Levine, defined antebellum sociality.[27] That is to say, the proslavery sense at the center of the theatrical and performance practices I consider in this book was, indeed, common. In the second volume of his magisterial *Democracy in America*, de Tocqueville explains the ways "drama" and "theatrical representations" archive mass thought in democratic polities:

> The literature of the stage . . . constitutes the most democratic part of their literature. No kind of literary gratification is so much within the reach of the multitude as that which is derived from theatrical representations. Neither preparation nor study is required to enjoy them: they lay hold on you in the midst of your prejudices and your ignorance. *When the yet untutored love of the pleasures of the mind begins to affect a class of the community, it instantly draws them to the stage.* [. . .] At the theatre alone the higher ranks with the middle and the lower classes; there alone do the former consent to listen to the opinion of the latter, or at least to allow them to give an opinion at all. At the theatre, men of cultivation and of literary attainments have always had more difficulty than elsewhere in making their taste prevail over that of the people, and in preventing themselves from being carried away by the latter. *The pit has frequently made laws for the boxes.*[28] (emphasis added)

Although later in the chapter de Tocqueville vastly underestimates how popular theatregoing was in the 1830s and 1840s, his observations regarding the "multitudes" and their effect on dramatic literature and theatrical performance betray how these cultural products functioned as a shared common sense. The knowledge he describes as "untutored" and lacking "study," Gramsci would describe as "spontaneous" and incoherent; when de Tocqueville declares "the pit has frequently made laws for the boxes," he anticipates Gramsci's argument that philosophy is common sense made "coherent and systematic," albeit in a different analytical context and rhetorical register. With performance culture, then, everyday Americans could become crafters and carriers of proslavery thought. From the dramas of the post-Revolution era that pondered the role of free African Americans and slaves in the new republic; to blackface minstrelsy of the Jacksonian period that helped foster a white working-class cultural identity and political consciousness amid the development of wage labor capitalism; to the racial melodramas of the 1850s that allowed audiences to weep over the sectional crises that would eventually rend the nation: all of these cultural projects, which I explore in *The Captive Stage*, chart out a chaotic ideological terrain that not only worked to defend chattel slavery or its underlying socio-racial theories in service of other forms of black captivity; they also stimulated and complemented the philosophical and elite-produced apologias of the institution that intellectual historians of proslavery thought study almost exclusively.[29]

My focus on performance culture also highlights the significance of embodiment to popular imaginings of new forms of racial subjectivity (e.g., free blackness or whiteness in a society without slaves). The speculative possibilities of the stage parallel those of racial performativity because, tautologically, race is performed. "Definitions of race, like the processes of theatre," Harry J. Elam, Jr. explains, "fundamentally depend on the relationship between the seen and unseen, between the visibly marked and unmarked, between the 'real' and the illusionary."[30] This is not to say, of course, that race is mostly an abstraction and lacks phenomenal reality; on the contrary, the affective, corporeal, and psychological materiality resultant to racialized social experience attests to the "fact" and "case" of racial life.[31] But those men and women who shaped several of the racial discourses I explore in *The Captive Stage* often went much further, arguing that their performances confirmed emergent theories of racial biologism. Thomas "Daddy" Rice, the period's most famous and influential blackface minstrel, made this claim most explicitly. Following an 1837 performance in Baltimore, Rice told his audience that his Jim Crow act "effectually proved that negroes are essentially an inferior species of the human family, and they ought to remain slaves."[32] This declaration, which I read in more detail in chapter 2, signals a central irony at the core of antebellum northerners' proslavery imagination: the performers and their publics who staged constructions of blackness as justifications of black captivity and racial inequality neglected to account for the fact their efforts were *staged*; that is, African Americans were not essentially or naturally (fit for) anything.

For their part, African Americans could not make such theoretical or critical claims and simply leave it there; they knew the importance of performance to the shaping of the public mind and decided to confront their (proslavery) detractors on that very cultural front. That is, because of the "democracy" of performance, they, too, used theatrical and civic stages (e.g., the street) to express their particular conceptions and demands—and they did so from the very beginnings of emancipation, as I explore in chapter 1. With virtually no recourse to the realm of formal politics, performance and other forms of cultural production offered the most viable and, in many respects, effective means with which to forge interventions of political significance. Thus looking back to the early national and antebellum periods does reveal what political theorist Richard Iton identifies as African Americans' "hyperactivity on the cultural front," but it is also to account for how and why aesthetic and cultural formations became perhaps the most fertile ground for the cultivation of black political identities and black engagements with the nation's democratic discourses and ideals.

Consider, for instance, Frederick Douglass' 1848 address at the National Negro Convention in Cleveland, with which I began this introduction. The speech and Douglass' leadership at the convention constituted a turning point in his public career and catapulted him to national stature, even though he had been a sought-after speaker on the abolitionist lecture circuit since 1841 and had published his popular *Narrative of the Life of Frederick Douglass, an American Slave* in 1845. According to the *Daily True Democrat* (Cleveland), Douglass presided over the convention with "dignity and ability," and in response to their rival newspaper's disparagement of Douglass' intellect, the same paper asserted: "Frederick Douglass is a man, who if divided into fifty parts would make fifty better men than the editor of the *Plain Dealer*."[33] Such appraisals of Douglass, both positive and negative, began to appear among (white) non-abolitionist syndicates with far greater regularity after the 1848 convention. Just as critically, Douglass' performance also solidified his place as a leading figure of the black public sphere. In the midst of Douglass becoming a self-determined sociopolitical actor and independent thinker—which his editorship of the *North Star* beginning in 1847 and his budding estrangement from William Lloyd Garrison signaled most decisively—the convention provided the stage upon which he demonstrated to those African Americans in attendance, as well as those who read the proceedings and reviews, how the combination of his singular talents and unique perspective (i.e., Douglass had escaped from slavery just a decade before and became legally free less than two years prior) expressed their demands for universal freedom and citizenship with uncommon power and urgency. Indeed, although delegates passed resolutions and crafted petitions as means to redress African Americans' collective grievances, it was most often the performances at the conventions that animated the most meaningful forms of ideological innovation and social change.

For all of their similarities to the processes and procedures of formal politics, the conventions are understood best as a form of cultural production. As I explore further in chapter 4, the performance and textual practices of the convention movement directly countered the proslavery formations that daily beset free black life. By the time Douglass performed his "Address" in 1848, African Americans had been holding national meetings for nearly twenty years (and state meetings for almost ten). Throughout that history, meetings functioned as training grounds for local, state, and national black leaders, but starting in the early 1840s they took a decidedly radical turn: with worsening forms of racial inequality, such as the disenfranchisement of all African Americans in Pennsylvania, and the rise of mob violence against black people and their property—all of which, I argue, proslavery performance culture stimulated—delegates to the conventions, and the black public sphere at large, became far more militant in their rhetoric and approach; that is, they doubted the efficacy of moral suasion and therefore dedicated themselves more forcefully to political and, in a few signal cases, insurrectionary action. This ideological and tactical transformation profoundly distressed the vast majority of white abolitionists and sympathizers. Notwithstanding their disapprobation of chattel slavery and racial terror, these men and women rejected full black equality in the political and social spheres, let alone violent black uprisings. In response, they fashioned their own dramatic and theatrical representations of complaisant and submissive blackness with which to offset the force and influence that Douglass and other fiery, self-determined African Americans performed. Proslavery ideology was critical to these renderings of free black subjectivity because, as chapters 4 and 5 show, it allowed white social reformers, abolitionists, and their northern publics to imagine African Americans as *necessarily* subordinated in the polity, though free from the horrors of chattel slavery. Indeed, even antislavery reformers were very often under the sway of the proslavery mind: "Opposing slavery and hating its victims has come to be a very common form of Abolitionism," Douglass proclaimed in an 1856 article he titled "The Unholy Alliance of Negro Hate and Abolitionism."[34]

As responses to the effects of African Americans' public performances of full black autonomy, which themselves were responses to the effects of other performances such as blackface minstrelsy, white reformers' imaginings of free blackness contributed to the back-and-forth dynamic that constituted the shape of the proslavery imagination of the antebellum north. Because of that dynamic, *The Captive Stage* forefronts the interplay between African Americans' culture of performance and that of their detractors. This method, which I employ both within and between chapters, best illustrates the ways multiple publics molded their shared ideological conviction—that is, free black people must remain captive in the American polity—to contest African Americans' "political aesthetics," which literary historian Ivy Wilson defines as their "various art forms [that] put into high relief the efficacy of affect to engender and sustain collectivities of social belonging" or what I would call full inclusion.[35] Put simply, northerners honed their proslavery common sense in direct opposition to the inclusionary claims African Americans embodied in their civil, oratorical, and theatrical performances.

In the nation's first decades, if not beyond, it was black performance that most captivated skeptical and antagonistic white onlookers. From the very beginnings of emancipation, for instance, African Americans staged parades to celebrate religious holidays, mourn the deaths of community members, and commemorate historical events. More broadly, the performances asserted their rights to public space, condemned structural and everyday racism, and laid claim to the U.S. as their own. The African Lodge of Freemasons in Boston was one of the first institutions to mount parades, as the protocols of Freemasonry dictated, and, given the acute exigencies of the city's free black population, they were necessarily political. White Bostonians "reacted to these black Masonic public activities with curiosity and mild satire," literary historian Joanna Brooks finds.[36] Yet as more and more legally emancipated and personally manumitted slaves flocked to Boston and other cities to build their lives as free people, institutions such as the black Masons and civic performances such as black parades acquired a phenomenal presence that could no longer be snubbed with simple parody.

To be sure, a large degree of the effect of this presence emerged from the sheer audacity and the conspicuity of a swelling collective of former slaves and their descendants. Yet just as critically, African Americans couched the parades in the nation's founding discourses and narratives, therefore endowing their performances with a rhetorical and symbolic potency that struck white publics to the core. In short, early national African Americans were too good at doing and being America. As one orator declared at a parade commemorating the 1808 abolition of the transatlantic slave trade: "That we are faithful to our country, we have abundantly proved: where her Hull, her Decatur, and Bainbridge, fought and conquered, the black bore his part, stimulated by the pure love of country, which neither contempt nor persecution can eradicate from his generous heart."[37] According to this view, black patriotism was unshakable, even in the face of white racism and violence, and black sacrifice for the nation was assured, as this testament to African Americans' participation in the War of 1812 suggests. (Earlier black orators made the same assertions citing black efforts in the American War of Independence.) Such avowals throughout the period affirmed African Americans' determination to be central contributors to the national project; as a consequence, white political figures, cultural producers, and invested publics began to reimagine northern society in such a way that maintained the dominant racial order (i.e., black captivity) but came to grips with the ineluctability of black freedom and the urgency of black politics.

The first chapter, "Setting the Stage of Black Freedom: Parades and 'Presence' in the New Nation," begins with one of those efforts: the work of playwright John Murdock. Murdock's plays, *The Triumphs of Love; or, Happy Reconciliation* (1794) and *The Politicians; or, A State of Things* (1798), constitute the earliest extensive consideration of the condition of free black people in U.S. theatre history. (In fact, *Triumphs* is the first American play to stage the emancipation or manumission of a slave.[38]) Always with an eye on his native Philadelphia, Murdock must have noticed how its free black population, the largest in the nation, more than tripled in the decade, going from less than 4 to nearly 10 percent of the city's entire populace.[39] He also must have taken note of the fact that ex-slaves and their descendants, both city natives and migrants, faced extremely limited economic opportunities and severe social restrictions.[40] For Murdock, the abject conditions African Americans continued to endure after emancipation belied the prospects of black freedom. Thus in his turn to drama, he envisions a role for African Americans in Philadelphia and, by extension, in post-slavery societies that denies them full freedom but, in so doing, safeguards them from its attendant "problems," such as procuring adequate employment, participating in politics, or engaging international affairs.

In their formal and everyday practices, African Americans dismissed such "solutions," and they did so most grandly in the parade culture they developed. Ironically, the means by which the parades enacted African Americans' claims for full inclusion were black nationalist. Unlike the better-known iterations of the 1850s and 1920s, the earliest formations of black nationalism in the U.S. did not seek racial separation but, rather, equal participation and shared stakes in the polity.[41] Using the tools of black nationalism such as racial solidarity and race language (e.g., us vs. them; descendants of Africans; sons of Africans), parade participants' inclusionary claims grew increasingly assertive over time. This swell of demands and rhetorical fervor provoked counter-responses from white publics, the most significant of which was the highly popular "Bobalition" series of broadsides. The first broadsides were published in Boston in the mid-1810s and circulated throughout the U.S. and in parts of England through at least the 1830s. Bobalition mocks the processional and sartorial manners with which black northerners commemorated the abolition of the transatlantic slave trade in their parades, rendering them as uniformed or well-dressed simians. But the broadsides are especially disparaging of black oratory and speech—hence "Bobalition," a contortion of "abolition." As I argue at the end of chapter 1, the ways in which Bobalition figures black orality draws on a proslavery logic that argues the African (American) lacks the oratorical, and therefore intellectual, abilities that mark those constituted for liberty and self-government in a republic. This effect relied on the mutually productive relation between embodied performance and print culture in the period, when, as Michael Warner notes, Americans "often insisted on seeing writing as a form of speaking."[42] The broadsides, in other words, were performative texts that enacted the reputed ridiculousness of black citizenship.

To be sure, the imagined orality of Bobalition drew on earlier forms of black derision such as those popular in late eighteenth-century almanacs and newspapers. But Bobalition is unique in the very direct ways it engaged black activism and sought to undercut its aims. Cultural historians have noted how this effort was "pedagogical" in that the broadsides taught "the white public to see black people as inherently different, unable to speak, and subject to public ridicule," but they have been less particular in terms of identifying how these racial lessons were, at bottom, proslavery.[43] If we attend to the ways proslavery ideology is at the core of Bobalition, we not only gain a better understanding of its effectiveness in the period but also of the animating force of the cultural practices it influenced. Of the practices for which Bobalition set the stage, blackface minstrelsy was the most instrumental and influential in terms of frustrating black inclusion. Like Bobalition, minstrelsy arose in direct contestation to black communal and institutional activism. In their caricatured and grotesque performances of black subjectivity, blackface minstrels and their audiences laughed off racial equality in any form as absurd; with corked-up faces, distorted physiognomies and gestures, and malapropistic diction, they upheld the propriety of black captivity *and* white freedom.

When blackface minstrelsy emerged in the late 1820s, the need for affirmations of white freedom mushroomed because of the unprecedented class-based stratification of American society that accompanied industrialization, urbanization, and the rise of wage-labor capitalism in the period. White workers (e.g., former artisans, journeymen, and simple mechanics) claimed their predicament was particularly acute because early capitalist production exploited their labor and concentrated the nation's wealth upward into the hands of the rich and the emergent bourgeoisie. As a result, they argued, they were losing their very freedoms. That the free black population was growing and black agitation was increasing in intensity only redoubled white workers' belief they were becoming the nation's new slaves, replacements for those freed from chattel slavery. With blackface minstrelsy, the white working class honed a theatrical practice with which to contest these economic conditions and socio-racial developments. Chapter 2, "Black Politics but Not Black People: Early Minstrelsy, 'White Slavery,' and the Wedge of 'Blackness,'" traces minstrelsy's origins and examines its early period (1829–43) to explore how and why proslavery thought charged its aesthetic formations and political interventions. I show how early minstrelsy esteemed the antiauthoritarian potentiality of black alterity and "opacity" as means to buffer the fears and uncertainties of the burgeoning white working-class consciousness.[44] But this regard did *not* signal a desire for an interracial working-class alliance, as some have argued.[45] Instead, early minstrelsy was as an especially crafty form of cultural expropriation with which white workers remonstrated economic and social elites and, at the same time, distanced themselves from their African American counterparts; that is, minstrel performers and their publics seized the power of black/slave *politics* but spurned black/slave *people*.

The incongruous relation between the closed texts and social effects of early minstrelsy reflected the broader antagonism between African Americans and their detractors. Black performances for citizenship and social belonging only widened the breaches in the polity's originary social contract that emancipation first inflicted. To that effect, and throughout the antebellum period, African Americans continued to craft a protest culture built on the nation's founding discourses, icons, and narratives. This method of historical repetition and revision, or what literary historian Russ Castronovo calls "deforming history," was a constant of antebellum African Americans' cultural formations and one of their most canny political tactics. Consider the following lyrics from "A Song for Freedom" from William Wells Brown's 1848 *The Anti-Slavery Harp: A Collection of Songs for Anti-Slavery Meetings*:

Come all ye bondmen far and near,
Let's put a song in massa's ear,
It is a song for our poor race,
Who're whipped and trampled with disgrace

Chorus. My old massa tells me O
   This is a land of freedom O;
   Let's look about and see if 't is so,
   Just as massa tells me O.

He tells me of that glorious one,
I think his name was Washington,
How he did fight for liberty,
To save a threepence tax on tea.

Chorus. My old massa, &c.

And then he tells me that there was
A Constitution, with this clause,
That all men equal were created,
How often we have heard it stated.

Chorus. My old massa, &c.[46]

These lyrics, which antislavery audiences would sing to a popular melody as was the standard practice for antislavery songbooks, deform history in at least two crucial, interrelated ways: one, the slave becomes an interpreter of the meaning of the nation's founding, which George Washington, a "threepence tax on tea" (i.e., the Tea Act of 1773), and the Constitution (which should be the Declaration of Independence) emblematize; two, and more obliquely, the democratic potential of that meaning is inextricably linked to the fate of the slave. That is, if colonists rebelled against Great Britain and founded the U.S. in response to the "political" slavery they suffered, then, surely *chattel* slavery, which subsumed political and all other types of human subjugation, legitimated black rebellion and full inclusion in the American polity.

The way in which Wells Brown and other African Americans deformed history rankled their antagonists who argued deploying Revolutionary-era history to press for black social and political rights was absurd and at odds with the Founders' intentions.[47] Chapter 3, "Washington and the Slave: Black Deformations, Proslavery Domesticity, and Re-Staging the Birth of the Nation," probes how this contest over the founding moment took shape in antebellum theatre and performance culture, paying particular attention to the functionality and value of proslavery conceits and conceptions in the practices of those who opposed racial equality. As theatre-makers and audiences re-staged the events and persons of the Revolutionary period — through performances like P. T. Barnum's widely popular exhibition of Joice Heth (1835–36), the purported 161-year-old former slave of the Washington family, or plays like *King's Bridge Cottage* (1826), *The Patriot* (1834), and *The Revolutionary Soldier or, The Old Seventy-Sixer* (1847, 1850) — they imagined a form of proslavery domesticity that benefitted blacks and whites alike. The figure of George Washington was central to these works because, as a kind of a demigod in the national imagination as well as life-long slaveholder, he endowed historical and almost sacred legitimation to the efforts of those who denied black inclusion on proslavery premises. African Americans, in turn, forged an ambivalent relationship to Washington, making sure to pay obeisance to the so-called father of the nation all the while remaining wary of his fraught iconicity. Wells Brown's "A Song for Freedom" succinctly captures that irresolution: "I think his name was Washington," the slave sings.

As noted, the backlash that Wells Brown's deforming history and other black cultural projects provoked came from all segments of the northern population, including social reformers and the white abolitionist establishment. The final two chapters of *The Captive Stage* analyze how these groups made use of, and therefore contributed to, the northern proslavery imagination as part of their efforts to restrain black autonomy and freedom. Although social reformers were strongly anti-theatrical, condemnatory of the lax and salacious sociality that normative theatregoing encouraged, by the early 1840s they could no longer ignore the considerable hold the stage maintained on the nation's collective imagination. Thus, they built their own theatres and developed their own performance ethic with which to promote their cultural and social ideals. Like the reformers themselves, these spaces and practices were bourgeois, dedicated to the principles of self-control, personal abstention, and collective efficiency. The rise of these entertainments constituted a "minor revolution" in American theatre, as theatre historian Bruce A. McConachie describes it; men like Moses Kimball of Boston and P. T. Barnum of New York City, for instance, pioneered the matinee as well as family-oriented museum theatres, which "promised their patrons chaste entertainments in environments closer to the church and the front parlor than traditional playhouses."[48]

Most accounts of mid-nineteenth-century reform theatre center on its role in large-scale movements such as those for temperance, abolitionism, and women's suffrage; yet scholars have paid little, if any, attention to the ways antebellum reformers used the stage to imagine and encourage new casts of free black subjectivity.[49] Thus chapter 4, "The Theatocracy of Antebellum Social Reform: 'Monkeyism' and the Mode of Romantic Racialism," explores how the aggressive and independent-minded black public sphere that began to materialize in the early 1840s, which white reformers viewed as another bothersome social ill, animated these theatrical efforts. The chapter begins with a reading of how performances by Frederick Douglass and ex-slave and abolitionist Henry Highland Garnet disrupted normative racial hierarchies and emphasized the importance of black leadership in abolitionism and African Americans' fight for citizenship. The collective of white social reformers rejected their acts, which one critic derisively termed "monkeyism."[50] Using Harry Seymour's temperance drama *Aunt Dinah's Pledge* (1850, 1853) as a case study, this chapter argues that romantic racialism emerged as white social reformers' favored mode with which to project new forms of black life. (That a temperance drama provided the occasion and frame with which to reimagine blackness is unsurprising because most antebellum reformers believed their movements intersected. *"All great reforms go together,"* Douglass declared in 1845.[51]) Romantic racialism, as historian George M. Fredrickson famously theorizes it, derives from proslavery thought and posits the African (American) as inherently docile, moral, and religious; it denies the viability of black self-determination in the modern world.[52] For their part, African Americans conceived of such racialisms, positive or otherwise, as the ideological basis of a broader effort to re-enslave them.

The final chapter, "Melodrama and the Performance of Slave Testimony; or, William Wells Brown's Inability to Escape," further interrogates how actual and imagined circumscriptions of black autonomy manifest in another reform performance culture: the staging of abolitionism.[53] As ex-slaves recounted their lives as chattel, they had to abide by a set of predetermined discursive protocols if they were to achieve legibility and legitimacy among their mainly white audiences. Operating within this circumscribed field of testimony, fugitive and former slaves such as William Wells Brown pragmatically, and perhaps unavoidably, deployed racial types (such as the "happy darky" and the foppish black dandy) and cultural forms and literary genres (such as blackface minstrelsy and melodrama) first fashioned to disparage black subjectivity and therefore delimit black freedom. One of the most illustrative of these performances is Wells Brown's melodrama *The Escape; or, A Leap for Freedom* (1858). In an extended reading of *The Escape*, this chapter contends that by means of the play's dramaturgical structure and narrative arc, Wells Brown dismisses the possibility that African Americans can achieve full inclusion in the north or anywhere else in the U.S. Such judgments, I argue, worked to strengthen the slaveholding status quo. Ultimately, *The Escape* prefigures a program of voluntary black emigration from the U.S. that Wells Brown increasingly championed in the years immediately following his first tour of the play in 1858.

By the late 1850s, the merits and historical necessity of black emigration were clear to men and women like Wells Brown, who once believed economic and so-called moral uplift would rectify racial inequities and catalyze national emancipation. As leading emigrationist Martin Robinson Delany memorably put it, "We love our country, dearly love her, but she don't love us—she despises us, and bids us begone, driving us from her embraces."[54] The chapters of *The Captive Stage* assemble a narrative of the ways multiple northern constituencies, by means of their respective performance forms and practices, spurned antebellum African Americans' love for the U.S. and its democratic principles and possibilities. Although these constituencies aimed their cultural projects toward different political and social ends, one proslavery notion linked them all: above all else, black people must serve the economic, moral, political, and social needs and interests of their white counterparts. This form of racial ascription dominated the collective American imagination in the first half of the nineteenth century and, as a result, ensured that the new stage of northern black life that widespread freedom inaugurated would be a decidedly captive one.

The archives, repertoires, and ideologies *The Captive Stage* engages were born of the most consequential institution of American life before the Civil War: chattel slavery. Although the U.S. abolished chattel slavery in 1865 and, therefore, negated the immediacy of defending the institution, the proslavery common sense that I recognize as constitutive of the antebellum north continued to shape American performance culture and racial signification in society at large. Despite universal emancipation and the enshrinement of black citizenship in the Fourteenth Amendment to the Constitution (1868), the dominant imagination still construed blackness as the mark of subjects who should be most captive, while whiteness marked those who should be most free. The emergence of sharecropping, the rise of lynching, and the instatement of Jim Crow in the second half of the nineteenth century, among other harrowing social realities, signified to those living in the wake of the Civil War that a good deal of the institutional practices and ideological premises of slavery remained very much in existence. As Hartman trenchantly puts it, "Slavery was both the wet nurse and the bastard offspring of liberty."[55]

With those practices and premises (seemingly) behind us, we would be remiss, I think, to argue they are no longer alive today. At the very least, they certainly *haunt* us. Haunting, sociologist Avery F. Gordon explains, "is one way in which abusive systems of power make themselves known and their impacts felt in everyday life, especially when they are supposedly over and done with (slavery, for instance)."[56] Avery's theory of haunting helps explain how Americans can, at moments, still feel held captive by chattel slavery's affects and meanings. The recent spate of white *and* non-white college students donning blackface (or at least the exposure of a practice that has always been popular) illustrates how the sociocultural force of the institution continues to shape twenty-first-century life.[57] In one instance from the University of Southern Mississippi (USM) in 2011, six white sorority sisters wore blackface to a costume party because they wanted to attend as the Huxtable Family of the "Cosby Show." It is most likely the case that these young women, like many in their generation, are big fans of the "Cosby Show" and believed their costumes were signs of respect for the landmark television program. But, as USM Dean of Students Eddie Holloway noted, their costumes signified far more than the Huxtables: "Though it is clear that these women had no ill intent, it was also clear that they had little cultural awareness or competency, and did not understand the historical implication of costuming in blackface."[58] Above all, these students were unaware of the fact that the fun they sought to have rested on a cultural history of racial derision and degradation that renders black people as the least worthy of human dignity in American society. It is no wonder, then, that African Americans and other invested persons condemned their blackface acts and those of other college students.

But the ire blackface engenders is about more than disrespect and the lack of decency. Its critics also recognize, however unconsciously, that blackface is a performance practice that is animated by race-based circumscriptions of freedom and citizenship in the American polity; it transmits the very proslavery common sense I delineate in the pages that follow. This is to say, although *The Captive Stage* confines itself to the late eighteenth and nineteenth centuries, a number of the performances, texts, narratives, figures, and modes that constitute the book's objects of analysis continue to signify beyond the time and spaces of chattel slavery; they have transmogrified into "ghosts" that still have "real presence" in American culture and society.[59]

| Setting the Stage of Black Freedom

*Parades and "Presence" in the New Nation*

In the aftermath of the armed conflicts of the American War of Independence, a series of "quiet" structural revolutions commenced.[1] The United States had to instate an untested system of democratic governance called republicanism; implement new economies of capital, exchange, and labor predicated on the individual's absolute right to property; and readjust to the large-scale demographic shifts the war produced.[2] The role of slaves and free people of color in the emergent polity surfaced as a markedly fraught question. On the one hand, dominant civic discourses rendered whiteness the precondition of citizenship. On the other, the prevalence of the rhetoric of egalitarianism threatened the permanence of such race-based civil circumscriptions.[3] That many slaves and free people of color had distinguished themselves in the Revolutionary cause and demanded full citizenship in return made questions of civil inclusion all the more pressing.

These demands helped quicken antislavery sentiment in the period, when many already doubted the viability of slavery in a new nation founded on principles of democratic freedom. Indeed, northern state legislatures enacted gradual emancipation statutes, and slaveholders in all regions (most notably the Upper South) manumitted slaves in vast numbers.[4] The increasing masses of free black people did not attempt to isolate themselves from their former masters; rather, they sought to expand the polity in such a way that included them as equal participants.[5] In this effort they crafted a protest culture that merged (inherited) African notions of community, institution-building, and personal obligation to Enlightenment discourses and political practices.[6] These doings, along with the patterns of black migration throughout the North American continent that emancipation instigated, laid the groundwork for what would become African America.

Throughout the early national period, African Americans continued to stress that their efforts toward the formation of the U.S. were at the core of their identity. As literary historian John Ernest writes, "In the pages of the early [black] historical texts, one encounters frequently both the history and prehistory of African American contributions to American military and political history."[7] The most venerated and recurring historical figure in this literature is runaway slave Crispus Attucks. Attucks was one of the first men British soldiers killed in the Boston Massacre, an initiating event of the American Revolution, and he quickly became the iconic signifier of selfless black patriotism.[8] His story appealed to early black writers and other "integrationist historians" because his martyrdom, as they would have classified it, and other contemporaneous acts of black sacrifice evidenced the ways African Americans had always been at the nation's center.[9]

Yet in official and normative accounts of the American Revolution from the period, Attucks' death is little more than a footnote, if that. For example, the most famous rendering of the Boston Massacre, Paul Revere's 1770 engraving *The Bloody Massacre Perpetuated in King Street Boston on March 5th*, does not graphically depict Attucks. Historian Marcus Rediker argues that Revere's engraving, which he contends "may be the most important political work of art in American history," excludes Attucks because he was "the wrong color, the wrong ethnicity, and the wrong occupation to be included in the national story."[10] But all stories—national or otherwise—invite us to read them against the grain, and the narrative Revere sought to tell with his engraving is a case in point. For instance, Attucks' name does appear in the subtitle of Revere's print as one of the Massacre's victims. Moreover, as cultural historian Tavia Nyong'o notes, "no one else is depicted either individually or realistically in the print."[11] Nyong'o suggests that "rather than see Attucks either included or excluded by Revere's print," we should "understand [Attucks'] status as an *exception*" because "it is impossible to say finally whether or not he is included or excluded, because he is clearly both."[12] Thus, Revere's listing of Attucks as one of the slain patriots destabilizes the narrative limits that the amorphous, yet racially all-white rendering presents visually. Even if Attucks is not discernibly "in" *The Bloody Massacre*, he is certainly there—throughout it, above it, under it.

Nyong'o's reading of Attucks as a figure of exception haunting Revere's engraving suggests an instructive way to frame free black life in the post-Revolutionary period. For African Americans living in the wake of the nation's founding, they lacked the *security* of being an American and the *surety* of being a non-American; instead, they were at once both, existing in what I would call the state of black exception.[13] This racial state has generated dialectics of desire and disgust, resistance and repression, and value and valuelessness that have beset black freedom since the nation's beginning and, for many, continue to trouble the viability of black freedom itself.[14] As theorist Lindon Barrett asks, "What are the particulars of negotiating social and civic relations in a society in which one remains part of a constantly expended present absence?"[15] In one form or another, this question has animated the ways African Americans have imagined the nation, their place within it, and the practical resources with which to overturn their condition as the excluded members who are also the included nonmembers of the American polity.

This chapter looks at some of the ways these imaginings crystallized into a culture of black parade performance that spurned the state of black exception and aimed to position African Americans as self-determined citizens and bearers of American possibility. More specifically, I explore how early national black publics across cities and towns in the north used commemorative parades to press for universal emancipation, black citizenship, and social equality. While African Americans grounded the parades' rhetorical, performance, and textual practices in the immediate concerns of black life, they were equally interested in the direction of the entire nation and of American democracy. Indeed, these civic performances mark the beginnings of a collectively honed political consciousness that draws from black struggle a set of imaginative and pragmatic resources with which to expand democratic possibilities for all Americans.

Hostile onlookers did not construe black parades as a kind of pedagogy that elucidated what the American polity could and should be; they viewed such acts as absurd at best and menacing at worst. That threat stemmed in large part from the fact that the parade, which was "the characteristic genre of nineteenth-century civic life," rendered ex-slaves and their descendants' demands highly legible and therefore potent.[16] Hundreds, sometimes thousands of African Americans participated, and their use of the nation's most cherished form of civic display signified to antagonistic white audiences an attempt to seize the nation. The parades, of course, were not projections of a black-controlled nation-state with a subordinate white population; rather, they were (re)presentations of African Americans as a free people deserving of the promises of American democracy.

The culture of parading that early national African Americans crafted also vexed certain antislavery northerners because its affirmations of American subjectivity pointed to an increase in the black presence. Many in the north, particularly in New England, supported emancipation because they hoped it would lead to the end of black people in their midst.[17] But, as the parades suggested in the grandest of scales, African Americans had no intention of disappearing. This reality became even more daunting for many in the region when they grappled with the fact that they no longer had the racial and social protections slavery once offered.[18] The question of what to do with a mass of free black people rarely arose before the 1780s because legislating bodies, slaveholders, and other invested white publics could not foresee large numbers of ex-slaves laying claim to the nation and demanding full inclusion therein. It took the realities of emancipation, notably including black activism, for them to begin to take seriously the overriding question of black freedom, which Thomas Jefferson succinctly articulated in his *Notes on the State of Virginia* (1781–82, 1787): "Why not retain and incorporate the blacks into the state, and thus save the expence of supplying, by importation of white settlers, the vacancies they will leave?"[19] With this query, Jefferson pinpointed the fundamental quandary of abolishing slavery. While northerners refused to incorporate the ex-slave into the state as an equal member, they did imagine new forms of black captivity with which to retain him. Some of the most representative of these efforts took shape in the plays of John Murdock, and, as I explore in what follows, they provided a model for future cultural producers to meld the assumptions of proslavery ideology with the realities of black freedom.

## "CITIZEN SAMBO": A PROBLEM FOR THOUGHT

John Murdock was a white hairdresser in late eighteenth-century Philadelphia. As a member of the artisan class, he was afforded time to contribute to the city's budding theatre culture. Theatre historian Heather S. Nathans argues that a "rise of class awareness" significantly informs Murdock's plays because of the "diminution in both [artisans' and mechanics'] political and economic influence." His dramas "presented the Philadelphia Murdock knew, a hodgepodge of recent German and Irish immigrants, slave and free blacks, Quakers, artisans, and wealthy elites."[20] Murdock's *The Triumphs of Love; or, Happy Reconciliation* (1794), for example, considers how these various groups attended to some of the period's most pressing concerns, including the slave uprisings in Santo Domingo and the parameters of political representation in the newly formed U.S. More relevant to the concerns of this chapter, *Triumphs* explores the conditions that led to and followed the onset of black freedom in Philadelphia, and it does so through a narrative of post-war intergenerational conflict. The older generation of characters, especially Jacob Friendly Senior, objects to the profligacy and sybaritism of the younger generation, particularly that of George Friendly Junior. Among George Junior and his peers' most troubling habits and practices, slaveholding is perhaps the most acute for Jacob Senior because, as a Quaker, it conflicts with his religious and moral convictions. Quaker antislavery activism dates back to the late seventeenth century and, institutionally, culminated in the creation of the world's first abolition organization, the Pennsylvania Abolition Society (PAS), which formed in 1775.[21] In Jacob Senior's view, which is to say the view of Quakerism, slavery is an institution that not only contradicts divine law but also nourishes the "rank weeds of vice [to] overgrow the seeds of virtue" in both man and society.[22]

Ultimately, George Junior accepts the way of his Quaker forebears, and manumits his slave, Sambo, after watching "the honest creature" perform an "untutored, pathetic soliloquy" on the physical and psychological wounds of the "barbarous, iniquitous slave-trade."[23] Before George Junior does, however, he recalls the so-called merits of being a slave; as he sees it, the life of the slave is hardly the worst lot one can endure: "And yet how many thousands of the poorer class of whites are there, whose actual situation are [sic] vastly inferior to his [i.e., the black slave's]."[24] Over the course of the first half of the nineteenth century, and especially in response to the rise in wealth inequality that early wage-labor capitalism produced, this claim became an ever-common refrain of proslavery ideologues. George Junior's use of it does not prevent him from freeing Sambo, but his comment does signal the ways white northerners believed slavery was something of a saving grace for the mass of black people; it also points to the qualms that accompanied statutory emancipations and personal manumission, the "moral" qualifications that prevented former masters and even non-slaveholding white people from treating their newly freed black counterparts as equals.

What is even more noteworthy about the use of this proslavery claim in *Triumphs* is that Sambo himself repeats a version of it in the very soliloquy that leads to his manumission.

Sambo what a gal call a pretty fellow.... Can tink so, so, pretty well. He tink; he berry often tink why he slave to white man? why black foke sold like cow or horse. He tink de great somebody above, no order tings so.—Sometime he tink dis way—he got bess massa in e world. He gib him fine clothes for dress—he gib him plenty money for pend; and for a little while, he tink himself berry happy. Afterwards he tink anoder way. He pose massa George die; den he sold to some oder massa. May be he no use him well. When Sambo tink so, it most broke he heart.[25]

Sambo is trapped, here, within a muddied logic. No sooner than he questions the bestial ways whites imagine and subsequently treat black people,
he expresses his gratitude that he has the "bess massa in [the] world."
Then, later in the scene, he takes another turn and makes clear that his assessment of George as a "good" master does not in any way dampen his
desire to be free. Sambo's equivocality, along with George's later reserve
regarding slave manumission, lays the conceptual and narrative groundwork for the play's ensuing speculation on what many saw as the wrong-
headedness of grounding abstract notions of liberty in the form of black
emancipation. In this effort, Murdock pursued a question that, in my view,
has shaped the course of American social history: "Sambo, suppose you
had your liberty, how would you conduct yourself?"[26]

After George asks this of Sambo and subsequently frees him, Sambo
declares, "O massa George, I feel how I neber feel before. God bress you.
(Cries.) I muss go, or my heart burst," then exits. He quickly returns, now
alone on stage, and tells the audience, "When massa George ax me how I
like go free, I tink he joke: but when he tell me so for true, it make much
water come in my eye for joy. (Sings.) Den Sambo dance and sing./ He more
happy dan a king./ He no fear he lose he head. He now citizen Sambo."[27]
Sambo's effusion in this solo act, it bears noting, is as much a celebration of
*white* freedom as it is his own. By means of the figure of manumitted black
slave, one happier "dan a king" (George III) in this case, the scene evoked
Americans' recent triumph over monarchial authority and commemorated
their (white) freedom from "political slavery." But immediately after hailing himself "citizen," Sambo exits, and only appears in *Triumphs* once
more. In that scene he is drunk and belligerent, and George remarks that
Sambo is in a "situation I never saw him in before."[28] Sambo's drunkenness
is not an instance of racial stereotyping, however, because in the previous
scene George and his white friend, Careless, are belligerently inebriated.
Thus, drunkenness and, by extension, other forms of intemperance emerge
in the play as problems of freedom rather than those of an essential racial
(i.e., black) disposition. The behavioral symmetry between Sambo and his
erstwhile masters, coupled with the paean to republican ideals he sings following his manumission, suggests that he has begun to wear the mantle of
American citizenship. In fact, Sambo's final line in *Triumphs* is "Liberty and
[e]quality . . . for eber."[29]

*Triumphs* offers no further clarification of the fate of "citizen Sambo";
but Murdock's 1798 follow-up, *The Politicians; or, A State of Things*, returns
him to the stage. In this play, Murdock explores the lingering partisan hostilities that stemmed from the ratification of the highly controversial Jay

Treaty of 1794, which helped the U.S. deter another war with Great Britain by strengthening economic ties between the two nations, and from American investment in the French Revolutionary Wars.[30] According to *The Politicians*, these tensions consumed all order of persons, from the wealthy merchant to the enslaved. Murdock's representation of slave investment in these affairs is hardly complex, as slaves simply ape their respective masters' views: Caesar "don't like" the French because his "massa no like 'em" and Pompey "dam[s]" the English because his "massa no like English."[31] But what about Sambo? How does he, as a "citizen," contribute to the discourses of American partisanship and international relations?

As if to avoid ambiguity, Murdock's play attends to these questions with striking clarity. To begin, Sambo refuses to favor the British or the French as the U.S.'s preferred partner in matters of diplomacy, trade, and war. Instead, he espouses American isolationism, a ready marker of personal virtue in the period that George Washington famously esteemed and encouraged in his 1796 "Farewell Address": "Europe has a set of primary interests, which to us have none, or a very remote relation," he argued.[32] But Sambo does not make such rhetorical or deliberative arguments to justify his isolationism; instead, he simply follows the lead of his former master: "I go we massa too. . . . Ah, for he country! massa say, dam French, dam English; he say, what e debil business have we do wi two bully nation? he say, let em fight and be dom'd."[33] Like his slave friends, Sambo does not rely on, or even seemingly possess, the democratic ideal of self-reliance. Thus, Sambo must remain captive, the play suggests, despite his freedom from chattel slavery. In fact, Murdock accentuates this resolution to the "problem" of free blackness by confining Sambo within the discursivity and spatiality of slavery: not only does he continue to call George "massa," but he also appears onstage with slaves only.

The value in turning to *The Triumphs of Love* and *The Politicians* to explore the concerns of free black life in 1790s Philadelphia rests on the fact that, as comedies, they produce a kind of historiographic effect. That is, the plays conform to what dramatic critic Alice Rayner theorizes as the ontology of comedy: plays that "function explicitly as social documents," "insist on being understood in the concrete and particular," and "present us with a socialized ethic."[34] Indeed, Sambo's plight within and across the plays evidences the ways African Americans in late 1790s Philadelphia did not live in a world very far removed from the one they endured while enslaved. Like other newly free black people across the north, black Philadelphians largely continued to work as domestics, often for their former masters with whom they sometimes continued to live, and in other unskilled jobs that

left them with little economic or social wherewithal to build fully autono-
mous lives. Even with the establishment of independent, black-led benevolent associations such as the Free African Society (FAS) in 1787 and religious institutions such as St. Thomas African Episcopal Church and Bethel
African Methodist Episcopal Church, both in 1794, the black condition was
"not so high that [African Americans] saw their interests as distinct from
those of the enslaved."[35] In the late 1790s and early 1800s, and especially in
cities like Philadelphia, free black life could look very much like slave life
because white northerners did not care to invest the energy and resources
necessary for its betterment. Their "overriding concern," writes historian
Gary B. Nash, "was to repair their war-torn society and secure a place for
themselves in the new republican order."[36] In fact, a great many of them
believed that the growing numbers of African Americans in the north hin-
dered both of these aims.[37] For observers like Murdock, the solution was a
new form of captive blackness for which his Sambo was its model "citizen."

However, the manner of "citizenship" Sambo represented repelled the
vast majority of African Americans, and they actively refused its limits.
Their demands for full inclusion heightened the urgency of Jefferson's
query: "Why not retain and incorporate the blacks into the state?" In the
dominant imagination, the ramifications of black retention and incorpora-
tion were worrying, if not frightful, because they ran counter to the economic, political, and social foundations upon which the ideology of American republicanism rested.[38] For this reason, the activism of ex-slaves and
their descendants induced an epistemological disturbance; they destabi-
lized and disrupted settled social knowledge. In their demand that Americans collectively re-conceptualize their relation to each other and, therefore, the nation itself, African Americans enacted what theorist Nahum
Chandler calls the "problem of the negro as a problem for thought."[39] That
is, their efforts necessitated re-imaginings of racial difference in/as social
life in the American polity.

Compounding the "problem" that early national African Americans
constituted for the broader public was their insistence that their labors and
their very nativity affirmed the nation as theirs. Ironically, the principal
strategy with which they cast their inclusionary strivings was racial solidarity. Philosopher of religion Eddie S. Glaude, Jr. explains that these solidaristic efforts and the "nation language" that emerged from them
"grounded common experiences and relationships in the effort to combat
American racism. No extra degree of particularity was required, for race
was merely an explanation that helped account for certain experiences in
order to respond more effectively to specific problems."[40] What early na-

tional African Americans inaugurated, then, was a tradition of black nationalism that forcefully asserts their rights to freedom, citizenship, and
social belonging.[41] They did so most generatively when they paraded in
commemoration of the abolition of the transatlantic slave trade, state emancipations, and the formation of black institutions.[42]

## FEELING THE (BLACK) NATION AND ITS TEXTUAL "PRESENCE"

The parade culture that African Americans crafted was not a simplistic
imitation of white Americans' parades. Instead, they drew on their African
and slave heritages, notably the festivals of Negro Election Day and Pinkster. From the mid-eighteenth to early nineteenth centuries, slaves in cities
and towns throughout New England annually elected "kings" or "gover-
nors" who wielded symbolic and, at times, material power over their black
counterparts. These elections were offshoots of whites' election celebrations, when, according to one late nineteenth-century account, slaves and
free people of color were "peculiarly alive to the effect of pomp and cere-
mony and not only made every effort to be present, but the imitative in-
stinct stirred them to elect a governor themselves."[43] Though Negro Election Day was derivative of several of the formalities of white elections, the
particulars of those doings "manifest African-derived style throughout, in
everything from structures of social organization to clothing practices," as
cultural historian Monica L. Miller argues.[44] The same is true of Pinkster,
which was contemporaneous with Negro Election Day but observed in
New York and New Jersey. Pinkster was originally a Dutch celebration of
Pentecost and the beginning of spring that slaves re-shaped to fit their particular psychological and social needs. (In his 1845 novel Satanstoe; or, The
Littlepage Manuscripts, James Fenimore Cooper described it as "the great
Saturnalia of the New York blacks."[45]) Both Pinkster and Negro Election
Day allowed slaves to dance, display fancy dress, and showcase oratorical
flair to the wider community; in all of these acts they merged African, European, and slave aesthetics. These processes of cross-cultural and interpersonal exchange mark the beginning formations of New World black
subjectivity, and the polyvalent sense of self that slaves fostered and performed in the festivals endowed them with expressive registers with which
to negotiate and, at times, withstand the harrowing and often alien world
of slavery.

But Negro Election Day and Pinkster were about just that: the world of
slavery. Masters and other white authorities sanctioned, subsidized, and

often participated in them. Thus, the festivals were carnivalesque, similar to those of southern plantations that Frederick Douglass characterized as "safety-valves" designed "to carry off the rebellious spirit of enslaved humanity."[46] Their immediate effect was to offer the slave something of a release from bondage, but ultimately they upheld the normative social order. So, while participants of Negro Election Day and Pinkster honed an aesthetic sensibility that influenced later affective, corporal, and sartorial forms of black expressivity and performance, the festivals themselves leveled little, if any, threat to the institution of slavery. If anything, they strengthened it.

Ex-slaves and their descendants knew this. As free people, they appropriated the aesthetic and performative habits of Negro Election Day and Pinkster but had little use for the festivals themselves; instead, as historian Shane White notes, they "expend[ed] their considerable energies elsewhere."[47] That elsewhere was in the formation of independent religious orders and secular institutions such as literary societies, mutual relief funds, and voluntary associations; it was also in the creation of a parade performance culture that united black communities across the north.[48] As concerted products and producers of black freedom, the parades constituted what Saidiya Hartman might call an "oppositional culture," a mutually constitutive set of affects, texts, and practices "poised to destroy [the] designs of mastery."[49] Oppositional cultures are intentional, strategic, and teleological; they project, and strive toward, heretofore non-normative futures. Although African Americans usually commemorated past actions in their parades, they always anticipated a future of universal emancipation and full black inclusion.

In their announcement of their parade to the public of Salem, Massachusetts, for example, the Sons of the African Society encapsulated the inclusionary aims that animated the culture of black parading in the period. Like other early national and antebellum African Americans who banded together to establish similar voluntary associations, the Sons of the African Society "formed [themselves] into a society for the mutual benefit of each other, behaving all times as true and faithful citizens of the Commonwealth in which [they] live, and that [accepted] no one into the Society who shall commit any injustice or outrage against the laws of their country."[50] When this group of thirty "well dressed" black men decided to parade in commemoration of the first anniversary of their association, they hoped their parade would make explicit its members' shared commitment to the U.S.[51]

If the Sons of the African Society's paraded affirmations of American nationalism did not immediately signify among the Salem public, the spectacle of it certainly struck the editors of the city's primary newspaper, the *Salem Gazette*. They called it "a novel exhibition," and its short review described the form and sequence of events:

> A number of Africans . . . paraded in procession through the street to Washington Hall, where a discourse was delivered to them by the Rev. Mr. Webb, of Lynn, and a contribution was made for their benefit. They afterwards returned in the same manner from the Hall to the Treasurer's house, where they dined. They were about 30 in number, were well dressed, wore the insignia of their brotherhood, and were accompanied with instrumental music. We are informed that their characters are respectable.[52]

This account outlines the standard structure of black parades in the first decades of the nineteenth century: processional ranks to and from the primary meeting place, orations, communal meals, sartorial accouterment, and musical accompaniment. Although they often celebrated different historical events or institutional milestones, the parades usually took this shape. With this reproduction of form, the parades functioned as rituals of continuity and rejuvenation that merged the resources of the past and the concerns of the present in order to cast a future of democratic possibility. In an 1865 remembrance of the parades, radical abolitionist and physician James McCune Smith described their regenerative function: "The colored people of New York [and elsewhere in the north], from an early date, carried themselves with a free air which showed that they felt themselves free, and on more than one occasion alarmed their best [white] friends with their bold action [i.e., parading]. . . . Secure in their manhood and will, they did parade, in large number . . . easily thrusting aside by their own force the small impediments which blocked their way."[53] Thus in their displays of black freedom, the parades simultaneously reinvigorated it, because freedom, like its denial, is performative: it does not rest on the page but must be embodied into actuality.

The spectacle of self-organized, civic-minded collectives of African Americans in northern cities and towns enacting their freedom by means of the nation's most meaningful symbolic frames markedly, and perhaps unavoidably, disturbed white onlookers. Unlike Negro Election Day or Pinkster, the parades were explicitly interventionist and political. This is why, as McCune Smith recalled, those black New Yorkers' "white friends" discouraged them from taking to the streets: black parades could not be deemed innocent or, like the slave festivals were, temporary loosenings of normative restraints with which subjects enter a new social order only to return to the older, often strengthened order. Instead, early national black parades became the "framework for the development of black politics," as White argues, and the politics that emerged most forcefully out of that framework were black nationalist.[54]

Black nationalism in the early national period was not a strategy with which to invert the prevailing racial hierarchy and to position black over white. Rather, it was a mode of action that, in its broadenings of the meanings and possibilities of American democracy, sought to alleviate the particular problems and sufferings that beset slaves, former slaves, and their descendants in the U.S. Henry Sipkins' 1809 "Oration on the Abolition of Slave Trade," for example, demonstrates how the rhetoric and practice of this form of black nationalism simultaneously affirmed the particulars of black experiences in the American polity *and* African Americans' deep attachment to the U.S. Sipkins was only twenty years old when he delivered the oration, but as the son of Thomas Sipkins, one of the founders of the African Methodist Episcopal Zion Church (AMEZ) in New York City in 1796, he belonged to a leading family in the black and abolitionist communities. In the "Oration," he used the phrases "my African brethren," "my beloved Africans," and "descendants of Africans"—just as Henry Johnson in his "Introductory Address" to Sipkins' speech employed "us Africans and descendants of Africans"—to distinguish black subjectivity from all others. Furthermore, he delivered the "Oration" at the "African Church in the City of New York" (i.e., AMEZ Church) and identified himself as "Henry Sipkins, a descendant of Africa" when he published the text in pamphlet form later that year.[55] Despite his avowals of black particularity, however, Sipkins argued that white effort was essential to the betterment of African Americans. In his laudation of whites' "philanthropic exertions" that led to the abolition of the transatlantic slave trade, he proclaimed: "To these [white men and women] we owe our preservation from a second bondage; and on these depend the prospect of future felicity. Their ever-memorable acts were such as the paternal hand rearing its tender offspring to mature years, and planning for its edifice of virtue and happiness."[56] Embracing the racially hierarchical paternalism that eventually prompted African Americans in the late 1820s to begin to separate themselves from white patronage, Sipkins imagines a world of democratic inclusion within which African Americans live peaceably and equitably alongside their white counterparts, a world in which *"slavery of every species* shall be destroyed."[57] The "species" of slavery that Sipkins condemned were not only the various manifestations of chattel slavery throughout the U.S., but also the very forms of political and social captivity that he and other African Americans endured in the free north.

The first iterations of black nationalism were not only thoroughly American in their ends but also in their means.[58] Its architects fused the singularity of black American experiences with normative figurations of national myths and ideals. In his 1808 oration at one of the first public celebrations of the end of the transatlantic slave trade, which took effect on January 1 of that year, abolitionist Peter Williams, Jr. modeled this approach:

> [At] that illustrious moment, when the sons of '76 pronounced these United States free and independent; when the spirit of patriotism, erected a temple sacred to liberty; when the inspired voice of Americans first uttered those noble sentiments [of the Declaration of Independence]; and when the bleeding African, lifting his fetters, exclaimed, "am I not a man and a brother;" then with redoubled efforts, the angel of humanity strove to restore to the African race the inherent rights of man.[59]

This reading tied the destiny of the "African race" to the progress of American history. For Williams and contemporaneous African Americans generally, black nationalism was a particular expression of American nationalism. That is to say, while the chief aim of black civic protest was citizenship and social inclusion, its architects understood the necessity of distinct political strategies because their race suffered from distinct forms of discrimination, exclusion, and violence. Glaude argues that a "moral obligation of we-intentions" animated these strategies, that is, "a sense of being one of us, the force of which is essentially contrastive in that it contrasts with a 'they' that is made up of violent white human beings."[60] While contrastive, early national African Americans' (moral) language of "us" against "them" did not reflect a desire for the permanency of these categories; that is, they sought to achieve an American "us," a new sociality free of race-based division and violence. Indeed, the realization of such a world was their overriding "we-intention."

Orations such as Sipkins' and Williams' as well as the wider parades were critical in this regard because they were what first allowed African Americans across the north to conceptualize and articulate their intentions as shared, as those of a "nation." Nationhood coheres around the terms of membership and identification, a set of criteria with which to determine who belongs and who does not. This imaginative bond of oneness, which "manifests" in performances such as parades or orations, upholds a nation's existence; it demands that its members accept particular discourses and mythologies, and that they do so *at once* across differences of place and space. In his foundational theorization of nation formation, Benedict Anderson emphasizes this notion of "simultaneity," which is "transverse, cross-time, marked not by prefiguring and fulfillment, but by temporal coincidence, and measured by clock and calendar."[61] Nation temporalities require its subjects make (national) meaning out of their shared embeddedness in a world that "ambles sturdily ahead."[62] Anderson argues that "the development of print-as-commodity [was] the key to the generation of wholly new ideas of simultaneity" and thus to the nation.[63] Yet his stress on print-capitalism is too limiting insofar as it does not account for the nontextual means with which simultaneities and nations are enacted. Slavoj Žižek helpfully explains the insufficiency of "symbolic identification" (i.e., print culture) alone to these formations: "To emphasize in a 'deconstructionist' mode that Nation is not a biological or transhistorical fact but a contingent discursive construction, an overdetermined result of textual practices, is thus misleading: such an emphasis overlooks the remainder of some *real*, nondiscursive kernel of enjoyment which must be present for the Nation qua discursive entity-effect to achieve its ontological consistency."[64] Žižek's turn to the affective and the aesthetic, what he calls the "*real*, nondiscursive kernel of enjoyment," takes into account the ways a nation is felt into being, how we corporeally "know" its reality. Thus, a nation emerges as the result of interdependent textual *and* performative affects.

When African Americans in and near New York City, Boston, Philadelphia, and other northern locales joined to parade in the early nineteenth century, they knew their (black nation within a) nation existed because they felt its actuality. It was with and through the parades that African and African-descended people (re-)united and (re-)committed themselves to the betterment of their own people and, by extension, the U.S. In fact, the parades functioned as rituals do, in that they aestheticized, formalized, and sustained structures of (national) feeling among their participants. As Žižek writes, "A nation *exists* only as long as its specific *enjoyment* continues to be materialized in a set of social practices and transmitted through national myths that structure these practices."[65] As a political affect, the "enjoyment" the parades offered black paraders and spectators was the assurance that they were *simultaneously* engaged in the struggle to abolish slavery and achieve equal participation in the polity.

The parades' structural similarities, which I outlined above, reinforced this feeling of affective and political simultaneity among geographically and even historically dispersed participants. Yet for my purposes, the texts of the orations archive their shared affects and aims most clearly. The orations were the climax of the parades, and they focused all attention on one sight, the speaker, who was nearly always a prominent member of the community. As cultural historian Geneviève Fabre notes, orators stressed that they and their black audiences were American above all, and, in notable respects, they were the nation's chosen people: "They tried to evaluate the contribution of black people in the building of the nation, to assess the progress of the race and its capacity for self-government, and to develop race pride as well as race memory. More significantly, the speakers were setting themselves in the place of the Founding Fathers, as those who could take the dream of liberty one step further and perhaps bring it to completion."[66] Orators couched these themes in diverse idioms, ranging from the theological to the sociological, and the political to the historical. For example, Episcopal minister and leading Philadelphian Absalom Jones analogized the end of the international slave trade to the deliverance of the Israelites in the Book of Exodus; Federalist Joseph Sidney of New York City used his oration to juxtapose what he recognized as the depravity of southern society with the enlightenment of New England; Sidney also exhorted black men who could vote to do so for Federalists rather than Democrats, whom he labeled "the enemy of our rights"; New York abolitionist and eventual board member of the American Anti-Slavery Society Peter Williams, Jr. traced slavery and black misery to European imperialism and material excess, what he called "the desire of gain."[67] This multiplicity of rhetorical modes indexes the expansiveness of early black political discourse as well as the ways in which African Americans contributed to the dynamism of what one antebellum chronicler of rhetoric termed "the golden age of American oratory."[68]

In her study of colonial and early national oratory, *Eloquence Is Power*, cultural historian Sandra Gustafson traces how women and Native Americans reshaped dominant forms and tropes of American political speech in order to foster equitable roles in the new nation's political and social orders. In their attempts to "remake forms of eloquence," Gustafson writes, these "figures of difference" were "met with real but sharply limited success in the public domains of the early republic."[69] This description, I argue, is equally apt for black orators at the time, who, as part of their parade culture, forged a tradition of politicized oral performance that achieved "real but sharply limited success": a language of black nationalism, on the one hand, but also a deepening of white antagonism that animated a counter-tradition of deriding black (political) speech, on the other.[70] In their efforts to remake American eloquence in their image and in the terms of their experiences, black orators, like women and Native Americans, sought to speak their race into the general body politic as equal contributors and beneficiaries. This strategy was extremely shrewd because, in the dominant imagination, one's worthiness for citizenship and indeed for freedom itself derived in large measure from his facility as a speaking subject. These cultural politics were what propelled African Americans to spotlight the orations at the parades; that is, they hoped to countervail the ways white publics used the racialized postulations animating the Anglo-American "oratorical revolution" (i.e., blacks lack "reason" and "sentiment," to use Jefferson's terms) to "define the distinctiveness of Americans, a distinctiveness that excluded African-Americans from that definition."[71] With their orations, African Americans sought to affirm the fact that the African (American) did hold what literary historian Jay Fliegelman describes as the "particular cultural code whose audibility signified the possession of a sensibility . . . of being an American, the principle of national differentiation."[72] No wonder, then, black orators greeted their audiences as "fellow citizens." Far more than a rhetorical flourish, this appellation was a performative speech act that engendered the very (affect of) American subjectivity that it expressed.

The hailing of ex-slaves and their descendants as "citizens" was only the initiating gesture in the orations' rebuke of assumptions of black oratorical deficiency. In their performances of critical memory, historical reasoning, and political theorization, orators invalidated the broader proslavery notion that the African (American) is incapable of literary or rhetorical genius and therefore his race is unfit for full inclusion in a free polity such as the American republic. Jefferson offered the most lasting formulation of this theory in his *Notes on the State of Virginia*, when he compared Native Americans to Africans and African-descended people: "The Indians, with no advantages of [the company and tutelage of whites], will often carve figures on their pipes not destitute of design and merit. They will crayon out an animal, a plant, or a country, so as to prove the existence of a germ in their minds which only wants cultivation. They astonish you with strokes of the most sublime oratory; such as prove their reason and sentiment strong, their imagination glowing and elevated. *But never yet could I find that a black had uttered a thought above the level of plain narration.*"[73] Of course, the oratorical praxis on display at the parades was well above the "level of plain narration." For example, in his January 1, 1808 "Thanksgiving Sermon . . . On Account of the Abolition of the African Slave Trade, On That Day, By The Congress Of The United States," Episcopal priest Absalom Jones brilliantly analogized the plight of black people in the U.S. to that of Hebrews in the biblical story of Exodus. With the end of the transatlantic slave trade as his most immediate "proof," Jones assured his Philadelphia audience that God was on the side of the oppressed and would deliver black people from captivity:

> The history of the world shows us that the deliverance of the children of Israel from their bondage is not the only instance in which it has pleased God to appear in behalf of oppressed and distressed nations, as the deliverer of the innocent, and of those who call upon his name. He is as unchangeable in his nature and character as he is in in his wisdom and power. The great and blessed event, which we have this day met to celebrate, is a striking proof that the God of heaven and earth is *the same, yesterday, and today, and forever.*[74]

Jones' stirring sermon fused the theological and politico-historical, a move in which, as Glaude puts it, "Africa is reread; the middle passage and slavery are reread; America is reread; and aspirations for freedom and citizenship are formulated as divinely sanctioned ends."[75] Indeed, the sermon, like all the speeches performed at other parades and freedom celebrations, dismissed Jefferson's proslavery logic in both its form and content, and those black "citizens" present helped bear those dismissals in and through their very bodies.

Organizers of the parades did not want the orations to affect only those in attendance, however. They sought to give the speeches a textual afterlife, so they published transcripts along with proceedings of the parades. (Jones, for example, published his sermon "for the use of the congregation."[76]) Historian Richard Newman argues that these textual forms of early national black protest "created a bridge to white leaders and citizens," but they were also a "bridge" among African Americans themselves, fortifying their sense of simultaneity.[77] They circulated transcripts and proceedings in their homes and in the social spaces of their voluntary and mutual relief societies, whose rolls were economically, politically, and religiously diverse.[78] Unlike newspapers and other textual matter that exacerbated personal and regional tensions among white Americans in the period, black print culture helped allay differences among black readers and listeners because it allowed them to recognize just how similar their experiences and concerns were.[79] With these small, yet crucial networks of print circulation, early national African Americans used textual formations to complement their performance practices of (black) nation-building.[80]

Although a discussion of the dynamics of this textual enterprise is beyond the scope of this chapter, it is important to note that, in their circulation of oration transcripts and parade proceedings, *ordinary* African Americans participated in the American Republic of Letters, the explosion of classically informed writing and print practices in the late eighteenth and early nineteenth centuries.[81] Theoretically, the Republic of Letters was a depersonalized, discursive public sphere built on an ideal of self-negation. As Michael Warner explains, "Persons who enter this discourse do so on the condition that the validity of their utterance will bear a negative relation to their persons. These perspectives are not to be separated: the impersonality of public discourse is seen both as a trait of its medium and as norm for its subjects."[82] Despite its seeming anonymities, the Republic of Letters was, effectively, racialized as white because, according to its dictates, one had to possess education, property, and a "modern" sensibility to participate fully—the very markers associated with whiteness. But if African Americans could distinguish themselves as reading and writing subjects in the Republic of Letters, they surmised, then they would have proved their fundamental *nature* was the same as that of white Americans or Europeans.[83]

Black orators were wary, however, that a Jeffersonian-minded skeptic would read their texts and assume a white man wrote them. When Peter Williams, Jr. published the text of his 1808 oration, for example, he had four influential white men attest to the authenticity of his authorship. As he put it, "Having understood that some persons doubt my being the author of this oration, and thinking it probable that a like sentiment may be entertained by others who may honour this publication with a perusal, I have thought it proper to authenticate the fact, by subjoining the following certificates."[84] With its paratextual apparatus, Williams' published speech instantiated the practice of white verification of black authorship, a literary convention in the period that ranged from at least Phillis Wheatley's 1773 book of poetry, *Poems of Various Subjects, Religious and Moral*, to antebellum slave narratives, which were often subtitled "Written By Himself."[85] With their respective certifications, Williams and other black writers sought to nullify doubts regarding their authorial and intellectual abilities—and therefore those of their race.

The four certifications Williams adjoined did more than identify him as the sole author; they also attested to his facility as a speaking subject, one capable of eloquence or "sublime oratory," to use Jefferson's phrase, by standing in place of his past/passed presence as a kind of ongoing presence. That is, each certification functioned as a signature might, which attempts to countervail the spatial and temporal realities of the signer's absence. As Derrida writes, "By definition, a written signature implies the actual or empirical nonpresence of the signer. But, it will be claimed, the signature also marks and retains his having-been present in a past *now* or present which will remain a future *now* or present."[86] In other words, signatures do more than alert us to one's former presence; more crucially, they work to *maintain* that presence as the graphic or textual trace of who is absent. Signatures are fundamentally performative in this sense in that they enact a kind of presence in the place of seeming absence. As such, the certifications Williams affixed when he published his address, including Williams' own, worked to (re)stage something of his presence, if not his performance, for future readers.

The texts of the orations and the wider proceedings also helped (re)enact the parade presence of their readers, including for those who did not attend. Reading these printed materials (out loud) worked to pull readers into the fold of the action, allowing them to take part imaginatively in the event and count themselves among the participants. At the end of abolitionist Joseph Sidney's published oration from an 1809 parade in New York City, for example, his publishers included the details of the parade: what associations participated, sartorial accouterments, the formation of the participants, and their route. They closed the text with the following *nota bene*: "The committee, after service, shortened their route on account of the numerous spectators, and dismissed at the place of rendezvous, with the greatest acclamations of joy."[87] Given the novelty of the event, and indeed of black freedom itself, the seemingly plain language of the text could do more than represent a past/passed action; at the very least, it might reproduce something of the affective bond of the parades. Thus, the contingently performative nature of the parade texts had the potential to transform their (black) readers and auditors into bearers of the event and its social and political force. Following Eve Kosofsky Sedgwick, we might think of this "reading posture" as a "sustained and intense engagement" that "simply *is* theatrical, trances themselves entrancing."[88] The texts that African Americans and their patrons published were attempts to do just that: namely, to *entrance* readers into the world of the parade performances.

In this way, the oration transcripts and parade descriptions were more than accounts of what happened; when read, they functioned as (intended) continuations of something of the happening itself. That is, the texts did not simply "save" or even "record" the parades; rather, they were the (affective) remains with which to extend the parades into future actualities. Embedded in each of the texts was a performative force, a script perhaps, that impelled its reading publics to *do* something. This force redoubled as the effect of the period's lack of aesthetic distance, if not distinction, between reading and listening. In other words, the written text as *read* became a text as *performed*, which is to say that the modes of writing and reading that structured early black literary aesthetics were fundamentally modes of action and transformation.

## THE "SENSES" OF BOBALITION

There is little evidence of what, if anything, the printed oration transcripts and parade proceedings compelled African Americans' detractors to do. But the parades themselves moved them to react, so they created their own textual responses that ridiculed black parades and its participants. The most important of these was the "Bobalition" series of broadsides that circulated throughout the north from the mid-1810s to the 1830s. The series drew on caricaturizations and satirizations of slaves and African Americans in late eighteenth-century newspapers and almanac literature, but differs in that it directly confronts black political culture. Indeed, the acute specificities of the broadsides attest to the potency of black nationalism in the first decades of the nineteenth century; that is, white publics could not ignore the re-imaginings of the nation that African Americans literally paraded on the streets.

The publication of Bobalition began in Boston following the War of 1812, when African Americans, like other constituencies, embraced the heightened nationalist fervor that swept the U.S.[89] Those printed in and near Boston quickly became the prototype. On the top third is an illustration of parade participants dressed in either militia regalia or their best formal wear, and a caption underneath that announces the occasion. The bottom two-thirds is usually divided into three columns: the first spells out the rules and route of the procession, and it is most often in the form of a letter from the president or secretary of a voluntary association to a participant in the parade; beginning somewhere in the second column is a series of historical and political toasts the paraders will raise; and in the third column are lyrics to a song, normally dedicated to a black woman, that will follow the toasts. This outline of the broadsides is admittedly rough, and there are exceptions such as an 1825 broadside that is divided into two columns rather than three.[90] Nonetheless, it gives a sense of the broadsides' shared form and, importantly, how its reproduction over time functioned similarly to the shared structure of the parades: both fostered a sense of simultaneity among its respective publics.

Consider, for example, the 1821 *Grand Bobalition, or 'Great Annibersary Fussible.'* It depicts twelve men, facing right and marching down a cobblestone road in two-by-two formation. The two men leading the procession clutch staffs, four more carry lances, and another hoists a flag. Each wears identical militia livery and regalia, featuring a braided tailcoat and prominent bicorn with plume. Their matching uniforms, though nondescript, denote they belong to the same voluntary or mutual relief association. Under the image, a caption reads: "ORDER OF DE DAY—Containing de CONSTRUCTIONS to de SHEEF MARSAL, de TOSE which will be gib on de GLORIOUS OCCASHUM, and ODER TINGS too many, great deal, to TICKLEISE. N.B All dis be rite not by de fist of de PRESIDUMPT, and gib to de Printer to be superdanglify in English."[91] Along with that of the title, the caption's orthographic excess renders the image absurd; despite the marchers' discipline and attention to detail, the parade is essentially a divertissement. The whole of the broadside, like that of others in the series, produces its own kind of presence that stands in for past/passed performances at the parades. In this case, that presence is a crude and vacuous blackness, which, in the dominant imagination, signified African Americans were unsuited for citizenship, if not for freedom itself.

The ideological force that Bobalition wielded was considerable, and it rested on the centrality of print-performance culture in the period.[92] As "print amplified the range of an oration," reasoned and sensible speech amplified legitimate citizenship.[93] Bobalition was not simply racist humor, then, but an attack on black verbal and literary expression that undermined African Americans' inclusionary demands. To be sure, the broadsides' "notations" of black speech were not wholly new; they derived in part from slave diction standardized in colonial and early national theatre cultures.[94] But these theatrical representations lacked the emphatically oppositional charge that animated Bobalition. In *Grand Bobalition, or 'Great Annibersary Fussible,'* for example, a letter to the appointed "Sheef Marsal," Cato Cudjoe, from the "Shocietee" President, Cesar Crappo, gives instructions on the formation, music, and order of the procession. Written in derisive and often nonsensical dialect, the letter features a header, "Bosson, Uly 14, 18021," a greeting, "Most superfluous Sir," and a "bosecrip" (i.e., postscript) that frame the letter; its transitions become "moreober" and "furder"; and it references "Massa Shakespole." Such representations of black writing and speech dismiss black intellect, functioning much the same way as black skin color did: as a sign of those who must remain politically and socially subordinate in the American polity.

The purported absurdity of black citizenship and patriotism that Bo-

# Grand Bobalition, or
## 'GREAT ANNIBERSARY FUSSIBLE.'

ORDER OF DE DAY—*Containing de CONSTRUCTIONS to de SHEEF MARSAL, de TOSE which will be gib on de* GLORIOUS OCCASHUM, *and ODER TINGS too many. great deal, to TICKLEISE.* N.B. *All dis be rite not by de fist of de PRESIDUMPT, and gib to de Printer to be superdaugtify into* English!

BOSSON, ULY 14, 18021.

TO CATO CUDJOE.

*Most superfluous Sir,*

IT hab once more become my duty to inform you dat dis be fourteenth day of de mont, spose you hab no slumsnack to find out de time of day by yourself. De recollecshums which be derivated mid dis day will neber be forgot so long as folks choose to member um. Dis be true as dat six and four be night, and he take jus two more to make out de dozen. But dis be not what I go to say. You muss know, dat dis day being de last of de week, de shocietee hab exoluded to postpone de celebrashum till nex Monday; as de various duty which convolve on de members to prepare for Sunday at home, make him no possible to hab time to sellybrate him in de most extrabonical and genman-like style. Derefore, you will take tickelar notice, and gubbern yourself discordiouly, as de lawyer say.

De Shochietee habin done you de mose gratest and big honor by pointing you as sheef Marshal for de day, it is wid pleasure dat I excommunicate to you deir destructions, by which you are to regulate de order of proceshum, and see dat dey all be carry into defect.

In de fuss place you hab full liberty to point your debilty Marshal—and tell um, if dey no mind what you say to um, dat dey may expeck de dignation of de whole body of dis honorable shochietee will tumble on he head, and like enough break he cocoa not fore he know what hurt you.

In de nex place, you muss be bery careful to point none to be Debility Marshal, sept de mose speckable character; such for sample as myself, and great many more, mose as good as I be;—less you bring disgrace upon de glorious cause of de Bobalition.

*Furder*—As you member lass year some little sturbance happen bout de Moose, it be proper to deform you, and trough you, de whole nation of Africa and he scandants, now libing in Bosson, dat we hab make derangement to prebent all sort of combombification on dat account.

*Moreober*—Let him be splicitly understand, dat de proceshum will mobe forward jus at de time which de committee of derangement say he shall, and not keep de people standing on Misser Expectation's tiptoes, as Massa Shakespeare say.

*Likewise*—You must destruct all in authority under your demand to deserve de, greatess punctuality, dat de forecoming order be carry into defeck, else you make me tell lie, and you swear to him youself. De time appointed hab been published in de paper, so if you hab no watch, you can tell dat how much soon you muss be on your pose, to tend to de various and portant duties of de occashum.

*Also*—I muss tell you, less. you forget all about um, dat de Shocietee hab full shurauce dat you will you mind ebery word I say, else dey no gib me de power to tell you do as I like.

Now name what I go to tell you—When de procesbum be all ready to march, you muss tep forrowd and go before, else dey none of um know whedder dey can follow after or no. When dey get fairly going, den you may make one of de Debility Marshal take you place, while you go one, side and tuddar, to seep all keep tune to de moosic; len if any need get out, you go right one follow on as soon as you can. If any outset order, and he no get in agin, when you tell um, you hab de authority of de shochietee for let him rap on de head. But you muss on no count take him on de shin, else you make he nose bleed, and so stain he ruffle shirt and he nice white trowsaloon. But from de well known lub of order and good principle which hab always been de character of de members of de Shocietee, I tink you will hab no need to exhort to such displeasant method of discumption. Dis part of you destructions, derefore, muss be examcise at skreshum.

When de posesbum shall arribe at de meetun-house, de orashum will be deliber of course; and as ebery one can den take care of heself, if you like you may go take a glass of wine by way of defreshment, and smoke a segar to wash him down. But mind and be back as soon as he ober, so as to scort de officers of de Shocietee, and your brudder Marshal to de dinner table, else he no look very dignify to see um going alone.

Some furder destruction specting your duty in de hall, I shall gib you in private. In de mean time, I hab de honor to be, Sir,

Your mose expedient,

Berry humble servant,

**CESAR CRAPPO,** *President.*

Misser Cato Cudjoe, Sheef Marshal.

## BOSECRIP.

Inclose, I send you de regular tose, wid de moosic to go long wid um, and good many Boluntear, which my friends say dey calculate to detain de company wid arter dinner. If you wish to gib a Boluntear yourself, mind and say someting to de purpose, and not beat about de bosh, and no catch the woodchuck arter all.

C. C.

## TOASTS.

De day we sellybrate—De be get here fuss Saturday, he jbs as good as any time. May he nebor forget to come once a year. *144 cheer, bery loud.*

De heart of Uly—No better day dan dis, spose he come tree monts ago. *1 laugh, 3 grin.*

Africa—De land of our fadders and mudders, and granfadders too; hope he soon find out we forget um in de country. *500 cheer, moosic, Our natile home.*

De Nited Tate of Merika—May he big Eagle fill all de hawk wise would bad he young chicken for he supper. *715 cheer, Moosic—Who come dare?*

Massachusetts—He de tate dat make dis country up gib American Liberty—Fifty more of um dont follow he xample. *50 cheer, Moosic—Hail de day.*

De Presidunt of de Nited Tate—Spose he dont dis way agin, we make Bobalition No. 2.

65 cheer and half—Moosic, President Marsh.

De Miilitia—He hab mudder selity uhbm nex fall, two years ago—spose some of um sell he uniform fore da time. *50 cheer, 2 grin—Moosic, De Soldier tir'd.*

De town of Bosson—Full of notion to clear—hope he keep de ule stock good, and not get so many new one he find out what to do wid um. *3 laugh and two thirds.*

De Primary School—Don't care how much he prime um, if he no snap und go off. *200 cheer—Moosic, When I was a little boy.*

De African School—De hope of Africa, and de glory of West Bosson. *300 cheer and hal, Moosic, Light in the East.*

De Chimical Shool—Don't understand um; hope he find out heself and tell ebery body else. *6 cheer and half, 3 grin and quarter.*

De Great Mill Dam—Some call him YOUNG; wonder if Cambridge Bridge de fore finger to um. *6 ober huck—Moosic, What you mean?*

De Fishs at de Boat End—All de clam lay flat as he buck wid his mouth open. *13 grin—Moosic, How come you so.*

Fort Independence—Guess dey felt independent nuf dare fourth of July. *20 cheer, 3 grin and half.*

Nantucket—Wonder if he mean to supply Bosson wid oil all nex winter. *10 cheer, 150 guesses.*

Uncle Sam—Spose he mean de Nited Tate—Dont see what dey call um Uncle for. *7 grin, all still.*

De Tate of Maine—He hoe he King—hope he WiN agate. *40 cheer, 100 laugs—Moosic, Possum up a gum tree.*

De African Fair Seck—De sparkling eye, de ibory teeth, and de crimson brush on de cheek of modesty, inspire de breast wid de mose hontitul destoration. *500 cheer, 90 sly grin, Moosic, Cupid among the roses.*

After dis toast, de following song, write specialy for de occashum, will be sung in honor of de fair sex, will be sung by any lady who stand by sing him, to jusenhat tune he like.

### SONG.

1 WHEN Phillis from de garden came,
I feel my bosom all in flame;
Wid my warm passion I perspire,
And beg dat she put out de fire.

2 De cruel maid to hear my prayer,
Den I get mad and almose swear,
Dat as she so destroy my hope,
I go and tie me up and rope.

3 Cluh! Phillis cried—why what a fool;
Cause I no like you, dat no rule
Dat you should take away your life,
And nebber, neber hab a wife.

4 So Phillis den I bid good bye,
And so I make anudder try;
De lubly Dinah kinder gnaws,
And sweetly all my juices more.

5 Phillis begin now to repent,
And bery soon for me she went:
O Pompcy, now forgiv what's past,
And my fond lub shall eber last.

6 No, no, Miss Phillis, den I say—
You recolleck, dat tudder day,
When faithful lub to you I swore,
Why you jam turn me out of door.

7 Such action so my temper suit:
And may I nebber clean a boot,
If I de lubly Dinah leave,
And you into my arms receive.

8 Den Phillis cry and faint awny,
But as I hear, on de nex day,
Radder dan he left in de lurch,
Wid Cesar she marsh'd off to church.

## BOLUNTEARS.

De Sea Serpent—Goten herring so no plenty dis way as dey use to be—Wonder if he gone up Taunton river. *40 cheer, 44 horse laugh.*

Misser Kean de Play actor Mun—How he sell tuken now—Guess he feel radder "astute." *50 grin, 4 grons, 900 Sier.*

De present time—Some say he hard time—but he better dan no time at all. *20 cheer and quarter.*

De King and Queen of England—Why dey so keep dele quarrel to themselves, and no sturb the whole neighbor. *600 cheer.*

Dis Shocietee—He stand like de light-house to show de African do way into snug-harbor—hope he light nober go out for want of oil. *[De last tose ought to given by de President—and after he be drunk, every one will take he hat and clear out de quietest-D muxer.]*

Figure 1: *Grand Bobalition, or 'Great Annibersary Fussible'* (1821). Library of Congress, LC-USZ62–40690.

balition's distorted renderings of black speech enacted was part and parcel of the broadsides' most fundamental claim: namely, black people lack full humanity. Although discourses of racial inherence did not take hold of the collective American imagination until after the 1830s, there were important meditations on the so-called nature of race in the late eighteenth and early nineteenth centuries.[95] These inquiries were often comparative, querying the existence of a common humanity between races. In *Notes on the State of Virginia*, for instance, Thomas Jefferson speculated on the "physical" differences between white and black; he considered questions of color, affect, figure, hair, renal function, pulmonary structure, and the brain.[96] Jefferson and his contemporaries' quasi-scientific approach to the study of race and racial difference culminated in the influential antebellum field of ethnology. Ethnologists worked within and across a range of disciplines in the natural sciences, including craniology, Egyptology, physiology, trichology (the study of hair), and zoology; they concluded that the races of mankind, as they would put it, were affectively, corporeally, and intellectually dissimilar in their very makeups.[97] (Darwin invalidated ethnology in the late 1850s.) The (pseudo-) scientific and quantitative approaches constitutive of ethnology and its anthropological antecedents do not figure in Bobalition, but the broadsides do contribute to the same intellectual genealogy: a tradition of thought that posits the African (American) is somehow lacking in his humanity and therefore must remain captive in a free society. Bobalition advances this claim, however obliquely, in its representations of black speech because the period's prevailing discourses posited that deficiencies in the faculty of speech signaled probable deficiencies in one's very humanity. Of course, the elocutionary and rhetorical shortcomings in Bobalition are intended to signify the human shortcomings of all black people, not just those of individual parade participants.

When producers first began to publish Bobalition in the mid-1810s, the U.S. was still an oral culture; thus, the immediacy of speech remained central to the ways Americans conceptualized forms of personal and collective subjectivity. The ongoing influence of eighteenth-century religious expression, most notably within evangelical Protestantism, accounted in large part for the continued emphasis on orality in the early nineteenth century (hence, the Second Great Awakening). But it was the collective of secular discourses, the so-called American Enlightenment, that most informed the socio-racial logics that structure Bobalition. Speech, these discourses held, is the medium of reason, and reason is what separates humans from all other beings in the natural world. John Quincy Adams, for example, emphasized this view throughout his theories of oratory and rhetoric, and he began with it in the "Inaugural Oration" to his influential *Lectures on Rheto-ric and Oratory* (1810):

> The peculiar and highest characteristic, which distinguishes man from the rest of the animal creation, is REASON. It is by this attri-bute, that our species is constituted the great link between the phys-ical and intellectual world. . . . It is by the gift of reason, that the hu-man species enjoys the exclusive and inestimable privilege of progressive improvement, and is enabled to avail itself of the advan-tages of individual discovery. As the necessary adjunct and vehicle of reason, the faculty of speech was also bestowed as an exclusive privilege upon man; not the mere cries of passion, which he has in common with the lower orders of animated nature; but as the con-veyance of thought; as the means of rational intercourse with his fellow-creature, and of humble communion with his God. It is by the means of reason, clothed with speech, that the most precious bless-ings of social life are communicated from man to man, and that sup-plication, thanksgiving, and praise, are addressed to the Author of the universe.[98]

As the "exclusive privilege[s]" of man, then, reason and speech become the qualitative markers of one's humanity; more specifically, defects in speech signify defects in reason, and the inability to reason fully marks those who are not fully human. This line of reasoning is the guiding premise of Bobali-tion, and its constitutive distortions of black speech, even if invented, sug-gest that black people are and will remain less human than their white counterparts because speech itself, Adams maintained, is "the source of all human improvements."[99]

In accounting for the ideological effects at work in Bobalition, Adams' theorization of the interrelation of reason, speech, and the human is also useful in terms of its implications regarding slavery and freedom in the U.S. Although neither volume of his *Lectures on Rhetoric and Oratory* di-rectly addresses the institution of American chattel slavery, Adams cham-pions the importance of rhetoric to the story of Exodus in the Bible. He writes, "When the people of God were groaning under the insupportable oppression of Egyptian bondage, and the Lord of Hosts condescended, by miraculous interposition, to raise them up a deliverer, the want of ELO-QUENCE was pleaded. . . . To supply this deficiency . . . another favored servant of the Most High was united in the exalted trust of deliverance [i.e., Aaron], and specifically appointed, for the purpose of declaring the divine will to the oppressor and the oppressed; to the monarch of Egypt and the children of Israel."[100] In Adams' exegesis, the deliverance of Hebrews from slavery in Egypt required both the spiritual authority of Moses *and* the rhetorical eloquence of Aaron; early national African Americans, for whom the story of Exodus powered their political imaginations perhaps more than any other biblical or historical narrative, also believed in the centrality of rhetoric in the fight to end the various forms of slavery they endured, which is why they initiated what would become a lasting oratorical tradition from the very beginnings of emancipation. With Bobalition, African Americans' detractors sought to blunt the power of black orality because they, too, believed the spoken word to be central to the production of (American) freedom. The history of the U.S. was the most meaningful and immediate testament to this view, as the rhetorical revolution that colonists waged against the British was just as critical as their armed revolution.[101]

Furthermore, Adams' *Lectures* contend that the spoken word does not simply produce freedom but, just as crucially, enhances it moving forward. Speech, he claims, promotes "progressive improvement," "individual discovery," and "rational intercourse [between] fellow-creature[s]."[102] For Adams and Americans in the early nineteenth century generally, these acts and conditions flourish most in democratic-republican polities, among which the U.S. was the exemplar. Their view suggests that the performance of eloquent speech distinguishes those subjects most capable and indeed those most responsible for the positive development of a free society; therefore, they should be the freest. By contrast, those who are the least articulate must remain the least free in that society because they retard its progress. This is the proslavery appeal at the center of Bobalition, an appeal its producers made most forcefully in their (mis-)representations of *how* African Americans spoke, more than what they spoke.

For its many admirers, Bobalition's graphic renderings of contorted black diction only redoubled its proslavery effect and ideological cogency. That the broadsides allowed Americans to *see* the purported defects of black speech worked to impress further the "truth" of those defects, and therefore the defects of black humanity itself. Indeed, the Aristotelian notion that sight is the most epistemologically productive of the senses remained operative in the period, and in the contemporaneous Anglo-American philosophical tradition, the Scottish aesthetician and philosopher Lord Kames gave it its most cogent articulation. In his influential *Elements of Criticism* (1762), which Jefferson and other American Enlightenment figures admired, Lord Kames argued that the "eye is the best avenue to the heart," and therefore "writers of genius . . . represent everything as passing in our sight; and, from readers or hearers, transform us as it were into spectators."[103] The "genius" of Bobalition, which it certainly warrants to be called, is precisely the way it visualizes the oral; that is, in confronting the broadsides' textual abundance, one has no choice but to "see" black speech as sounded. Bobalition's graphic representations of the sounds of blackness reinforced the "truth" of blackness that those sounds were meant to convey because, according to the period's prevailing aesthetic theories, the visual "both strengthens the illusion of an immediate engagement and more effectively influences future behavior."[104]

The most common ways in which Bobalition visualized deficient black orality were catachresis, misspellings, malapropisms, and puns. But the broadsides also relied on other techniques. For instance, the *Grand Celebrashun ob de Bobalition ob African Slabery!!!* (1825) renders black oral maladroitness by way of its word arrangements. At the top of the broadside is an image of two black men standing face-to-face, both wearing top hats and tailcoats. By means of a speech bubble, which were popular in the political cartoons of the period, the man on the right asks, "What is de day ob de grand CELEBRASHUN [?]" The other answers, "BOSSON, ULY 14, 1825, and little arter."[105] The placement of their words in this exchange renders their already ridiculous speech doubly preposterous; the man on the *right* initiates the dialogue, therefore upsetting the normative procedure of reading left-to-right. Furthermore, his words wrap around the speech bubble in such a way that all but "Celebrashun" is upside down. The resultant interplay of aural and visual derision undercuts the men's seeming refinement and success that their accouterment and clothing might otherwise signify. Indeed, the visual representations of black speech in *Grand Celebrashun* render the prospect of racial equality as the potential of black freedom utterly incongruous.

The production of this effect was the predominant aim of Bobalition. But across the individual broadsides there is no single demand regarding what role African Americans should fulfill in the north. Some broadsides express proslavery arguments. *The Grand Celebration! Of the Abolition of the Slave Trade"* (1817), for example, includes the toast, "'Tis better to be a well fed SLAVE den a damn poor half starve FREE negur."[106] Others, like *Grand Bobalition, or 'Great Annibersary Fussible'*, cheer antislavery sentiments, toasting "Massachusets" because "He de fuss tate in dis country to give African liberty—Pity more of um dont follow he sample."[107] *Bobolition of Slavery!!!!!* (1818) is more biting in its reproof of the U.S., "[To] De Nited Tate—de land of liberty, sept he keep slave at de South," but nonetheless affirms the nation as African Americans' rightful home: "[To] Massa

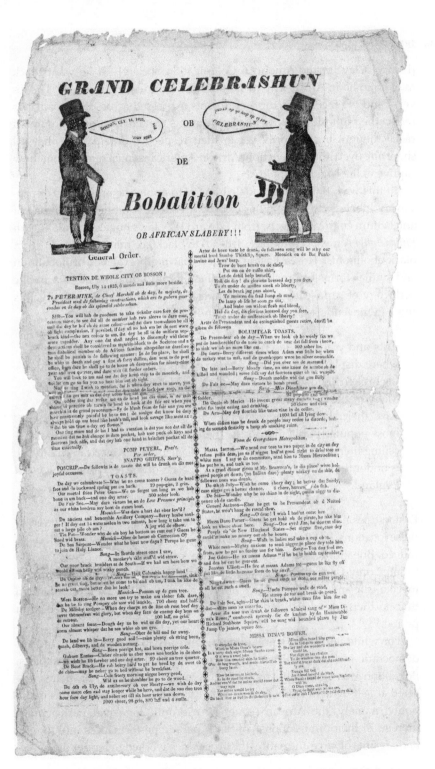

Figure 2: *Grand Celebrashun ob de Bobalition ob African Slabery!!!* (1825).
Library of Congress, LC-USZ62–40688.

[Henry] Clay [of the American Colonization Society]—If he want brack man to go lib in Africa why he no go show him de way heself."[108] The diverse and often contradictory sentiments expressed across the broadsides reflect the multiple ideological commitments that characterized dominant racial thought in the north, yet in their respective articulations they all share one overriding conviction: African Americans must remain somehow captive in the American polity.

In this way, Bobalition modeled a way to apply the arguments of proslavery ideology to the realities of black freedom; it influenced a range of antebellum cultural projects, from Edward W. Clay's hugely popular *Life in Philadelphia* series of cartoons (1828–30) to blackface minstrelsy.[109] In 1837, black abolitionist Hosea Easton argued that the prevalence of Bobalition and similar forms of proslavery graphic literature functioned as a public pedagogy of sorts, categorizing them as part of a "baneful seed which is sown in the tender soil of youthful minds."

> Cuts and placards descriptive of the negro's deformity, are every where displayed to the observation of the young, with corresponding broken lingo, the very character of which is marked with design. Many of the popular book stores, in commercial towns and cities, have their show-windows lined with them. The barrooms of the most popular public houses in the country, sometimes have their ceiling literally covered with them. This display of American civility is under the daily observation in every class of society, even in New England.[110]

Easton does not specify the particular "cuts and placards" he observed in these locations, but Bobalition's influence on whichever they were is clear. Indeed, Bobalition was "simultaneously a technology and a trope," as historian Corey Capers aptly describes it, and the broadsides' fusion of the mechanistic and the imaginative offered a manner of racial representation that northerners craved and appropriated for the rest of the antebellum period.[111]

For white northerners unwilling or unready to expand the bounds of democratic inclusion and extend citizenship to their black counterparts, Bobalition was especially compelling because it produced or, better, enacted a "self-evident truth" that upheld race-based circumscriptions in the polity: namely, the African (American) is unfit for equal participation therein. In their "translations" of black parade performances into the generic realms of farce and satire, the broadsides worked to render the neces-

sity of black captivity axiomatic.[112] Thus, Bobalition was not simply something northerners laughed at, but, more important, something they acted
from. With its emphasis on black speech and linguistic incompetence, Bobalition tapped into, and consequently boosted the currency of, a set of
ever-common racial theories positing black people's constitutional—that
is, human—deficiencies vis-à-vis other races; most notably of these, the belief that African Americans were inherently lacking as speaking subjects
and therefore unqualified for full freedom in the increasingly modern
world. The "broken lingo" constitutive of Bobalition, to use Easton's
phrase, became the lexicon with which white northerners both heard and
saw black speech in the early nineteenth century, despite the rhetorical flair
that early national African Americans performed at the parades as well as
in pulpits and in other public spaces. Put another way, Bobalition conditioned the "ear" and "eye" of the dominant racial imagination of the north,
both set to deride black political speech and reject the inclusionary appeals
of black political formations. These proslavery "senses" did not amount to
a demand for the reinstitution of chattel slavery in the region; rather, they
strengthened and "legitimated" white northerners' resolve that African
Americans must remain captive in the realm of existential indeterminacy
that would characterize free black life throughout the antebellum period.

# TWO

# Black Politics but Not Black People

*Early Minstrelsy, "White Slavery,"*
*and the Wedge of "Blackness"*

During an 1833 anti-abolitionist riot in New York City, a mob of an esti-
mated two thousand people descended on the Chatham Street Chapel,
where they found the entrance blocked by locked iron gates. Inside the
chapel, a committee of abolitionists was busy laying the foundation of an
"association to oppose slavery, and reaffirm the doctrine of their revolutionary forefathers," as one member put it.[1] That association would become
the New York City Anti-Slavery Society, a regional precursor of the American Anti-Slavery Society that formed later that year. After the adoption of
resolutions concerning the group's function and structure, the abolitionists
gave the keys to the janitor and instructed him to allow the mob to enter the
chapel. When the rioters discovered their targets had escaped by way of
private passages, and therefore violence against the abolitionists was no
longer possible, they resolved to "amuse themselves" another way.[2]

Thus the mob decided to hold a mock antislavery meeting. Several of
the rioters forced a black bystander to assume the role of white abolitionist
Arthur Tappan, chair the proceedings, and deliver a speech. Although the
conscripted participant resisted performing, "his audience would take no
denial." He eventually addressed the mob, and he did so in a stunning, yet
dangerous improvisation that recalled the orations at black commemorative parades:

> I am called upon to make a speech! You doubtless know that I am a
> poor, ignorant man, not accustomed to make speeches. But I have
> heard of the Declaration of Independence, and have read the Bible.
> The Declaration says all men are created equal, and the Bible says
> God has made us all of one blood. I think, therefore, we are entitled
> to good treatment, that it is wrong to hold men in slavery, and
> that—[3]

The rioters halted his speech with "yells and curses" then "broke up their meeting and dispersed"; they did not anticipate such daring eloquence in the face of their violent multitude.[4] Indeed, the mob made the mistake of allowing "Tappan" to speak for himself, and he refused to do so in the fatuous, grotesque, and obtuse ways that typified black characters in dominant performance culture, which was what the mob expected from him.

Of all the antebellum cultural practices that shaped normative expectations of how African Americans should conduct themselves, blackface minstrelsy was the most formative. During its early phase (1829–43), when the "Tappan" incident occurred, minstrelsy's points of articulation between free black life were particularly strong. But after 1843, in response to the economic depression of the late 1830s and early 1840s as well as its own commercialization, the form began to solidify its pro-plantation ideology and nostalgia.[5] For critics like cultural historian Eric Lott and especially musicologist Dale Cockrell and cultural historian W. T. Lhamon, this periodization best represents the course of antebellum minstrelsy; that is, "an early radical phase followed by its co-optation by commercial and middle-class interests by the 1850s."[6] In their highly influential accounts, these scholars suggest that much of what made early minstrelsy "radical" is that it "asks poor [and disaffected] whites to align themselves with blacks against the civil sense that it was 'a gross outrage' to do so."[7] This proposed alliance, they contend, reflected white workers' desire to forge bonds of working-class solidarity with their black counterparts. This chapter disputes that claim, which has become an "increasingly orthodox" one; instead, I argue that, with early minstrelsy, white working-class northerners expropriated black performance culture and developed a distinct strand of proslavery thought with which to bring about their socioeconomic betterment at the expense of African Americans'.[8]

To be sure, early minstrelsy poses a complex set of analytical challenges because of its polyvalent and ostensibly contradictory enactments. Although the form's texts and practices register an admiration for its antiauthoritarian and crafty black characters, its extra-theatrical contexts undercut, or even nullify, the esteem its figurations accord African Americans and slaves. These contexts, which I explore throughout this chapter, manifest in early minstrelsy's white supremacist Jacksonian politics as well as its discursive and visual reliance upon the battered and bruised black body for its humor.[9] Furthermore, the particulars of production also trouble the notion that those who crafted and craved the form sought solidarity with their black working-class counterparts. Perhaps more than any other factor, white actors and managers barred the onstage contributions of actual African Americans, even though their performances usually took place near black communities.[10] Black performance by black people would have subverted the mechanisms of identification and structures of (inter)racial feeling that white audiences (predominately male) worked out for themselves in minstrelsy—structures they used to buffer the ongoing vicissitudes of industrialization and the entrenchment of wage labor capitalism. Instead, African Americans remained outside the theatrical frame, and blackface minstrelsy emerged as a performance form for, by, and about the white community.

To begin to untangle early minstrelsy's complex and seemingly antithetical implications, I turn to its origins in order to grasp the aesthetic foundations and social impulses that charged its formation. An examination of these underlying conditions explains how early minstrelsy was, indeed, a "form of engaging the black 'Other,'" but not one "supportive of action to correct the Other's social plight."[11] Rather, white working-class performers and publics relied on the ideological and spatial propinquity they shared with African Americans to fashion minstrelsy in such a way as to sustain their distinctive race- and class-based ends. In this effort the rejection of African Americans as performers was crucial, and "Tappan's" improvisation at the Chatham Street Chapel reveals why: there was always the threat they might move off script and subvert early minstrelsy's ideological thrust.

## RASCALITY AND THE SURPLUS OF BLACK/SLAVE PERFORMANCE

Within the gestures, music, and narratives of minstrelsy, the traces of black performance praxis are evident. Lhamon has done the most thorough job of charting the cross-racial pollination that characterizes minstrelsy's prehistory. He argues that this exchange was fostered most decisively in sites of market and labor, in sites such as New York City's Catherine Market "and other early spots for the performances of American culture [where] there was an eagerness to combine, share, join, draw from opposites, play on opposition. An enthusiasm for the underlying possibilities in difference continually reappears in this popular-folk culture of the Atlantic diaspora."[12] What made this interplay of difference possible was something of a concentration of slaves, ex-slaves, and their descendants in the public spaces of northeastern markets and town squares.[13] In fact, this concen-

trated, cross-racial cultural reciprocity took place in other locales throughout the country, too, in places such as the ports of Baltimore and Charleston, sites of early canal construction, and the haunts of rivermen along the
Mississippi River system.[14]

Within these spheres of cultural interchange, what most attracted those
white participants who would eventually hone early minstrelsy was what
black rivermen called "rascality." This unofficial code of living among
black men working the rivers and at ports combined legal and extralegal
action for personal advantage and collective benefit. As one historian puts
it, "While these men were not above occasionally swindling other working-
class people, for the most part their actions were directed at the region's
elites. They lied to, cheated, and stole from bankers, shopkeepers, plantation owners, and merchants—the people who possessed the wealth they
coveted. . . . But money was not the only thing that mattered to these men.
[Black riverman] Charles Brown, for instance, combined the pursuit of
ready money with efforts to liberate runaway slaves."[15] Yet illegality did
not constitute all of rascality. It was also a way of life that stressed un-
abashed expressions of individuality in which black men "lived by their
own wits as confidence men and tricksters. This independence was an important part of their black masculine identity that prized not only the more
common working-class virtues of toughness and strength but also cleverness, dexterity, and flamboyance."[16] It is clear why rascality appealed to
young white workers: its dual, often simultaneous function—to defy elites
and enact pride in oneself and one's class—provided them a mode of performance with which to decry their new position as maltreated wage earn-
ers and those men of capital who created it.

The terms of rascality, particularly its emphasis on "cleverness, dexterity, and flamboyance," are undoubtedly related to the gestural and rhetorical lexicons of the interracial performances at markets that prefigured
blackface minstrelsy. For scholars of early black cultural production, if not
for contemporaneous observers themselves, one of the most productive
sites of rascal performance was Catherine Market, which was located in
lower Manhattan directly across the East River from what is now Brooklyn
Heights.[17] Starting sometime in the late eighteenth century and lasting until at least the 1820s, Catherine Market constituted a stage where slaves
displayed their mercantile and performative goods for black and white
consumption. According to Thomas De Voe's famous retrospective 1862
account, slaves who had "leave of their masters for certain holidays,
[would], for 'pocket-money,' . . . gather up everything that would bring a
few pence or shillings . . . and bring them in their skiffs to [Catherine] Mar-

Figure 3: *Dancing for Eels at Catherine Market* (1820). Unknown Artist, Private Collection (Sotheby's Inc., 1973 auction).

ket." In addition to selling their small wares, slaves "were ever ready, by their 'negro sayings or doings,' to make a few shillings more." In fact, De Voe claims, "the first introduction in this city of public 'negro dancing' no doubt took place at this market."[18] He goes on to describe the stages and music of the dances: slaves performed on their own "shingles," a "board [that] was usually about five to six feet long, of large width, with its particular spring in it," and "their music or time was usually given by one of their party, which was done by beating their hands on the sides of their legs and the noise of the heel." When money "was not to be had" for the best dancer, he received fish or eels.[19]

De Voe's description outlines enactments of the canny, improvisational, and inventive aesthetics that form liberatory black performance—a rascal aesthetics that has marked radical black performance ever since.[20] These aesthetics resisted easy accounting and legibility because, under the gaze of the performers' masters, overseers, and other observers, they signified on multiple and at times contradictory levels. Because of its significatory abundance, then, slave performance attracted diverse constituencies.

Slaves' dancing for eels as well as their "Negro sayings and doings," which prefigured the wordplay and tricksterism of early minstrelsy, were popular because audiences found "different values in the [performances] at the same time."[21] The sheer talent of slave performers attracted many in the audience.[22] For other spectators, the political material of the performances was what most enticed them: namely, a fleeting yet affective corporeality that resisted captivity itself. Thus, slaves' performances for money or eels at Catherine Market were also rascal-radical enactments of freedom and selfhood.

Following performance theorist Fred Moten, we might think of these liberatory significations as the surplus of black/slave performance. When slaves sang and danced at Catherine Market, there was more at stake than competition and the possibility of material gain. This surplus is subject to what Moten terms a "material reproductivity" that pursues "another liberty waiting activation."[23] Slave dancers and doers at Catherine Market and other contemporaneous performers of rascality pursued liberty in their productions (in addition to money or eels). Their performative, political materiality marks one of the beginnings of a black radical (performance) tradition, a history that runs from slavery to freedom.

Yet there is a cutting, ultimately ghastly twist to this story of reproduction. Those who donned burnt cork grasped the unruliness and therefore sociopolitical potentiality of the surplus of black performance; that is, they used that surplus to activate *their* "liberty waiting." White performers and publics latched onto the disorderly material of rascally black performance and expropriated it to create blackface minstrelsy, the nation's first popular entertainment.

## "WHITE SLAVERY" AND BLACK INSURGENCY: TWO DISCOURSES

As a bracketed theatrical form, blackface minstrelsy began to emerge in the late 1820s. To be sure, blackface performance appeared well before this period, but what we now recognize as the choreography, figures, forms, music, and narratives that constitute minstrelsy cohered as a kind of theatrical whole in the early Jacksonian period. For instance, it was at this time when actor George Washington Dixon performed his signature song, "Coal Black Rose," in New York City over a span of three nights in 1829, each time at a different venue—The Chatham Theatre, the Bowery Theatre, and the Park Theatre.[24] Although Dixon had already successfully toured the country by that point, performing from Charleston, South Carolina, to Salem, Massachusetts, these three performances of his blackface act at New York City's iconic theatres catapulted him to stardom and fostered the craze that surrounded "Coal Black Rose."[25] Also in the late 1820s, Thomas Dartmouth "Daddy" Rice, who became the most famous blackface minstrel before the Civil War, honed his "Jim Crow" in the western theatres of Louisville, Cincinnati, and Pittsburgh.[26] Rice's time in what was then the west marks how the cultural world of the frontier also contributed to early minstrelsy's performative vocabularies and parabolic structures.

Dixon's popularity and Rice's frontier acts, therefore, simply reinforce the widely accepted notion that minstrelsy was an invention of the north and west, not of the south. As Lott puts it, "One might begin by recognizing that the minstrel show most often glossed not white encounters with life on the plantation (minstrel-show mythographers to the contrary) but racial contacts and tensions endemic to the North and the frontier. The chiefly working-class orientation of cultural interchange in the North and Southwest was responsible both for installing this new entertainment in its northern class context and for the kinds of racial representation to be found there."[27] These "racial contacts and tensions" of the north and the frontier emerged from the practice and gradual end of slavery in these regions, a process that started in the late eighteenth and early nineteenth centuries. Slavery in these two regions centered most on domestic service, small-scale farming, and artisanship rather than on the plantation regime that was ubiquitous in the south.[28] Nonetheless, the fact that the staging of slaves and ex-slaves took hold in the north, where slavery was (for the most part) no longer practiced, suggests something about the institution's importance to how that region constructed and understood itself. Put simply, minstrelsy became a kind of aesthetic surrogate for the loss of slavery in the north.

That said, early minstrelsy was not a nostalgic attempt to theatricalize a "history" of slavery. Rather, its intent and appeal rested on its explicitly imagined futures. The deliberate and marked differences between actual slave life, in the north and elsewhere, and representations of slaves on the minstrel stage reflected the economic, political, and social desires of white northerners *looking forward*. Lott calls this psychic energy the "social unconscious of blackface"; that is, "the conflicts and accommodations that lay behind the transformations" that white artists and their publics made to black cultural formations.[29] Certainly their psychological and sociopolitical needs powered the dynamism of those transformations. The most important of these changes was the substitution of actual blackness with the "blackness" that would typify the minstrel stage. Yet white desire and effort alone did not charge that transition; the actions of an increasingly assertive free black community in the north also contributed to this change, yet few critics of early minstrelsy have taken that public into account.[30] Black agitation helped precipitate the social turmoil that characterized the late 1820s and early 1830s, and blackface minstrelsy became one way to attenuate and regulate its pressures.[31] That is, the form functioned simultaneously as a conduit of white assertion and as a buffer against black protest.

But what were some of the circumstances of the period that framed the inception of blackface minstrelsy and therefore help make sense of its fluctuating and at-times-contradictory negotiations? To begin, a rhetoric and praxis of "common man" politics resulted in the inauguration of Andrew Jackson in 1829 as well as the formation of a "radical popular movement [the Working Men]—led by a committee composed primarily of journeymen mechanics."[32] At the same time, black activism was reaching national proportions: in 1829, when the first African American newspaper, *Freedom's Journal* (New York), shut down after a remarkable two-year run, another, *The Rights of All* (New York), quickly began publication. That same year, Richard Allen, founding bishop of the African Methodist Episcopal Church and one of the most powerful African Americans in the nation, and his cohort began plans for a national convention of black delegates to explore strategies of collective uplift; and David Walker published his jeremiad, *Appeal, in Four Articles, Together with a Preamble to the Coloured Citizens of the World, but in Particular, and Very Expressly, to Those of the United States of America*, which prophesied a murderous racial reckoning and circulated in the north and the south.[33] Although scholars of the period often treat white working-class Jacksonianism and contemporaneous black political ideology in isolation, these historical formations were not as separate as the historiography suggests. Indeed, one place of intersection was minstrelsy, and not least because those who crafted its aesthetics, figurations, and spaces consciously avoided the sociopolitical consequences of black politics.

The popular allows for such a (dis-)junction because, as Antonio Gramsci remarks, the contents of common culture are always contested; its borders are never settled but always in process.[34] Because common culture operates on a shared popular level where everyone (believes he or she) is a legitimate contributor, it is not subject to philosophical or formalist coherence and systematization. Lott notes that "popular forms and popular audiences are less fixed referents than sites of continual reconstitution[;] the popular [is] less an object than a space."[35] He finds that the spaces of early minstrelsy allowed for such interchange of cultures and therefore of the belief systems of blacks and whites. Yet even in his groundbreaking study of blackface minstrelsy, *Love and Theft*, Lott hardly attends to black responses to the form, not to mention wider, concurrent black social and political formations that also framed minstrelsy's inception. The vast majority of the literature on early minstrelsy follows this example, tracing what I view as an unfortunate instance of historical continuity in which scholars borrow the model of those who crafted minstrelsy itself: they refuse black people except when they are advantageous to one's particular narrative. But what happens when we admit black doings into the historiographic frame? How did they figure (within) the popular spaces of early minstrelsy? In terms of the writing of the history of those spaces and their contents, in what ways do the actions and discourses of African Americans in the late 1820s and early 1830s refocus the claim that early minstrelsy imagined a cross-racial alliance of disaffected workers?

To begin to answer these questions, I want to consider the rise of white working-class discourse vis-à-vis black political discourse in the period because this method helps clarify how and why minstrelsy's white working-class publics aligned themselves with black politics but refused black people. Starting in the late 1820s, white workers began to conceive of their relation to capital, wage labor, and private enterprise as one of enslavement.[36] This conceptualization engendered and unleashed a set of discursive and ideological resources that animated and fortified their politics throughout the Jacksonian period.[37] One of the most conspicuous of these was the notion of "white slavery," which eventually helped foment Free Soil politics in the late 1840s and early 1850s.[38] As a general hermeneutic, the discursive figuration of "white slavery" allowed white workers to imagine themselves as free republican citizens who controlled the rights to, and fruits of, their labor. [39] They framed that figuration in historical terms, declaring that developments of capitalism contravened American ideals. "White slavery" evoked the forfeitures and perils that workers and, by extension, the nation suffered in its feverish and unrelenting processes of industrialization (i.e., the move from agrarian economies, and the shift to wage labor and centralized manufacturing) in the first decades of the nineteenth century.[40]

This historical narrative was a nostalgic and, in significant respects, fanciful vision of a precapitalist past that, along with the rhetorical figure of the "white slave," helped align white workers with their revolutionary forefathers, especially Thomas Paine and Thomas Jefferson who most forcefully outlined the rights and virtues of independent artisanship. The Founding Fathers, of course, used the metaphor of slavery to conceptualize the colonial relationship to Great Britain. The key difference was that their "slavery" was based on the lack of *political* representation, whereas Jackso-nian workers believed theirs stemmed from *economic* concerns such as the rise of wage labor and the increasing concentration of property in the hands of the few. There was, though, one crucial similarity: the Founders and the white working class after 1829 both declared that their respective "enslave-ments" violated republicanism. And, as Edmund Morgan has famously argued, black slavery was critical to the ideological formation of American republicanism: "The presence of men and women who were, in law at least, almost totally subject to the will of other men gave to those in control of them an immediate experience of what it could mean to be at the mercy of a tyrant. Virginians [and others who witnessed slavery] may have had a special appreciation of the freedom dear to republicans, because they saw every day what life without it could be like."[41] Yet one could argue that that "special appreciation" of freedom and republicanism did not rely on the *continual* enslaving of black people, especially by the 1830s. If republican identity in the late eighteenth century depended on the darker negatives of slavery to expose the very terms of that identity, hadn't the conceptual, definitional work of black bondage run its course?

The discourse of "white slavery" remains one of the fundamental con-cerns here. Critics of early minstrelsy find that "ragged white publics hoisted [early minstrel figures] to flag their own, even their mutual, condi-tion" with blacks and that "when not distracted by the class makeup of some abolitionist organizations . . . [they] were quite ready to hear the mer-its of antislavery"; they suggest that the discourse of the "enslaved" white worker was an objection to slavery in *any* form, black or white.[42] Eric Foner, in a foundational article on abolitionism and the labor movement, makes the case most clearly:

> After all, inherent in the notion of 'wage slavery' [or 'white slavery'], in the comparison of the status of the northern laborer with the southern slave, was a critique of the peculiar institution as an ex-treme form of oppression. . . . The entire ideology of the labor move-ment was implicitly hostile to slavery; slavery contradicted the cen-tral ideas and values of artisan radicalism—liberty, democracy, equality, and independence.[43]

In this view, normative white working-class discourses condemned slav-ery, racial or otherwise, because it was anathema to free labor and Ameri-canness itself.

But there were two significant factors that troubled the material and political functionality of these discourses as censure of *black* bondage: the prevalence of the term "white slavery" and the ubiquitous comparisons of the conditions of the white northern worker vis-à-vis that of the black southern slave. When white workers conceptualized their condition as one of slavery, they used the term "white slavery" much more frequently than "wage slavery" (and "wage slavery" was also used less often than "slavery of wages").[44] For one, "wage slavery" was too ambiguous because it left the possibility that black workers and even slaves would use it. As historian David Roediger writes, "The advantages of the phrase 'white slavery' over 'wage slavery' or 'slavery of wages' lay in the former term's vagueness and in its whiteness, in its invocation of *herrenvolk* republicanism."[45] Moreover, the usage of "white slavery" fostered a qualitative valuation of the white laborer alongside the black slave, an approach that ultimately performed a kind of proslavery work. Such comparisons "computed rates of exploitation that putatively showed that a much greater proportion of the value produced by a Black slave was returned to him or her than was returned to the white slave in the North," Roediger finds. In contrast to "white slavery," then, chattel slavery was rendered a benevolent institution, and proslavery ideologues circulated this judgment in legislatures, newspapers, and pulpits in order to defend black bondage and boast of its goodness.[46] Thus the discourse of "white slavery" constituted an apology for chattel slavery.

Moreover, the comparisons between northern labor and southern slavery suggest that those who adopted the discourse of "white slavery" did not believe that their situation was at any time the same as black bondsmen's. Despite the belief among the majority of small artisans and wage-workers that the destruction of the apprentice system and the rise of capitalism signaled a form of enslavement, to reduce their definition of freedom to one understood solely in the terms of political economy is to miss the dynamism of class formation and racial ideology. Such crude economism ignores other modes of being and self-definition (such as the emphasis on manliness, street honor, and drinking) that antebellum urban workers used to enact their freedoms. Although these modes were at times related to changes in labor conditions, economic factors alone do not account for how those practices might have shifted or signified. Furthermore, that the discourse of "white slavery" was able to materialize in the first place and take hold as it did, and that many of those who fought for the claims it denoted and connoted would later form the Free Soil movement and political party, certainly signaled the political and social subjectivity of the free—precisely what the (black) enslaved lacked.

My focus on "white slavery" is an attempt to come to grips with how white labor racialized questions of slavery. It unsettles the argument that early blackface minstrels and their working-class publics opposed slavery in any form because the institution subverted democracy in its concentration of economic and political power in the hands of wealthy elites and catalyzed oppressive labor conditions that all races had to endure. Or, as Cockrell claims, early minstrelsy enacted their audiences' "contrary [positions] to the interests of middle- and upper-class Americans" and was more interested in problems of class rather than those of race.[47] As the discourse of "white slavery" makes clear, however, this characterization of white working-class political economy (and, by extension, ideologies of slavery) misses the very complex ways in which that thinking was fundamentally a *racialized* one. White labor's objection to slavery was an objection to *their* "enslavement"—that is, the steady dissolution of artisanship and workers' weaknesses against the strongholds of northern men of capital and southern slaveholders. It is specious to forefront issues of class over those of race in early minstrelsy: race *and* racism influenced white workers' understanding of their rights as citizens and as a class; their whiteness denoted their political and economic freedom. Concerns of class and race were so intertwined in early minstrelsy that separating them for the purposes of historical analysis is methodologically inappropriate and leads to erroneous conclusions about the form.

Thus, despite the fact that the interracial origins of minstrelsy flaunted black rascality as embodied resistance to enslavement, white audiences of early minstrelsy rejected racial equality because it would severely curtail the economic and political promise they affixed to whiteness. Furthermore, the white public had long fostered a collective fear of universal black freedom on the basis that widespread violence would be the cause and/or effect of such a goal. (The Civil War, it seems, bore out this prognostication on the grandest of scales.) In his *Notes on the State of Virginia* (1787), Thomas Jefferson offered a lasting summation of this view: "Deep rooted prejudices entertained by the whites; ten thousand recollections, by the blacks, of the injuries they have sustained; new provocations; the real distinctions which nature has made; and many other circumstances, will divide us into parties, and produce convulsions which will probably never end but in the extermination of the one or the other race."[48] From Jefferson's time through at least the Jacksonian period, the high number of personal rebellions among slaves as well as the belief that black criminality was a natural or social inevitability signaled to many, particularly proslavery ideologues and proponents of African colonization, the social danger of realizing racial equality.[49]

African Americans themselves considered the role of violence in the amelioration, or lack thereof, of their condition. The most vocal and influential in the Jacksonian period was David Walker, whose *Appeal* outlined the destruction that a racial reckoning might cause. Walker published the *Appeal* in Boston, and sailors, churchgoers, and other free African Americans smuggled the pamphlet into all parts of the eastern seaboard, including the south. The treatise marked the birth of a militant antislavery politics.[50] Like the vast majority of other black thinkers in the north, Walker conceived the abolitionist struggle as inextricably bound to the fight for full black inclusion. His revolutionary and bloody exhortations are not confined to the world of the south and its networks of slaves and slaveholders; that is, the *Appeal* outlines an apocalypse of the nation as a whole because of the universal shortcomings of rights discourses.[51]

What is most remarkable about the *Appeal* is its explicitness in this regard. Walker's plan of destruction is plain and unequivocally racialized. For example, he cautions, "If you can only get courage into the blacks, I do declare it, that one good black man can put to death six white men; and I give it as a fact, let twelve black men get well armed for battle, and they will kill and put to flight fifty white men. . . . Get the blacks started, and if you do not have a gang of tigers and lions to deal with, I am a deceiver of the blacks and of the whites."[52] Although Walker's rhetoric was not as publicly echoed among African Americans, white publics feared that the kind of bloodshed he envisioned was within the realm of possibility. When the *Appeal* was smuggled into slave states and read in secret meetings throughout the nation, authorities worried that Walker's words would instill "courage" in slaves and African Americans, who would then turn to slay their masters and oppressors. In fact, some contemporaneous commentators believed that Nat Turner had heard or seen the *Appeal* and that it played a role in his epochal 1831 slave rebellion in Southampton, Virginia.[53]

Of course it is impossible to quantify in any exact measure how the *Appeal* affected black insurgency. Historian Peter Hinks writes, "Walker's *Appeal* made appearances in the United States from New Orleans and Boston. The scale of its identifiable circulation is impressive, but it still leaves open questions about how much further it penetrated in Southern slave society and just what [was] the impact of that penetration."[54] The same can be said of the *Appeal* in the north. But the point is not so much to establish that the *Appeal* directly caused bloody acts of black resistance; rather, it is to note how the text marked the boundaries of the performative field of black oppositionality and ideology in the period. Hinks is correct to note that "Walker was a product of [the black/slave] tradition of resistance rather than the other way around. Yet the pamphlet was nevertheless a rallying point in several locations for conspiring and resistance and could have sustained other efforts."[55] Thus, the *Appeal* and its popularity signify the antebellum black public sphere's horizon of possibility and its ever-forming national collectivity. As literary historian Elizabeth McHenry explains, "The story of the *Appeal* points to the tentative beginnings of a cooperative system for the distributions of knowledge and pertinent information in antebellum black communities, through which printed texts were primarily consumed collectively rather than individually."[56] Though these beginnings were not so tentative by 1829, as I explored in the previous chapter, the epistemological and material functionality of the *Appeal* and the budding forms of African Americans' institutional activism reveal how black striving against oppressive, often violent normative relations—protest practices that ranged from literacy to rascality, from moral reform to massacre—was strikingly multiple and at times contradictory.

What is also clear is that the *Appeal*, or at the very least the structures of radical black oppositionality from which it borrows, also functioned as a kind of rallying point for *white* observers, from common people to political elites. After authorities in Virginia and Georgia discovered copies of the *Appeal* shortly after its publication, the mayor of Boston, H. Gray Otis, wrote letters to alert his southern counterparts that he and "the New England Population" held Walker's "vile pamphlet" in "absolute detestation." Otis told William Branch Giles, governor of Virginia, that he believed the *Appeal* "is disapproved of by the decent portion even of the free coloured population in this place, and it would be a cause of deep regret to me, and I believe to all my well-disposed fellow-citizens, if a publication of this character and emanating from such a source, should be thought to be countenanced by any of their number." To the mayor of Savannah, William Thorne Williams, Otis admitted that although "he ha[d] no power to control the purpose of the author," the city of Boston is "determined . . . to publish a general caution to Captains and others, against exposing themselves to the consequences of transporting incendiary writings into your and the other Southern States."[57] Both letters were subsequently published in the *Enquirer* of Richmond, Virginia, an attempt to provide evidence to a wider southern audience that the white north was united in its opposition to black insurgency.

What I am suggesting here is that racism was not the only factor that inhibited black inclusion in the theatres of early minstrelsy and other contemporaneous white working-class sociocultural formations. White workers were also uneasy about the chance that the emancipated slave and the fully incorporated African American might release from their breasts "the unconquerable disposition" of vengeance that white oppression put there in the first place.[58] If we recognize the conceptual and material implications of the interrelation of race, class, and performance in the 1830s and early 1840s, the fraught ideological field that the producers and publics of early blackface minstrelsy negotiated becomes clearer. On the one hand, black performance offered them a set of gestural, linguistic, and narrative resources with which to confront and ultimately contest the brutalities of a changing economy and the resulting oppression of the working class. On the other hand, whites feared that emancipation and the expansion of equal rights to African Americans might lead to violent reprisals and an abrogation of the legal and extralegal rights that whiteness granted. These conditions regulated the development of minstrelsy and its "black" politics, a politics that was both anti-capital and proslavery.

## THE POLITICS OF "BLACK" PERFORMANCE AND BLACK WORKING-CLASS POLITICS

The "black" politics that early minstrelsy fostered was the product of white working-class publics' need to position themselves as a mistreated, yet singular community. For them, Lhamon observes, "the metaphor of blackness came to signal a worst-case condition that others who were neither black nor fully empowered could join and deploy to signal their own disaffection."[59] Yes, but the identificatory bond audiences had with early minstrel figures was not linear or one of direct equivalence; white spectators did not simply see their (blackened) selves on stage. The aesthetic and cognitive relation between staged "black" identities and their audiences was fraught with antagonism, coercion, and equivocation. In fact, *any* process of identification (or purposive copying) can never be wholly mimetic but is always modified by the producer's desire, expectation, and fear. These revisions become clearer within the representational (e.g., theatrical) frame because there the conscious alterations and disavowals of the object are emphasized. The most meaningful change the producers of early minstrelsy made to the origin(al)s was the removal of black people and the restyling of their politics for those of "blackness." In short, the pragmatic and strategic overlay of the blackface mask allowed early minstrel publics to operate both within *and* outside the oppositional materiality and significations of black culture.

As these performers and publics invested in the modes of alterity and antiauthoritarianism constitutive of black (political) culture, they simultaneously expanded the bounds of that culture to the point of near unrecognizability. Their "exaggerations" of black life and refusals to "represent the colored man . . . as he is," to borrow Frederick Douglass' description of blackface minstrelsy, resulted in casts of grotesque blackness that were essential to antebellum processes of self-making; that is, they allowed Americans to define themselves as a *this* in contradistinction to a (black) *that*. The appeal of minstrelsy's grotesque blackness emerged from its elasticity, that it respected few affective and figural bounds. Bahktin's gloss on the grotesque is useful here because it helps explain the multiple lines of gratification early minstrelsy extended its audiences, on the one hand, and its audiences' ability to withstand the most objectionable of its representations, from racial amalgamation to black revolution, on the other. Bahktin writes, "In the example of the grotesque, displeasure is caused by the impossible and improbable nature of the image. . . . But this feeling is overcome by two forms of pleasure: first . . . we find some place for this exaggeration within reality. Second, we feel a moral satisfaction, since sharp criticism and mockery have dealt a blow to these vices."[60] Throughout the antebellum period, performers and critics sought to establish minstrelsy's authenticity. One of the most revealing of these efforts was that of actress and diarist Fanny Kemble, who claimed northern blackface minstrels did not go nearly far enough in their portrayals of slaves. In her 1838–39 journal, she declares: "Oh, my dear E—, I have seen Jim Crow—the veritable James: all the contortions, and springs, and flings, and kicks, and capers you have been beguiled into accepting as indicative of him are spurious, faint, feeble, impotent—in a word, pale Northern reproductions of that ineffable black conception."[61] Such pseudo-anthropological estimations, coupled with the traces of black/slave performance praxis at the origins of minstrelsy, endowed the form's grotesqueries with a seeming veracity that made them not simply palatable but irresistibly pleasurable.

Even if certain spectators believed that the representations of slave and free black life they witnessed onstage were somehow real, they nonetheless deflected the actualities of blackness that black people had to endure (i.e., being the slave or the noncitizen) in service of their own betterment; that is, they used blackness as a *metaphor* for the lowest condition whites endured in the polity. To be sure, a number of the texts of early minstrelsy do seem to be concerned with the fate of slaves and free African Americans; but this is only on the page. In performance, these texts signified in radically different ways. The theatrical and social contexts (over-)determined how early minstrelsy made its aesthetic and sociopolitical sense. For example, white men performed in blackface, thus the words did not come out of black mouths before white and black audiences. As well, the gestural and linguistic contortions that defined early blackface minstrel performance unsettled its physical and ideological threats. "Exaggerations or distortions of dialect, or gestures meant to underscore the complete nonsense of some songs," Lott explains, "might effectively dampen any too boisterous talk."[62] Performance, in other words, cut short the full meaning of those black political structures at the core of early minstrelsy.

Consider, for instance, the 1835 song "Jim Crow Still Alive!!!!" In it, Jim Crow sings instructively of the differences between whites and his "race":

> What stuff it is in dem [i.e., whites]
> To make de debbil brack
> I'll prove dat he is white,
> In de twinkling of a crack.
> So I wheel about, etc.
> [. . .]
> Now my brodder niggars,
> I do not tink it right,
> Dat you should laugh at dem,
> Who happen to be white.
>
> Kase it dar misfortune,
> An dey'd spend every dollar
> If dey could only be
> Gentlemen ob color.
>
> It almost break my heart,
> To see dem envy me,
> And from my soul I wish dem
> Full as brack as we.[63]

To Cockrell, Lhamon, and similar-minded critics, these sentiments signal a real desire of Jim Crow's white working publics to band with their African American counterparts. But what about the fraught theatrical and social contexts that fueled the composition and performance of this song and others like it? In my view, Jim Crow and his white "brodder niggars" were not so interested in the African Americans they excluded from the stage and the pit, the treasured spot in the audience of white working-class men. Rather, their investment was in black performance and political material,

Figure 4: T. D. Rice as Jim Crow and His "Black" Public, Bowery Theatre, New York City, Nov. 25, 1833. Collection of the New-York Historical Society.

not black men. When white "gentlemen ob color" and "brack" men reveled with Jim Crow in the spaces of early minstrelsy, they performatively and socially constructed their own "race": the "blacks."

In the event that black spectators, who were restricted to the gallery, might have looked past minstrelsy's racial derision and interpreted the pro-"black" sentiments as pro-black, T. D. Rice made sure they knew his performance practice was not evidence of antislavery sentiments or evidence in favor of black inclusion. In a curtain speech during an 1837 performance in Baltimore, Rice cleared up any ambiguity (if there was any) about his Jim Crow acts. *The Baltimore Sun* reprinted the words of "Mr. Crow":

Before I went to England, the British people were excessively ignorant regarding "our free institutions." (Hear) They were under the impression that negroes were naturally equal to the whites, and their degraded condition was consequent entirely upon our "institu-

tions;" but *I effectually proved that negroes are essentially an inferior species of the human family, and they ought to remain slaves.*—(Some mur-
murs of disapprobation from the boxes, which was quickly put
down by the plaudits of the pit.) You will never again hear of an
abolitionist crossing the Atlantic to interfere in our affairs.—
(Tremendous applause.) I have studied the negro character upon the
southern plantations. The British people acknowledged that I was a
fair representative of the great body of our slaves, and Charles Kemble attested the faithfulness of my delineations.—(Three Cheers)

Ladies and Gentlemen:
It will be ever a source of pride to me that, in my humble line, I have
been of such signal service to my country. (emphasis added.)[64]

Here, Rice affixes specific proslavery meanings to his work, which the
dominant audiences of early minstrelsy, white working-class men in the
pit, applauded. His admission, I argue, should serve as an interpretative
frame for his (and others') blackface performances before 1843, one that
topples Cockrell's claim that "one of the most curious features of 'Jim
Crow'" was the "sympathetic, even respectful, expression of what it was to
be black in a country with slavery."[65] In addition, the speech wholly repu-
diates Lhamon's argument that, with Jim Crow, Rice (and his audience)
"never requests nor assumes higher status than society allows its lowest
figures. Grotesquerie of blacks is [Rice's] vehicle, not his target."[66] As this
curtain speech made clear, however, black grotesquerie was both Rice's
vehicle *and* his target; he imagined his work not simply as anti-abolitionist
but as patently proslavery. To claim Jim Crow as a champion of antebellum
blackness is, at best, to work within a too-rigid binary of black and white.
Instead, it is critical that we admit "blackness" into the social fold, and position Jim Crow as its "racial" icon. (It bears noting that neither Cockrell
nor Lhamon engages Rice's proslavery curtain speech in their respective
studies.)

Since Rice delivered this speech after his performance at the Holliday
Street Theatre in Baltimore, one of the primary port cities of the slave south,
it makes sense that his audience cheered his words. But Rice's ties to southern audiences and his proslavery affirmations did not hamper his or other
Jim Crow delineators' appeal in the north, notwithstanding the nation's
steadily escalating sectional crisis. Samuel Cornish, co-editor of the *Colored
American* (New York) with Philip Bell, hoped Rice's admission in Baltimore
might, at the very least, dissuade his paper's black readership from attend-

Figure 5: "Mr. T. Rice as The Original Jim Crow" (1830s). John Hay Library, Brown University Library.

ing minstrel performances. He reprinted Rice's speech as it appeared in *The Baltimore Sun*, and introduced it with a firm denunciation of minstrelsy and the theatres that produced it: "I sincerely hope after reading the following no colored American will ever again so disgrace himself, or his people by patronizing such performances, nor even the theatres where they are exhibited."[67] While the immediate impact of Cornish's remonstrations is unclear, such exhortations had no long-term effect in terms of steering black audiences from blackface minstrel performances.[68] What, then, prompted African Americans to continue to patronize performances built on derisive representations and grotesque figurations of their race?

One way to account for this seeming incongruity might be to look beyond the stage and its enactments of black disparagement and ridicule, but to the broader milieus of early minstrelsy. These spaces, such as the Bowery Theatre in the 1830s and the Chatham Theatre in the early 1840s, celebrated and encouraged manly ways. This masculinist ethic appealed to many African Americans, especially the black working class.[69] Like their white counterparts, black workingmen and workingwomen embraced rascality and flouted Victorian mores. They rejected bourgeois ideals such as temperance and somber displays of community and selfhood, charging that the reformers who espoused these ideals were out of touch with the realities of black life and ignorant of effective political action.[70] For example, the Stewards' and Cooks' Marine Benevolent Society served alcohol at their third anniversary celebration in 1840, even though it knew the *Colored American* would be there to cover the event. In his article, the reporter for the *Colored American* assured his readers that "of the wines we did not partake," but, despite his objections, he wished that if "the angel of temperance could wink at any indulgence, it would be over a scene like this, where men, spared by the perils of the sea, united after long separation, sit down to enjoy a fleeting hour which, in too many cases, may to them never return."[71] Of course, the stewards and marines cared little for the approval of the *Colored American* or of other bourgeois institutions and outlets; they were going to have their drink and toast their labor and mutual relief efforts because drinking was an integral part of their social ethic. Indeed, the Stewards' and Cooks' Marine Benevolent Society refused to change its ways merely because bourgeois reformers deemed it necessary for personal salvation and therefore collective racial uplift.

That the *Colored American* and its syndicates might bend on temperance did not somehow make their sociopolitical measures more appealing to the black working class. Besides, as historian Leslie Harris notes, black bourgeois reformers very often "viewed other objections to moral reform as more threatening to the cause of racial equality."[72] One of their most hard-line convictions was that African Americans should be somber in their per-formances of community and selfhood, obtain a classical education, and train in a skilled profession.[73] But many black workers objected to such prescriptions, charging that a man like Cornish knew little of what they endured, and, therefore, he was ill equipped to dictate behavior and offer solutions. The most eloquent and vocal defender of black working-class mores in the period was porter Peter Paul Simons, whose ideological bat-tles with Cornish and other black middle-class reformers gripped the free black community in the late 1830s. Simons' labor-based activism and his refusal to renounce the habits of black common life betray the sharp cul-tural and ideological differences that stratified African Americans in the Jacksonian period.[74] These differences trouble Cockrell's central argument that middle-class reformers' efforts "to scapegoat white, common Ameri-cans by painting *them* the racists" drove the "wedge in the real and reason-able alliance between white and black common Jacksonians."[75] Black work-ingmen and workingwomen largely separated themselves from bourgeois reform and rejected its claims, and white workers in northern cities knew that.[76] In my view, the wedge that forestalled an alliance between black and white working-class Jacksonians was the explosion of discourses that ques-tioned a shared humanity between the races and positioned African Amer-icans as the (inherently) inferior race, discourses that the disaffected white populations used for their own social and political gain.[77] The cultural ma-chinery of early minstrelsy helped define that wedge and drove it deeper.

Analytically, though, Cockrell's image of a wedge is useful because it connotes a beginning mutuality, a shared *mentalité*, between the black working class and the white working class that might have deadened par-ticular antagonisms of racial difference. As labor theorist Stanley Aronow-itz explains in more general terms, "Social movements consist of more than their immediate demands for the redress of grievances. The precondition of sustained protest and contestation is a congealed community, broadly shared perceptions and values upon which agreement to act may be reached. Participants may retain their individual views, may be in conflict about many aspects of the movement's goals and program, but what marks their unity is not only shared enemies, but a strongly held sense that they share the same worldviews."[78] Because black labor held similar world-views with white labor, the *potential* for a kind of antiauthoritarian inter-racial solidarity was there, as the social and theatrical worlds of rascality suggest. But rather than inculpate the work of the bourgeois or middle class as that which stalled the alliance, I argue the deciding factor was white workers' promulgation of whiteness and its "racial" offshoot, "blackness," as cultural, historical, and "scientific" legitimation of the singularity and supremacy of their own economic and sociopolitical claims. Early minstrelsy was central to this effort, as its enactments of "blackness" hypostatized innate black inferiority and provided the most extensive cultural defense for the entrenchment of black captivity—"I effectually proved that negroes are essentially an inferior species of the human family, and they ought to remain slaves," Rice proclaimed.

In effect, then, black workers found themselves in a race-based struggle with white society and a "class"-based struggle with bourgeois black reformers. African Americans have always been engaged in such internal dialogues, as black sociopolitical struggle has never turned exclusively on a black-white axis. In the 1830s, the primary concerns of this internal debate involved the protocols of personal behavior and collective proprieties. For example, Simons advocated for the inclusion of women in the political sphere; he took particular issue with African Americans who claimed that women should not be intellectual and social leaders.[79] Their insistence on female docility and domesticity, Simons argued, reflected the worst of bourgeois politics, which in his view were ineffective and perpetuated racial inequality. He contended bourgeois reform was too passive a sociopolitical project, and African Americans who adopted its tenets were waiting for a liberty that would never come. As Simons explained in an 1839 speech before the African Clarkson Association, a mutual relief society, "The basis of the [New York Manumission Society, which was founded in 1785] was to elevate Africans by morals, and this has been upwards of half a century, and what has been done? *Our people were slaves then and are the same today; this northern freedom is nothing but a nickname for northern slavery.*"[80] Simons went on to argue that a program of austere personal conduct, Sabbatarianism, and temperance would not deliver freedom or racial equality, but, instead, produce just quieter and more somber slaves. In fact, Simons believed proponents of moral reform purposely sought to keep African Americans acquiescent: "Yes Brothers, this moral elevation of our people is but a mere song, it is nothing but a conspicuous scarecrow designed expressly, I may safely say, to hinder our people from acting collectively for themselves."[81] In this view, which Simons couched in a rhetorical register strikingly redolent of Walker's *Appeal*, moral reform impeded the realization of black solidarity and black freedom itself; it produced new forms of black captivity operating under the "nickname" of "this northern freedom."

Because moral reform had run what he thought was its largely ineffective course, Simons called for "physical and political efforts [as] the only methods left for us to adopt."[82] He pushed for more direct means of agitation such as petitioning, grand displays of black freedom and antislavery struggle, and, like David Walker before him, maybe even violence. At the end of the African Clarkson Association speech, he exhorted his listeners to "ACTION! ACTION! ACTION!" because "moral elevation suffers us to remain inactive," and "your children will curse the day of their birth . . . and the almighty himself will spurn you, for the lack of courage and not using properly your agency."[83] Simons' brand of agitation, both in its tenor and its tactics, was democratic or, at least, bottom-up. As Harris argues, he "pointed the way to alternative political actions on behalf of abolition and black equality that could involve greater numbers of blacks across class lines."[84] Along with figures like David Ruggles, who co-founded the New York Committee of Vigilance, Simons encouraged acts that everyday black workers could perform, such as strikes for higher wages or harboring and aiding fugitive slaves. With these efforts, black workers flouted the dictates of moral reform, just as their white counterparts had with their institutional and sociocultural formations.

Thus, the ever-normative view in the study of early minstrelsy that white patrician elites and black middle-class reformers separated black labor from white labor is far too reductive and somewhat specious because black labor largely rejected elites and reformers. Had early minstrelsy's white working-class audiences wanted to forge an interracial labor alliance, they might have clutched the economic condition and sociocultural disposition they shared with black workers and united to combat class- and, perhaps, race-based oppression. What these audiences did do, however, was simultaneously isolate themselves from the black working class and the white establishment; within the minstrel frame and behind burnt cork, they fashioned their own race, the "blacks." As "blacks," they resisted elite oppression from above with black material from below. They did not seek "an ally in the black laborer against their common superiors," as Cockrell claims, because they believed their oppression was singular: namely, white slavery.[85] The grotesque figurations of early minstrelsy allowed its working-class audiences to forge a cultural and political identity that buttressed their own inclusionary efforts as well as to foment proslavery sentiment and racial inequality, a process they employed in response to their fears of black insurgency and the loss of the rights of whiteness.[86] (Racism is always informed by some kind of fear.)

For their part, and as the literal and figurative refuse of the nation's first popular entertainment, African Americans had to endure the pervasive reach and unceasing appropriation of early minstrelsy's affects, characters, and conceptions. As minstrelsy's critics have maintained since its very beginnings, their struggle was about far more than literary and theatrical proprieties; theirs was a campaign to blunt the force of the cultural practice that, more than any other in the period, undermined efforts for black inclusion. (It's no coincidence that the system of *de jure* and *de facto* racial segregation that lasted from the end of Reconstruction in 1877 through the late 1960s was known as "Jim Crow.") The increasing recuperation of early minstrelsy as an attempt to forge bonds of interracial solidarity too quickly moves past this effect because it minimizes how and why the form's actors and audiences used the minstrel stage to fashion their own racial structure: white, black, and "black." If we take this triad as seriously as its creators did, we discover a story almost as "tired" as Cockrell feared, one that is not nearly as "positive" as Lhamon seeks to tell: in matters of class politics, early minstrelsy enacted revolutionary impulses, but in the process it exacerbated the many forms of black captivity in the antebellum north.

THREE | Washington and the Slave

*Black Deformations, Proslavery Domesticity,*
*and Re-Staging the Birth of the Nation*

In October 1838, Pennsylvania voters approved amendments to their constitution that enfranchised all "white freeman" in the state, regardless of
their property holdings or tax receipts.[1] Pennsylvania's new constitution
was one of many post–War of 1812 civil, juridical, and statutory decrees
throughout the nation that led to near universal white male suffrage by
1840.[2] These same efforts very often stripped the franchise from the few
black men who theretofore held it, and the 1838 Constitution of Pennsylvania became the most notorious case: not only was the state home to one of
the largest and most politically active free black populations, but also the
designation of "white freeman" made black disenfranchisement a total affair. (By contrast, the 1821 Constitution of New York gave the vote to all
white men in the state but retained prohibitive property qualifications for
black men that disenfranchised *nearly* all of them.[3]) When black Pennsylvanians first got word of the Constitutional Convention's proposal to restrict
the franchise to "white freemen," they immediately began a campaign to
defeat the amendment's passage. Robert Purvis, a leading figure in the Underground Railroad and future president of the Pennsylvania Anti-Slavery
Society, crafted the most eloquent and influential remonstrance of the
amendment, "Appeal of Forty Thousand Citizens, Threatened with Disenfranchisement, to the People of Pennsylvania." In the "Appeal," Purvis declared African Americans were especially qualified for the franchise because, above all else, they upheld the nation's highest ideals and values in
the face of state-sanctioned inequities and everyday terror.[4]

Along with its rhetorical power, one of the most remarkable details of
Purvis' "Appeal" was just how broad its audience quickly became: opponents of the amendment circulated the tract among their syndicates, and,
more crucially, the *Public Ledger*, Philadelphia's first penny paper and its
most popular daily in the antebellum period, reprinted it.[5] The editors' decision to publish the "Appeal" in the *Public Ledger* reflects how the cam-

paigns for black citizenship and full inclusion increasingly gripped multiple northern publics, particularly those in urban centers.[6] If Purvis' white readers were to accept the premises and pleas of his "Appeal," for instance, they would have had to repudiate the race-specific arguments they used to expand the nation's participatory frameworks. That is, as white common people from the 1820s onward worked to dislodge the hold that the class of economic and political elites maintained on the levers of governance, an undertaking that constituted the dominant ideological and rhetorical engine of Jacksonian democracy, they most often based their claims on the related beliefs in the natural equality of white men and the natural inferiority of black people. Yet Purvis' "Appeal" ran counter to such notions.[7]

Indeed, the collective of African Americans rejected these budding discourses of racial inherence, which became more "biological" or "scientific" as the nineteenth century progressed, and their implications for black participation in the polity. Instead, they continued to claim the mantle of American republicanism as their own, often doing so by appropriating what literary historian Ivy G. Wilson terms "the established rhetoric of the national vernacular."[8] The dominant affects, figures, and narratives of the national vernacular were most often those related to the history of the nation's founding, and African Americans made sure to stress their role as prime agents in that history. In his "Appeal," for example, Purvis recalled the shared sacrifices of the American War of Independence to substantiate his entreaties for black enfranchisement: "In which of the battles of the revolution did not our fathers fight as bravely as yours, for American liberty? Was it that their children might be disfranchised and loaded with insult that they endured the famine of Valley Forge, and the horrors of the Jersey Prison Ship?"[9] As Purvis' interventionist reading instantiated, antebellum African Americans affirmed themselves as architects and, thus, legitimate beneficiaries of American possibility and promise; it was a political strategy they learned from their early national predecessors.

Antebellum black publics were not the only ones looking back to the beginnings of the U.S., however. White northerners, too, returned to the nation's founding events to project the polity's (racial) future. As Ralph Emerson proclaimed at the beginning of his magisterial book, *Nature* (1836), "Our age is retrospective. It builds the sepulchers of the fathers. It writes biographies, histories, and criticism. The foregoing generations beheld God and nature face to face; we, through their eyes."[10] Scholars of antebellum cultural production have been particularly attuned to the ways in which these retrospective acts manifest in the great literary and philosophical works of the period, but they have been less attentive to how those acts took shape in theatre and performance culture, the representational domain where most antebellum Americans would have "revisited" their revolutionary and early national pasts.[11] This chapter explores a number of these less studied performances, centering on a set of theatrical works that reimagined the people, places, and events of the Revolutionary era as means to theorize the place of free blackness in the nation going forward. Several of these texts and practices admitted the historical significance of black people to the formation of the U.S. but refused to accept them as worthy of full and equal participation therein. In the process, these works enacted a uniquely northern strand of proslavery thought: namely, black people as slaves were pivotal to the nation's founding and are therefore most useful to the nation as slaves.[12]

## DEFORMING HISTORY: BLACK LEADERSHIP
## AND AMERICAN REVOLUTIONS

Within these re-stagings of the birth of the nation, the figure of George Washington emerged as audiences' most favored. In the dominant imagination, Washington, above all others, epitomized the virtues of republicanism and mitigated the sectional differences and social and political developments (e.g., the acceleration of capitalism, the entrenchment of essentialist discourse, and hyper-partisanship) that were steadily fracturing the nation. As historian Robert S. Cox explains, "Washington charted a spiritual terrain that linked individuals affectively, not only to kin and kind, but to the extended nation." He was "a way to *think* and *feel* the nation, to create a constellation of love that consolidated family and state in mutually cognizable dependency and that offered a reformist map of the structures of the sundered body politic."[13] Although Cox's primary interest is Washington's "postmortem career" within Spiritualism, the mid-nineteenth-century religious movement built on communing with the dead, his reading applies equally to the ways in which Washington signified within normative theatrical formations. (Of course, theatre is its own "dubious spectacle" within which the living encounters the dead.[14])

African Americans were far more ambivalent toward Washington. As a lifelong slave owner, he too readily upheld proslavery arguments and race-based inequities.[15] Because Washington offered "messages of freedom" *and* "examples of proper domestic management of one's slaves," an aporia beset his figuration; his was a "confused identity" that, as cultural historian Russ Castronovo puts it, "functioned as a telling symptom of a national inconsistency, of an incoherent American body."[16] African Americans remained well aware of the narrative and symbolic problematics Washington posed their struggle toward citizenship and full inclusion, but, given his preeminence in the national imaginary, they could not wholly jettison him, either. Frederick Douglass' manipulation of the name "Washington" in his personal life and literary work is illustrative of this negotiation. While enslaved, Douglass dropped Washington (along with Augustus) from his name, thus rejecting the supremacy of his master and, more obliquely, the Founding Father himself. Yet the mutinous slave protagonist of his 1852 novella, "The Heroic Slave," is "Madison Washington," a character that Douglass modeled on his ideal combination of intellect, righteousness, and passion. Castronovo argues, "Douglass' changing attitudes not so much represent an acceptance of the national legacy as they indicate the development among nineteenth-century African Americans of a narrative strategy that repeats history in order to deform it."[17] The move to "deform" history was one of the primary tactics antebellum African Americans used to revise the national vernacular and craft what literary historian John Ernest brilliantly terms a "liberation historiography," a mode of writing and a body of texts with which to bring about universal emancipation and citizenship.

Washington was a significant figure in black deformations of history because he functioned as something of an epistemological hook that conjured two interconnected ideals that engrossed antebellum African Americans: charismatic leadership and revolutionary possibility. With a more conspicuous national black public sphere materializing in the late 1820s and early 1830s, the desire emerged for magnetic leaders who could maintain some sort of cohesion among African Americans across the north, west, and even some parts of the south.[18] Unlike the imaginative ties that early nineteenth-century print and performance practices fostered among newly freed slaves and their descendants, black agitation from the Jacksonian period through the Civil War—not to mention unprecedented advances in steam, rail, and print technologies—brought geographically disparate African Americans into far greater material contact. Indeed, the circulation of the first black newspapers, national and intra-state conventions composed of black delegates dedicated to racial uplift, and a more radical abolitionism made the "national" of a black public sphere more actual than notional. These developments brought into relief the signal differences of behavioral sensibility and reform strategy that split along lines of class, complexion, and region. Accordingly, the call for black leadership surfaced more as an appeal for negotiators and translators of this ideological polyvalence rather than a desire for a single master vision.[19]

The archival predominance of the class of antebellum black leaders obscures this dynamism. Political and sociocultural "thinking" among the masses of black communities most often took place in more ephemeral and performative sites, through what historian Patrick Rael aptly describes as "shared daily experiences and participation in a cultural milieu of words and rituals that united them and gave meaning to their lives."[20] Those black men and women who became leaders and spokespersons emerged from this milieu, within which they honed their individual personas. The rhetorical praxis they developed was the product of the way their singular talents were collectively conditioned by a people hardly, if at all, removed from slavery. In other words, the public voice of antebellum black politics was not only a speaking *for* the race, but also a speaking *from* it. Thus, we should not treat even the most contentious of African Americans' entreaties as idiosyncratic; rather, we should approach it as the consequence of some sort of widely shared aim. Calls for continued revolution, for instance, reflected African Americans' desire to see the nation extend to all segments of the population the democratic possibilities American independence actualized. For them, the American Revolution was not past or complete; that is, the rhetorical and perhaps some of the armed interventions colonists waged against Great Britain in the eighteenth century were necessary to end black captivity in its multiple forms in the nineteenth.

Much like their parents and grandparents had in the wake of the nation's founding, antebellum African Americans classified black revolutionary action as thoroughly American, and they often relied on the figure of George Washington to signify as such. For example, in his 1843 "An Address to the Slaves of the United States of America," ex-slave and radical abolitionist Henry Highland Garnet argued that slave insurrection was in the tradition of the best of Western freedom struggles. Praising Denmark Vesey's 1822 attempt to lead his fellow slaves in an uprising in South Carolina, Garnet proclaimed, "He was betrayed by the treachery of his own people, and died a martyr to freedom. Many a brave hero fell, but history, faithful to her high trust, will transcribe his name on the same monument with Moses, Hampden, Tell, Bruce and Wallace, Toussaint L'Ouverture, Lafayette and Washington."[21] This list of exemplary leaders who delivered their people from physical or sociopolitical subjection maintained considerable purchase on the nation's collective consciousness. But Washington is unique here because he is the only American. As such, he validates the promise of (black) revolution on domestic soil.

Despite its complications, the imaginative relation African Americans fostered with Washington was stronger than that between them and the

other men Garnet lists, with one possible exception: Toussaint L'Ouverture.
L'Ouverture was the leader of the late eighteenth-century slave uprisings
that culminated in the independent nation of Haiti, the first black-led republic in the Western Hemisphere. Throughout the antebellum period, African Americans exalted him as the epitome of black freedom, sacrifice, and
self-governance, though they remained wary of identifying with the bloody
Haitian Revolution itself too much because they did not want to disquiet
the white men and women around them.[22] Perhaps the weightiest of these
black-authored encomiums of L'Ouverture was that of ex-slave, abolitionist, and literary pioneer William Wells Brown, "St. Domingo: Its Revolutions and its Patriots." Wells Brown first delivered this lecture in London in
May 1854, then later that December in Philadelphia, and published it in
Boston in 1855.[23] In the address, he detailed the first slave uprisings that
L'Ouverture commanded, subsequent battles Haitians waged with France
to establish and maintain their independence, and the turbulent internal
strife that strained the nation during its first decades of existence. Throughout, Wells Brown maintained that only black leadership such as that
L'Ouverture performed could lead to the alleviation of black suffering.

For Wells Brown, the necessity for black leaders was both urgent and
historically legitimated. To ground his argument, he contrasted the examples of Toussaint L'Ouverture and George Washington:

> And, lastly, Toussaint's career as a Christian, a statesman, and a gen-
> eral, will lose nothing by comparison with that of Washington. Each
> was the leader of an oppressed and outraged people, each had a
> powerful enemy to contend with, and each succeeded in founding a
> government in the New World. Toussaint's government made lib-
> erty its watchword, incorporated it in its constitution, abolished the
> slave-trade, and made freedom universal amongst the people. Tous-
> saint liberated his countrymen; Washington enslaved a portion of
> his, and aided in giving strength and vitality to an institution that
> will one day rend asunder the UNION that he helped to form.[24]

The comparative structure of this prescient exposition functions both histo-
riographically and prospectively; it suggests that the decisions of the past
do not disappear but accrete to produce future presents. Wells Brown understood his historical moment as bound up with the nation's first moments because, in his estimation, those moments never ceased. As he proclaimed at the end of the lecture, "The indignation of the slaves of the south
would kindle a fire so hot that it would melt their chains, drop by drop,

until not a single link would remain; *and the revolution that was commenced in 1776 would then be finished.*"[25]

William Cooper Nell, a leader of the black Boston community and the most notable black historian of the antebellum period, also understood the American Revolution as ongoing. He believed how Americans wrote the history of their revolution was central to its eventual outcome. In 1855, the same year Wells Brown circulated the text to his lecture on Santo Domingo, Nell published *The Colored Patriots of the American Revolution, with Sketches of Several Distinguished Colored Persons: to which is added a Brief Survey of the Conditions and Prospects of Colored Americans.* He begins the narrative of *Colored Patriots* in 1851, when he and his associates unsuccessfully petitioned the Massachusetts legislature to erect a fifteen-hundred-dollar "monument to the memory of CRISPUS ATTUCKS, the first martyr of the Boston Massacre of March 5th, 1770."[26] (The recognition of Attucks as a national martyr was central to Nell's literary and performance activism, and throughout the late 1850s he pressed for a Crispus Attucks Day.[27] In fact, *Colored Patriots* opens with a rendering of Attucks' death that Nell would use later for a broadside calling for that day of recognition.) Nell's decision to start *Colored Patriots* with his failed effort to raise the monument is no mere anecdotal point of departure. Rather, the account establishes Attucks as the leader of the revolution the text subsequently details. In this sense, the book itself becomes the monument to Attucks; that is, he is "honored as a grateful country honors other [i.e., white] gallant Americans."[28] Furthermore, the 1851 start of *Colored Patriots* initiates the temporal disorder that characterizes Nell's methodology; the book is structured around geography rather than chronology, with each chapter detailing men and women from a specific state. Nell's refusal of a chronological spine helps produce a textual locus of contemporaneity within which "several distinguished colored persons" who did not take part in the armed conflicts of the American Revolution become "Colored Patriots" of it. These include writers and poets, and Nell interpolates samples of their work into *Colored Patriots.*[29] Despite Nell's dating of events, the book's subjects coalesce into a kind of synchronicity or "present" that seeks to bring about a future of universal freedom and black citizenship.

Chapter XII of *Colored Patriots*, "North Carolina," typifies this effect. Nell offers sketches of four men from the state: David Walker, Jonathan Overton, Delph Williamson, and George Horton. Like the structure of the book itself, the arrangement of these brief portraits defies chronology. Walker is listed first followed by Overton, but Overton was born before Walker and the order of their deaths is unclear. (Williamson and Horton were still alive at the time of Nell's writing.) The flow from sketch to sketch is indiscriminate and lacks transitions; it moves from Walker, writer of the *Appeal* (1829), to Overton, a soldier who served under George Washington in the Continental Army, to Williamson, a slave who witnessed the Revolution, to Horton, the esteemed slave poet. In all, the chapter includes biography, criticism, written testimony, newspaper accounts, and poetry. This diversity of authorial voice and literary genres redoubles Nell's deforming history: that is, to repeat but revise the national past with signal differences of *form* in addition to those of content. As a result, these four North Carolinian men become colored patriots fighting alongside each other in the ongoing American Revolution.[30]

*Colored Patriots* encapsulates the conceptual, methodological, and narrative tactics with which African American cultural producers and historians deformed the American past as means to reorient the nation's course going forward. They fostered a *positive* view of their shared history, however circumscribed it might have been. More broadly, they anticipated Walter Benjamin's assessment of the stakes and struggle of historiographic representation: "Only that historian will have the gift of fanning the spark of hope in the past who is firmly convinced that *even the dead* will not be safe if the enemy wins."[31] Garnet, Wells Brown, Nell, and other African Americans who deformed history knew the dead could not be left alone but were central to the battle over the meaning of the nation's past and the progress of its future; so, too, did their antagonists.

## THE PASTORAL AND PROSLAVERY DOMESTICITY

The embrace of the dead as "present" and instrumental in American life was ubiquitous in the antebellum period. Spiritualism, for example, was a fast-growing religion in the mid-nineteenth century and was based on its devotees communicating directly with the dead.[32] In addition to the affective and phenomenological bonds that Spiritualists forged with the dead, Americans also used death as a heuristic with which to conceptualize ideal American citizenship. To conceive of democratic participation in terms of death is to strive for a polity without contingency and volatility. As Castronovo explains, "The final release from embodiment plays a resonant role in the national imagination by suggesting an existence, posthumous as well as posthistorical, that falls outside standard registers of the political. . . . The afterlife emancipates souls from passionate debates, everyday engagements, and earthly affairs that animate the political field."[33] The material and corporeal differences that divided Americans quickened this theory of "necro citizenship," which "incites a necrophilic desire to put democratic unpredictability and spontaneity to death"; it was a way to project a world free of the unrest and vagaries that racialized and other differently marked living bodies incur.[34]

The problem, of course, is that a democracy is lived, and therefore its particulars are necessarily dynamic, temporal, and variable. But necrophilic antebellum publics claimed otherwise. They argued that the nation's first dead already spelled out those particulars, and it was the living's responsibility to recall the dead's intentions—literally so, if one was a Spiritualist—and fashion the nation accordingly. Others, like the young Abraham Lincoln, were less yielding to their dead (national) fathers and mothers. In the most absolute instances, these men and women committed what Castronovo terms "figurative parricide"; that is, they "abandon[ed] deference to either historical beginnings or continuity."[35] For example, in his 1838 "Address before the Young Men's Lyceum of Springfield, Illinois," Lincoln warned of the dangers of conceding the direction of the future to the dictates of the past. Such an approach, he presciently argued, would devastate American political institutions and rend the nation. In particular, Lincoln claimed that the "interesting scenes of the Revolution" and the "passions . . . against the British" they produced "must fade" because they stymied the affective and imaginative resources necessary for the nation's ongoing functionality and betterment. He went on:

> I do not mean to say that the scenes of the Revolution are now or ever will be entirely forgotten, but that, like everything else, they must fade upon the memory of the world, and grow more and more dim by the lapse of time. In history, we hope, they will be read of, and recounted, so long as the Bible shall be read; but even granting that they will, their influence cannot be what it heretofore has been. Even then they cannot be so universally known nor so vividly felt as they were by the generation just gone to rest. At the close of that struggle, nearly every adult male had been a participator in some of its scenes. The consequence was that of those scenes, in the form of a husband, a father, a son, or a brother, a living history was to be found in every family. [. . .] But those histories are gone. They can be read no more forever. They were a fortress of strength; but what invading foeman could never do, the silent artillery of time has done—the leveling of its walls. They are gone.[36]

Lincoln's historiographical absolutism rendered his particular moment singular, a beginning both distinct and divergent from what came before. He pressed his audiences to unmoor themselves from the past and project their future using their own terms and with their own aims in mind; that is, he urged Americans to seize control of their democracy because they were the ones living it.

Lincoln's entreaty was not only a political intervention but also something of a cultural one. He objected to the way Americans raised the dead in their cultural formations as means to deal with the turbulent newness the Jacksonian period engendered; he argued for the gritty and uncomfortable work of grappling with and through the living. African Americans agreed with Lincoln up to a point but could not fully abandon the dead because the nation's social and political shortcomings proved to them that the revolutionary events of the late eighteenth century were unfinished. Several of their antagonists also refused to concede the past, and looked back to the very same historical moments African Americans did to legitimate their opposition to black freedom and inclusion.

One of the earliest of these re-stagings was Samuel Woodworth's play *King's Bridge Cottage* (1826). Woodworth worked in all areas of literary production as an editor, printer, publisher, and writer.[37] Patriotic renderings of American history and historical actors abound in his body of work, from *Champions of Freedom* (1816), a novel based on the events of the War of 1812, to *Forest Rose; or, American Farmers* (1825), one of the most popular dramas of the antebellum period. *Forest Rose* featured the hugely popular character Jonathon Ploughboy, a stage Yankee that, as theatre historian Bruce McConachie notes, "embodi[ed] republican virtues [and] told stories with a New England twang and balanced rationalistic calculation with sentimental action."[38] Jonathon is Woodworth's most lasting contribution to American cultural history. For its part, *King's Bridge Cottage* was nonetheless significant in its historical moment because it both registered and stimulated the cultural and racial politics of the 1820s north. The play offered a kind of blueprint with which to reconcile the practice of black inequality with the principles of American liberty by means of dramatic retellings of the Revolutionary era.

*King's Bridge Cottage* premiered at the Amateur Theatre in New York City and resurfaced at least once in the 1830s, when the city's fashionable Richmond Hill Theatre restaged it in celebration of George Washington's birthday.[39] The play follows the capture and subsequent rescue of an American ingénue from her British abductor, a not-too-subtle metaphor for its broader setting of the American War of Independence. Though its characters report on several events that marked the war's end, it is impossible to tell exactly when *King's Bridge Cottage* takes place: its subtitle notes it is "founded on an incident which occurred a few days previous to the evacuation of N. York," which would date the play in 1783, but the action ends with "despatches from the Commander in Chief" that proclaims Cornwallis' surrender, and that would set *King's Bridge Cottage* in 1781. The play's lack of historical specificity was not the result of haphazard dramaturgy. Rather, Woodworth, like many early American playwrights, took liberties with the past because his was project was not historical precision but, instead, socio-national invention and vitalization, the necessary cultural work of a still new republican polity.

With the play, Woodworth suggests black captivity was essential to the preservation of the U.S. The slave character, Cato, declares his worth to the patriot causes of political freedom and national independence but defends the propriety of chattel enslavement, including his own. (Slavery would almost entirely disappear from New York in 1827, when the course of the state's gradual emancipation laws would reach its endpoint. Woodworth and his audiences knew this, so it is possible to read *King's Bridge Cottage* as a kind of yearning for an institution free New Yorkers depended on to legitimate their freedoms.) In his defense of slavery, Cato spells out a form of racial paternalism in which "families" composed of masters and slaves thrive when they maintain bonds of complementarity, mutuality, and reinforcement. Black people needed such care and protection from their white "fathers," according to this view, because they lack the mental and physical wherewithal to function and survive in an increasingly modern world. Throughout the antebellum period, opponents of black inclusion marshaled this "biological" argument, just as proslavery ideologues did in defense of chattel slavery; what makes Cato's iteration of it particularly noteworthy is the way in which he melds it with a nationalist rhetoric.[40] In soliloquy he declares:

> Lad-a-massy, what sabbage scoundrel Ingrish soger be. . . . I wonder Ginerl Washington don't abbertise in de paper, for brack soger? I speck he tink do dat white soger got pluch 'nuff, and dat de nigger run 'way same as if de debill after him. He mistaken if he tink so bout me, for I bin used to berry hard using and terrible sight ob up and down, 'fore good old massa Richardson buy me at de hoss auction; he berry kind to Cato, and I must go gib him little comfort, or cry 'long with him.[41]

At the end of the speech, Cato runs off to take care of his master. Just as he tends to the diurnal needs of Richardson, Richardson keeps Cato from a life of "berry hard using and terrible sight ob up and down." Master and slave live together in a "country dwelling" with its tranquil environs (the other settings in the play are a cottage and the woods). If not for the war and the villainous British officer who kidnaps the play's ingénue, the Americans would enjoy an unending bucolic bliss. But they do not shy from the fight. Cato aids and protects his masters from the British, actions that suggest the slave's role is the maintenance of the home *and* of the nation. What emerges in *King's Bridge Cottage*, then, is a figuration of black-white domesticity that is at once pastoral and historicist.

The pastoral was the prevailing idiom of racial paternalism. As Saidiya Hartman contends, "The pastoral renders the state of domination as an ideal of care, familial obligation, gratitude, and humanity. . . . As a mode of historical representation, the pastoral seizes upon the strains of song and story, invariably part of slave life, as precious components in the depiction of the moral landscape of slave life, in order to give voice to values of the social order in the appropriately simple tones of the enslaved."[42] Though the most enduring inscriptions of this form of the pastoral recur in the discourses, melodies, and narratives of nineteenth-century minstrelsy, works such as *King's Bridge Cottage* also performed the kind of "historical representation" that Hartman describes here.[43] The problem, however, was that such representations of slave contentedness and reciprocity were clearly spurious. That is, if enactments of the pastoral were "emblems of an integral moral economy," the ethicality of that economy was dubious at best because of the actuality of boundless injury and psychic brutality intrinsic to the institution of chattel slavery—those very "scenes of subjection."

As historiography, then, slave domesticity rendered in terms of the pastoral was largely easy to dismiss, but that figured in nationalist terms was not. Slaves *did* play an important part in the fight for American independence and the building of the nation, and Cato's contemplation of black involvement in the war conjures those actions. He asks, "I wonder Ginerl Washington don't abbertise in de paper, for brack soger?"[44] Although Washington might not have advertised in newspapers for black soldiers, there were certainly many who fought as part of the Continental forces, not to mention those slaves and free people of color who provided necessary provisions and support away from the battlefield.[45] Unlike the vast majority of these men and women, however, Cato pledges himself to Washington *and* to a life of slavery; the prospect of freedom for his service does not figure into his calculation. His deeds and words evoke the proslavery figuration of the captive black and the free white working toward the establishment of an enduring national harmony. The facts of black involvement in the revolutionary cause matter little to the socio-racial politics *King's Bridge Cottage* articulates. Instead, the significance of Cato's rumination and of his actions throughout the play, including his efforts to foil the machinations of a British officer, depends on their effect as domestic fantasy: namely, the projection of the mutually constitutive home-family and nation-family.

A romanticized Burkean conservatism animated this fantasy. This set of principles holds that men are not created equal but nature endows, indeed obliges, the talented very few to govern the intellectually and socially inept multitudes. Familial metaphors often express this hierarchy (e.g., "The Father of the Country," "Big Daddy," or "Uncle Tom and Aunt Chloe"). Its advocates claimed it to be a sociality of reciprocating protection, ensuring the strong would protect the weak, the weak would provide some necessary service to the strong, and, thus, all parties would thrive "molecularly," as a unit, despite the vicissitudes of the outside world. For proslavery paternalists, race-based chattel slavery was the ideal institution with which to achieve this communal order because, in their view, it fortifies blacks and whites from the perils of bourgeois liberalism, capitalism, and other modern social and political developments. This theory, Eugene Genovese explains, "extended and reinforced the bonds of family life. Accustomed to treat slaves as members of a larger family, the master has his sense of natural family enormously strengthened," just as his slaves should feel protected as part of that family.[46] Sustained by ties of affectivity and affinity, this form of proslavery domesticity seeks to insulate masters and slaves from the uncertainties of change and the menace of time itself.

Of course, emancipation negated the possibility of this slave-based sociality in the north. Nevertheless, northerners transmuted its underlying theories of innate yet complementary differences among the races to shape their expectations of the way the course of black freedom should unfold in the region. From proscriptions on employment and civic inequities to the struggle over leadership in abolitionism and other reform movements, normative treatments of free black life steadily turned on burgeoning discourses of biological essentialism and racial inherence, theories that rendered the African (American) as a "pathetically inept creature who was a slave to his emotions, incapable of progressive development and self-government because he lacked the white man's enterprise and intellect."[47] Plays and performances like *King's Bridge Cottage* instantiated this discourse of inherent black inferiority, but they did so while granting black-people-as-slaves a critical role in the sustenance of interpersonal and national domesticity. Yet no other cultural event in the period enacted this "compromise" more forcefully than did P. T. Barnum's exhibition tour of Joice Heth, a performance that brilliantly synthesized the biological, the historical, and the pastoral in its defense of black captivity.

## BARNUM'S HETH: EXHIBITING OWNERSHIP, WRITING MASTERY

From August 1835 to January 1836, Barnum exhibited an elderly black woman called Joice Heth, whom he advertised as "the Nurse of Gen. George Washington (the Father of Our Country) Now Living at the Astonishing Age of 161 Years and Weighs only 46 Pounds."[48] Audiences throughout the northeast thronged to see Heth, who regaled them with tales of raising and even suckling the infant George Washington; sang hymns and other devotions; and engaged in spirited banter. They also marveled at her anatomical peculiarities, which were, as one representative account puts it, "eyes . . . entirely run out and closed," "nails . . . near an inch long and on the great toes horny and thick like bone and incurvated, looking like the claws of a bird of prey," and "nothing but skin and bones."[49] Barnum advertised her as a "natural & national curiosity," and he exhibited Heth at all manner of establishments, from the genteel and Whiggish to the rowdy and Jacksonian.[50] The veracity of her story, or lack thereof, captivated journalists, scientists, and lay audiences during the tour and even more so in the years following her death. Without question, Heth was "one of the first true American media celebrities" and catapulted Barnum on his way to becoming the most famous entertainer of the nineteenth-century U.S.[51]

Though the exhibition's affective and ideological meanings were manifold, I want to focus on two of its interrelated features that most tellingly enacted the fantasy of proslavery domesticity I have been tracing in this chapter: Heth's corporeal link to a mythical national past and the ambiguity of her slave/free status. Barnum's staging of Joice Heth as the pious, at times cantankerous wet nurse of George Washington theatricalized a fantastical coalescence of living history and tranquil black captivity. These relations became vividly material because Heth's wizened body and most intimate of acts were on display: audiences watched her eat, drink, sleep, smoke, and talk; they asked about her bowel movements; they also imagined her suckling Washington—and maybe even themselves. The projection of the self onto Heth's breasts instantiated what performance scholar Uri McMillan calls "mammy-memory," which was "a strange dependence on, and perhaps even nostalgic longing for, . . . black wet-nursing, a social

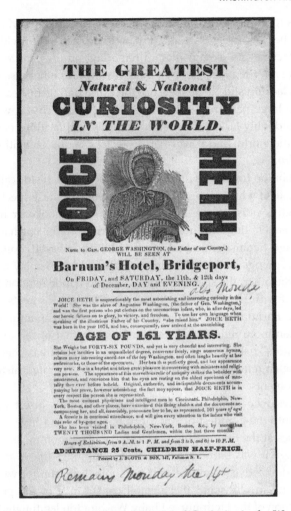

Figure 6: "The Greatest Natural & National Curiosity in the World.
Joice Heth, Nurse to Gen. GEORGE WASHINGTON, (the Father of
Our Country,)" (1835). Courtesy of Somers Historical Society, Somers
New York.

practice that was predicated on white infants' vulnerability and dependence on their black maternal care-takers for survival."[52] In this way, "Aunt
Joice," as Barnum and his co-manager Levy Lyman called her in the promotional pamphlet biography they circulated during the tour, signified as
the nation's mammy because she was the national Father's mammy.

The "familial" relation Heth evoked is a fundamentally reciprocal one:

the loving support that she and other slaves give their young white masters is returned because these masters grow up to protect and provide for their slaves. In fact, several commentators remarked on the care and comfort that Barnum afforded Heth, who in their view would otherwise have been a helpless black invalid.[53] The pleasure the exhibition furnished spectators emerged in large part from this paternalist relation. To her white audiences, Heth doubly lacked the mental and physical faculties necessary to survive in the world, and it was her protectors' moral obligation to safeguard her from it.

The exhibition framed its paternalism in biological, historical, and pastoral terms, all of which became far more tangible for those spectators who checked Heth's pulse, fingered her wrinkles, and shook her hand. This staging, it bears noting, was in some ways daring: on the one hand, Heth's purported age, her anatomical oddities, and the bombastic promotion and theatrical trappings of the exhibition established her display as a "freak show"; on the other, the spatial propinquity and haptic relation that audiences shared with Heth undercut the antebellum freak show's normative architecture. Barnum's refusal to erect barriers fostered an intimate spectatorial relation more redolent of a visitation than that of the theatre, and Heth's "visitors" risked the contagions of a perceived "freak" because they were one touch removed from the nation's most venerated historical figures and moments.

Audiences who sought to touch history and thus insert themselves physically into the grandest of American narratives had little concern for what skeptics at the time rightly declared the exhibition to be: a veritable sham. Though it was Barnum's first major "humbug," Heth *qua* national body offered affective, cognitive, and psychological calm for white northerners seeking to withstand the turmoil constitutive of the period. The soothing fiction of the Heth-nursed baby Washington legitimated the even more soothing fiction of a Washington-birthed nation of a people blessed over all others.[54] The ability to touch Heth grounded these fictions into a (black) material reality, and the shaking of Heth's hand was perhaps the most meaningful of those touches. The handshake, as cultural historian Benjamin Reiss neatly puts it, was "for nineteenth-century Americans a fleshy gesture of republicanism."[55] Shaking hands with Heth was hardly an acknowledgment of her republican subjectivity, though; rather, it was a corporeal gateway for her audiences to return to the U.S.'s beginnings. Thus, in addition to the vast interest audiences took in Heth's gnarled physiology—so much that Barnum staged a public autopsy of Heth, which nearly 1,500 people paid the high price of fifty cents to attend—the imaginative networks audiences crafted on and through her body were just as appealing as that body itself.[56]

For Reiss, this affective and fantastical labor amounted to a "figurative public servitude to the northern whites who visited her and followed her story."[57] In other words, Heth was the nation's slave, a slave whose bodily acts sustained the emotional, narrative, and even somatic bonds of American mythologies. Because they saw Heth as a living monument to the birth of the nation, men such as Henry Cole, a patron of the tony Niblo's Garden in New York City, objected to the way in which Barnum produced the exhibition. (Niblo's Garden was where Barnum first staged Heth.) Cole wrote to the *New York Sun* in order to "ascertain why SHE who nursed the 'father of our country,' the man to whom we owe our present happy and prosperous condition, should at the close of her life be exhibited as 'our rarer monsters are.'"[58] These "rarer monsters" were the *lusus naturae*, or "nature's freaks," that captivated audiences and a steadily growing class of scientists that would go on to create the field of teratology, the study of congenital and acquired abnormalities.[59] For Cole, Heth did not deserve the gaze of the popular eye or the scalpel of the scientific hand because of what she performed and embodied: she was, as he proclaimed, "the sole remaining tie of mortality which connects us to him who was 'first in war, first in peace, and first in the hearts of his countrymen'—and as such, we should protect and honor her, and not suffer her to be kept for a show, like a wild beast, to fill the coffers of mercenary men."[60]

Cole's censure of the exhibition rested on the question of ownership. He argued that Barnum and his associates had no right to profit from displaying Heth because they had no right to Heth. Instead, she belonged to all Americans—literally so. "She is the common property of our country," Cole declared.[61] Given the socio-racial context of his assertion, Cole's notion of Heth as "common property" is closer to an actual designation than a figurative one. Heth was born into slavery, so the feasibility of her (or any black person, for that matter) as chattel was anything but far-fetched. Cole and similar-minded critics of the exhibition did not specify how collective ownership of Heth might take shape, but their view of her as "common property" evidenced northerners' willingness to tolerate, indeed encourage, black captivity.

The public servitude that Cole imagined for Heth reflected how northern attitudes and laws permitted her personal servitude to Barnum. Even though Barnum exhibited Heth in a number of free states—including in Pennsylvania, New York, Massachusetts, and Rhode Island, all of which were home to abolitionist strongholds—there was no absolute dictate, statutory or juridical, that would have freed her once she entered their borders. Moreover, the irregularity and frequent disregard of interstate comity rendered slaves who traveled north "neither fugitive nor free" but positioned them within a kind of existential limbo.[62] To be sure, those slaves who went before courts had their fates settled, but these decisions did not culminate in a body of case law that states adhered to. In Heth's case, evidently no one, including abolitionists, made a challenge on behalf of her freedom. As Reiss points out, "Few questioned the propriety of [Barnum's] relationship to her, and even fewer latched onto the potential legal issues involved in a Yankee's participation in chattel slavery on free ground. . . . No abolitionist paper seems to have commented on her exhibit, and no abolition society took her up as a cause célèbre."[63] That African Americans did not concern themselves with Heth's cause is surprising, though the years of her tour coincided with a profound fracturing of black leadership; perhaps her case was lost in these cracks.[64] Nonetheless, black silence on Heth's captivity was secondary to the larger chorus of white acceptance of it, an acceptance that Barnum tapped into to promote his tour of Heth and boost his reputation as a deserving cultural idol after her death.

In the exhibition's promotional pamphlet, *The Life of Joice Heth, the Nurse of George Washington*, there is no mention of whether the Heth that northern audiences went to see was free. The pamphlet simply notes that she is extremely pleased with her present condition, particularly in light of the history of her enslavement: when she was "at the age of fifteen," her captors snatched her from the "Island of Madagascar, on the Coast of Africa" to work on plantations in Virginia, where she "was the first person to put clothes on the unconscious infant . . . little Georgy," and in the fields of Kentucky, where she "had been very much neglected, laying for years in an outer building, upon the naked floor."[65] Even more than a marketing effort, Barnum and Levy's published retelling of Heth's personal history, with its affixed "certifications" that purportedly substantiate that history, amounts to a kind of slave narrative. Specifically, *The Life of Joice Heth* is an example of what literary historian Robert Stepto theorizes as an "authenticating narrative" because its "machinery [e.g., letters, newspaper accounts, and testimonials] either remains as important as the tale or actually becomes, usually for some purpose residing outside the text, the dominant and motivating feature of the narrative."[66] What the entire accompanying materials supposedly authenticated was, indeed, extra-textual: namely, the touring exhibition and Heth's ongoing captivity. Thus, the structural apparatus of *The Life of Joice Heth* was similar to that of the vast majority of antebellum slave narratives, but the economic and sociopolitical aims of

Barnum and Levy's text differed radically from the latter's customary anti-slavery intentions.

If *The Life of Joice Heth* reads as proslavery slave narrative, then it was only the first text in a number of antebellum literary renderings of the Heth affair that Barnum wrote (or authorized) that are structured around the binary of white mastery and black captivity. Given Barnum's patent striving and singular ability to gratify public demand, his decision to write repeatedly about Heth and his interactions with other black people using this binary signals just how meaningful northerners' proslavery imagination was. For example, one of the earliest biographical (perhaps autobiographical) portraits of Barnum details his travels with a circus company through "every portion of the Union," and it was "during these peregrinations, [when] he came across the famous Joyce Heth, in Kentucky." When he reached Vicksburg, Mississippi, he "purchased a negro . . . to attend him as a servant." After "several hundred dollars [went missing] from his pocket . . . Barnum suspected the 'nigger,' searched him, found the money, gave him fifty lashes, and took him to New Orleans, where he was sold at auction." While in New Orleans, he visited the nearby town of St. Martinsville where "he sold his streamer and all his horses, receiving in payment cash, sugar, molasses, and a *negro woman and child*."[67] Written in 1845 by an anonymous "foreign correspondent" (most likely Barnum himself) for the *New York Atlas*, a long-running Sunday-only Jacksonian paper, this account makes plain Barnum's thorough involvement in the capital and social economies of slavery, including trading in the New Orleans slave market, which was the nation's largest and most brutal. Yet the narrative does so with a remarkable ordinariness. Its tonal dispassion in its descriptions of the slaveholding Barnum suggests that his exploits in the south would not have upset the paper's principal readership, the urban white working class of the north. In my view, these readers countenanced the brutality intrinsic to chattel slavery not only out of an apathy and, in some cases, desire for broken black bodies, but also out of a yearning to identify with the mastership wielded by one of their very own, the Yankee Barnum.

By the time Barnum (or his amanuensis) published this story of his time in the south, he knew his readership well, and they him, because he had been writing for the *Atlas* since 1841. His first major piece, *The Adventures of an Adventurer*, was an autobiographical novella the *Atlas* serialized over twelve weeks, and he wrote it under the *nom de plume* Barnaby Diddleum. The most anticipated chapters of *The Adventures* were those that recounted the circumstances of the Heth exhibition. Relating his first encounter with the "black beauty," Barnum explains that he "thought this woman a great curiosity, and that she might be turned to some account by being exhibited." As a result, "a bargain was immediately struck and aunt Joice *became the property of Diddleum* and . . . contributed very extensively to the principal adventurers of an adventurer." For the rest of her life, Heth was then "commanded at my *sovereign will* and *pleasure*."[68] *The Adventures* limns Barnum as an omnipotent and omniscient master, yet that description lacks the turgidity with which the novella frames his talents as a showman and businessman. Instead, the plain diction renders his slaveholding an uncontentious and unexceptional practice.

Barnum broadened the slave owner persona he delineated in the *Atlas* when he turned to Heth in his 1855 autobiography, *The Autobiography of P.T. Barnum: Clerk, Merchant, Editor, and Showman*, to describe his assumption of the slave buyer's gaze.

> I was favourably struck by the appearance of the old woman. So far as outward indications were concerned, she might almost as well have been a thousand years old as any other age. . . . She was apparently in good health and spirits, but former disease or old age, or perhaps both combined, had rendered her unable to change her position; in fact, although she could move one of her arms at will, her lower limbs were fixed in their position, and could not be straightened. She was totally blind, and her eyes were so deeply sucked in their sockets that the eyeballs seemed to have disappeared altogether. She had no teeth, but possessed a head of thick bushy gray hair. Her left arm lay across her breast, and she had no power to remove it. The fingers of her left hand were drawn down so nearly to close it, and remained fixed and immovable. The nails upon that hand were about four inches in length, and extended beyond her wrist. The nails upon her large toes also had grown to the thickness of nearly a quarter of an inch.[69]

Barnum's quasi-ethnography of Heth instantiates the hyper-scrutiny that buyers and traders performed on and through enslaved black bodies in their search for profit—though, unlike most, Barnum searched for decrepitude in his potential chattel rather than vitality. Their gawking, poking, and prodding along with their subsequent recording of those actions in writing helped produce what historian Walter Johnson calls "an aesthetics of domination," that is, the "language and categories and objectifying gaze" essential to chattel slavery and white supremacy.[70] Barnum contributed mightily to these aesthetics, and his antebellum theatrical displays, from Heth to his

1860 "What Is It?" in which he exhibited an African American man in a wooly costume as the potential link between humankind and the animal kingdom, reflected the ways proslavery categories and conceptions were constitutive of antebellum northerners' socio-racial imagination.[71]

Consequently, biographer A. H. Saxon's brusque dismissal of Barnum's racial politics is far too shortsighted. He insists, "Let us be candid about the matter and have done with it: Barnum's opinion of blacks during the pre–Civil War era was no higher than that of most of his countrymen, whether Southerners and Northerners."[72] On the contrary: we certainly should not "have done with" the fact that Barnum shared prevailing racial views, but, instead, turn to his supremely popular performance and literary practices as appeals to, and evidence of, the collective (northern) hearts and minds that produced those views. As for his exhibition of Joice Heth and subsequent literary accounts of it, Barnum tapped into a desire for a form of domestic harmony that aligned audiences with Washington and affirmed magnanimous white mastery as an ideal of Americanness. This sort of racial paternalism, inextricably nationalist and proslavery, remained popular in northern performance culture because it included African Americans in the republican project but excluded them from equal participation therein. And just like with Barnum's Heth, the citation of George Washington was very often the critical hinge.

## THE PROSLAVERY ICONICITY OF WASHINGTON IN PAINTING AND PERFORMANCE

While Barnum's exhibition of Heth rested on fancifully invented narratives of Washington's infancy, other Washington-based performances of proslavery domesticity such as George Jaimson's *The Revolutionary Soldier; or, The Old Seventy-Sixer* (1847, 1850) relied on ignoring the ways Washington questioned slavery later in his life.[73] In *The Revolutionary Soldier*, an icon of Washington upholds chattel slavery as a boon to both the family and the nation. In his important theory of signs, Charles Sanders Peirce's description of the icon helps account for the phenomenological force and semiotic heft of Washington's proslavery iconicity in *The Revolutionary Soldier* and, more generally, of the use of icons in performance. He writes, "An *icon* is a representamen [i.e., sign] which fulfills the function of a representamen by virtue of a character it possess in itself, and would possess just the same as if its object did not. . . . For a pure icon does not draw any distinction between itself and the object. It represents whatever it may represent, and, whatever it is like, it in so far is. It is an affair of suchness only."[74] The icon, then, fosters an immediacy of feeling and a certainty of recognition. These temporal and epistemological aspects, among others, differentiate the icon from the *index* (something like a hydrometer or weathervane, which necessitates an existential or causal relation with its object to make meaning) and the *symbol* (something like a word or document, which has an arbitrary relation with its object and relies on social habits and conventions to signify). In *The Revolutionary Soldier* the icon of Washington that affirms the play's racial and national appeals is a portrait, and, according to Peirce, portraits, along with statues, are classic examples of icons.

   *The Revolutionary Soldier* premiered at the historic Federal Street Theatre in Boston in 1847.[75] The play, which takes place at the Goodwin estate ("a scene near Boston"), opens with Mrs. Peabody, the estate's chief housemaid who is probably Irish, and Enoch, the Goodwins' slave, discussing why their master, a decorated veteran of the American War of Independence, has been firing his gun early that morning. They remember that the day is the sixteenth of October and, as Enoch puts it, "massa Nathan always up at five o'clock" on that date to "kind o'circumcelebrate de fuss time he shake hand wid Massa Washington."[76] Goodwin then enters, wearing his Continental Army uniform, and Enoch asks if he should take the overcoat and clean the "ole seventy-six buttons." Goodwin tells him no, because it is his daughter Fanny's wedding day, "so I shall keep it on." He continues, "It will serve to keep up my spirits; and with this on I can more easily console myself for the loss I sustain in parting with my daughter. I've parted with many good friends with this coat on."[77] Despite Goodwin's sadness from the "loss" of his daughter, the scene is essentially a joyous one, and George Washington is central to its production.

   But the tenor of the play takes a swift turn in the following scene, as Goodwin starts to wonder whether he will lose his estate. When he was younger, his rival stole and signed his own name to the estate's original deeds. At the beginning of the third scene, we learn those papers are in the possession of the thief's son, Augustus Fritz Marson, who has travelled "three or four thousand miles from home" (i.e., London) to the "land of half-civilized beings" (i.e., the U.S.).[78] With the help of a mercenary American lawyer, the aptly named "Mr. Leechy," the British Marson lays claim to the property as his "by law," and Goodwin cannot prove that Marson's father illegally took the documents decades ago. (In soliloquy, Marson admits his father stole them: "This deed, however, I have heard him mention was taken to England by him through mistake. I believe my father was in the habit of taking things through mistake."[79]) Consequently, Goodwin tells his servants to "stop your preparations for the wedding" and "commence packing up" his belongings because he will soon have to hand over the estate to Marson.[80]

Later in the play, as she is busy "removing pictures from the wall" of one of the estate's apartments, Mrs. Peabody comes across a portrait of George Washington. While unhanging it she cries out, "O! this picture, that has hung here so long!—immortal Washington!—I never thought I should take you down! Well, well! (Wipes her eyes)."[81] In this moment, the icon doubly focuses the (ostensible) tragedy of the Goodwins' impending penury because its removal from the walls marks not simply the loss of their property, but, more critically, a loss at the hands of an Englishman; in this battle the British are victorious, usurping even "Washington." Yet in the midst of Mrs. Peabody's lamentation, Enoch runs in "almost out of breath." He asks for "Massa Nathan," then commands, "Stop, Misse Peabody; you can stop luggin' de tings out ob dere places. Place ole Massa Washington back in he place again."[82] Enoch just learned that the deeds to the estate have been stolen back, therefore "Massa Nathan [can] lef de tings along whar dey is, 'case all [is] right!" Before Mrs. Peabody can return anything to its former place, however, Enoch declares his adoration of Washington by way of performing with the icon.

(Dancing and capering, goes to the portrait of Washington, and dances round it, singing) Old Massa Washington a berry good man.[83]

Given Enoch's satisfaction with his existence as the Goodwins' slave, his dance with the portrait does not intimate antislavery sentiments; it is highly untenable that his affection for Washington stems from Washington's gradual embrace of abolition at the end of his life and the course of manumission and care he laid out for his slaves that was to take effect after his wife died. Even at the time of Washington's own death in 1799, historian Richard Newman notes, "very few white Americans commented on" the change in his view of the propriety of chattel slavery.[84] Instead, and certainly by the early 1850s, Washington's iconicity reached its greatest force in proslavery thought and cultural production. In fact, The Revolutionary Soldier was so firm in its defense of slavery that it played at the Holliday Street Theatre in Baltimore, and it was the particulars of this run in a major slaveholding city that provided the production details that Jaimson included in the script when he published it in 1850.

For audiences in Boston where The Revolutionary Soldier premiered, Enoch's dancing and capering with the portrait of Washington, which the black-faced actor almost certainly performed using the choreographies of the minstrel stage, might have reminded them of a similar moment in another play that also premiered in Boston, George Lionel Stevens' *The Patriot* (1834). A dramatic paean to the American Revolution and the formation of the U.S., *The Patriot* was Stevens' attempt to reinvigorate national unity at a time of increasing sectionalism, an attempt that was somewhat ironic given that Stevens was British. The play's subtitle reads, "A Drama, in Three Acts, Wherein is Introduced A *National Chant*, Containing the Names of the Signers of the Declaration of Independence. Adapted to Be Represented in All Theatres of the Union on Public Days of Rejoicing."[85] Hoping to appeal to northern and southern audiences, Stevens renders slavery a benevolent institution of domestic reciprocity, where slaves affirm their allegiance to the home and to the nation. The play's slave character Sambo, for example, claims a special relationship with Washington because his ancestors were slaves of the president. When Sambo's master tells him to clean and prepare a bust of Washington for an Independence Day display, he exclaims, "Yes, mass—de big Washinton, me lub him, massa! were he 'live, me would hug him massa, as him Sambo do."[86] Sambo's embrace of the bust, like Enoch's dance with the portrait, performed the romance of master-slave life that proslavery ideologues and their sympathizers contrived to shroud the brutality of chattel slavery.[87]

The forms of proslavery domesticity enacted in *The Patriot* and *The Revolutionary Soldier* bring to mind American neoclassicism of the late eighteenth century, especially the decorative and visual arts. Portraits of George Washington were central to this movement because, as Federal man *par excellence*, he seemed to embody the classical ideal: order, solemnity, and the consummate blend of physical power and intellectual cogency. Indeed, Washington and other leaders of the American Revolution served as perfect models for the neoclassical painter and, later, sculptor because they proved not only more favorable than pagan, pre-Christian figures from antiquity, but also more relevant in that they were the ones, in normative accounts, most responsible for the birth of the new nation. These works—especially the paintings and studies of Benjamin West and his students Gilbert Stuart, John Trumbull, Edward Savage, and others of the so-called American School—were crucial to the development of a national sense of self, providing the visual complement to the classically informed philosophies and political theories that animated the American Revolution and shaped the constitutionality of the U.S. Their aesthetic and representational effects reached beyond the eighteenth century because, as historian Caroline Winterer argues, "next to Christianity, the central intellectual project in

America before the late nineteenth century was classicism."[88] Of course, one of the most significant aspects of that project was the way Americans reshaped the classical institution of slavery into its *neo*-classic form: namely, race-based chattel slavery. And despite its brutalities, chattel slavery could be an important subject for neoclassical artists, ranging from Revolutionary-era poet Phillis Wheatley to antebellum sculptor Hiram Powers.[89]

Two of the most significant neoclassical paintings of Washington—John Trumbull's *George Washington* (1780) and Edward Savage's *The Washington Family* (1789–96)—feature slaves in their settings. Trumbull was the son of Jonathon Trumbull, who was governor of Connecticut from 1769 to 1784, and he served in the Continental Army, in which he rose to the ranks of aide-de-camp to Washington and other American generals. He drew on these personal experiences and observations for his painting of a number of the nation's most influential historical actors and events, such as the Battle of Bunker Hill and the signing of the Declaration of Independence.[90] Trumbull conceived of his artistic practice as "paying a just tribute to the memory of eminent men, who had given their lives for their country."[91] Washington did not perish in battle like others whom Trumbull sought to memorialize in his paintings, but he certainly qualified as one who sacrificed greatly for the American cause; ultimately, Washington became Trumbull's most favored personal subject. George Washington Parke Custis, Washington's adopted son, argued that Trumbull's representations of Washington were the most true to life: "Hence, *for the correct figure of Washington we must refer, in all cases, to the works of Trumbull.*"[92]

Perhaps the exactitude Trumbull achieved in his paintings of Washington was an effect of the special bond Trumbull believed they shared. In his autobiography, Trumbull calls Washington his "fast friend"; accordingly, *George Washington* is the most intimate of all his works.[93] While it shares many of the formal properties that characterize his other portraits, *George Washington* stands apart in its composition: it is, I believe, Trumbull's only full-body portrait in which the subject looks straight ahead at the viewer. Further, *George Washington* is direct and lively, and lacks the careful wistfulness that typifies the works he produced after 1784, when he began to study closely with Benjamin West in London.[94] Trumbull's deep personal affinity for Washington manifests in the portrait's vibrancy, particularly in the ebullience of Washington's countenance. The source of this affective register is not restricted to Washington's relation to Trumbull and the viewer, however; it is redoubled by the portrait's depiction of another pair of "fast friends": Washington and his slave, William "Billy" Lee.

Washington purchased Lee, whom he called "mulatto Will" in his led-

Figure 7: *George Washington* (1780). John Trumbull. Oil on Canvas.
Metropolitan Museum of Art, Bequest of Charles Allen Munn, 1924
(24.109.88).

ger, in a lot of four "sundry slaves," which included Lee's brother Frank, in May 1768 from a Mrs. Mary Lee of Westmoreland County, Virginia, for a total of one hundred forty-nine pounds and fifteen shillings. Lee was the most expensive at sixty-one pounds and fifteen shillings, but he turned out to be the most valuable of all Washington's slave investments.[95] He was Washington's huntsman and riding companion, which was a testament to Lee's riding prowess, as many Virginians agreed with Thomas Jefferson that Washington was "the best horseman of his age and the most graceful figure that could be seen on horseback."[96] Moreover, by 1770 Lee had distinguished himself as a valet, so much so that Washington started referring to Lee in his diary as his "mulatto manservant," his "boy" and his "body servant."[97] Throughout the American War of Independence, Lee stayed by his master's side, serving as Washington's "Revolutionary attendant" who, as one early nineteenth-century account described him, "periled his life in many a field, beginning in the heights of Boston, in 1775, and ending in 1781, when Cornwallis surrendered, and the captive army, with unexpressible chagrin, laid down their arms at Yorktown."[98] In his *Recollections and Private Memoirs of Washington*, which he began to compile in 1826, George Washington Parke Custis dubbed Lee the "ancient follower, both in chase and in war, [who] formed a most interesting relic of the chief," who had died in 1799; Custis also noted that, with "his master having left him a house, and a pension of one hundred and fifty dollars a year, Bill became a spoiled child of fortune."[99] Upon his death, Washington offered "his mulatto Man William" something far more valuable than these and other material conveniences, however; he granted Lee "immediate freedom," which made Lee the only one of Washington's 124 slaves freed by the will, and he did so "as a testimony of my sense of his attachment to me, and for his faithful services during the Revolutionary War."[100]

*George Washington* pays tribute to Lee's "attachment" to Washington, which Trumbull witnessed during his dealings with both men during and following the war. In the portrait, Lee sits astride a thoroughbred to Washington's left. Both men are in the foreground, against a backdrop of sweeping strokes of neutral colors. While Trumbull dedicates most of his attention to Washington's appearance and mien, he does delineate features of Lee's aspect. The most conspicuous of these details is Lee's ornate and deep red turban, the most eye-catching use of color in the entire painting. There is no indication in Washington's or his contemporaries' writings that Lee practiced Islam, but there is a very good chance that he descended from Muslims. The Spanish brought Muslim slaves to Florida beginning in the mid–sixteenth century; thus, as historian Michael A. Gomez notes, "the

Muslim presence in North America antedates the arrival of the English colonists."[101] Moreover, seventeenth-century British and American slavers often preferred slaves from heavily Islamic areas in West Africa because they believed those Africans were more exploitable and compliant than other Africans.[102] In the U.S., the records and runaway advertisements of Georgian and South Carolinian slaveholders evidence a strong Islamic presence in those states, Gomez finds, while Virginian planters "were not as discriminating."[103] Washington himself held no ethnic or tribal preference for his workforce. In a 1784 letter to his former aide-de-camp and friend Tench Tilghman, Washington wrote, "If they are good workmen, they may be of Assia, Africa, or Europe. They may be Mahometans, Jews, or Christian of any Sect—or they may be Athiests."[104] Lee was most likely a descendant of other "good" Muslim slave "workmen" in Virginia, and his wearing a turban would have been a practice he inherited from them, even if he did not know its religious and ethnic meanings.

Another striking detail is Lee's face. With his head slightly raised, he looks admiringly at Washington yet ready to heed his master's command. Trumbull paints Lee's face with remarkable specificity, which was certainly an act of respect for Lee and his service to Washington and the future American republic. This careful treatment distinguishes *George Washington* from other contemporaneous renderings of Lee. In French engraver Noël Le Mire's 1780 *Le Général Washington*, for example, Lee wears his turban but his visage is more imprecise and racially stereotypical, particularly around the eyes and nose. *Le Général Washington* is also noteworthy compared to *George Washington* because in the engraving Lee does not look at Washington but stares off into the distance. To be sure, Lee is an integral part of Le Mire's work, but its primary interest is Washington's political triumphs, as Washington holds a copy of the Declaration of Independence and the Treaty of Alliance with France, and stands atop torn copies of post-war reconciliation documents with Great Britain. In *George Washington*, however, the focus is on the charismatic Washington and his attachments to Trumbull (i.e., the viewer) and Lee. The portrait is as familiar as it is stately, and Lee is inseparable from its memorialization of Washington. Its gallant tones and corporal particularities yield an intimate, complementary relation between master and slave, a relation that was indispensible to the formation of the (future) nation itself. Thus, complementing the "distinction" *George Washington* achieved as "the first portrait of [Washington] in Europe" was the fact that it also introduced him to the world as a magnanimous slaveholder, one whom proslavery ideologues could champion as a caring master whose efforts demonstrated the grand potential, indeed necessity, of the institution of chattel slavery.[105]

Figure 8: *Le Général Washington* (ca. 1785). Noël Le Mire. Engraving.
Library of Congress, LC-USZ62–102494.

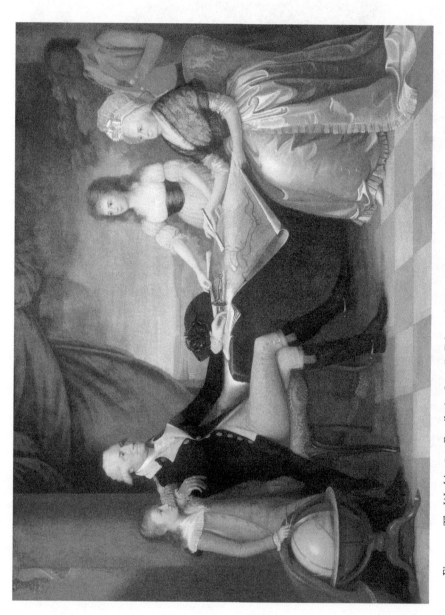

Figure 9: *The Washington Family* (1789–96). Edward Savage. Oil on Canvas. National Gallery of Art, Andrew Mellon Collection, 1940.1.2.

The (seemingly) idyllic relationship between Washington and Lee in *George Washington* is taken from the battlefield and resituated in the home in Edward Savage's *The Washington Family*. In 1789, Harvard University commissioned Savage to paint a portrait of now-president Washington; and from 1789 to 1790 Washington, his wife Martha, and her grandchildren Eleanor Parke Custis and George Washington Parke Custis, both of whom Washington adopted, sat for the Harvard and other private commissions. George and Martha Washington gave Savage new sittings in 1795, and he used these and the earlier sittings to complete the nine-foot-wide *The Washington Family* in 1796.[106] The painting lionizes Washington's virtues as a patriarch, one who presides comfortably over his sober and dispassionate nuclear family and, more implicitly, the newly constituted United States at large. Indeed, against a backdrop of the Potomac River, George wears military garb; Martha and Eleanor consider plans for the under-construction capital city, the District of Columbia; and George Custis holds a pair of navigational dividers and leans against a globe: *The Washington Family* affirms Washington's place as the "father" of the newest world power. But the portrait also attests to the fundamental source of the U.S.' power, chattel slavery, because, behind Martha Washington's chair, Billy Lee stands in waiting.

In full livery and without his turban, Lee nearly recedes into the background of *The Washington Family*. Unlike its representation in *George Washington*, his face in Savage's portrait is listless and lacks particularity. Moreover, Lee does not look at his master but stares off in a different direction than any of the Washingtons. He seems to share little human relation with his masters; if Trumbull paints Lee's role as Washington's close companion, Savage paints it as Washington's chattel. To be sure, the representational disparities of Lee in *George Washington* and in *The Washington Family* betray differences of emphasis between the two artists; but they also evidence how, in the postrevolutionary era, "natural rights–style arguments [against] slavery . . . no longer had the kind of strategic purchase they had a decade earlier," as literary historian Eric Slauter describes it.[107] With its lack of interest in Lee's visage and disregard of his contributions to the founding of the nation, Savage's portrait suggests the slave (in the painting) could be any black person because, despite the claims of natural rights discourses, blackness qualifies *all* black people for bondage. Further, Savage's erasure of Lee in *The Washington Family* reflects the increasing racialization of dominant American neoclassical theory: not only were black people incapable of producing satisfactory forms of classically informed art and inquiry, but also they lacked the intellectual and physical ideals worthy of aesthetic treatment.[108] In this view, even the singular and valiant Lee did not deserve visual individuation and, by extension, freedom in the new nation, despite his status as a "member" of the Washington family.

When antebellum cultural producers looked back to the revolutionary era to legitimate their opposition to black inclusion, they often did so with the sort of historical haziness that Savage visualized in his painting of Lee, all the while maintaining the familial tenor of his work *The Washington Family* and the heroic tones of Trumbull's *George Washington*. These works, including *King's Bridge Cottage*, Barnum's exhibition of Heth, and *The Revolutionary Soldier*, enacted a form of proslavery domesticity, both of the home and of the nation, which seemed true to the intentions of the nation's founders and, consequently, rebuffed the inclusionary claims of African Americans. The figure of George Washington anchored these re-stagings of the birth of the U.S., all of which championed productive and obedient slaves above all other forms of black subjectivity. These performances did not project a future of earned freedom and full inclusion for slaves' descendants, as African Americans argued they deserved; rather, they functioned as cultural and "historiographic" justifications for ongoing forms of black captivity in the antebellum north.

FOUR  |  The Theatocracy of Antebellum
Social Reform
*"Monkeyism" and the Mode of*
*Romantic Racialism*

The tremendous instrumental value the theatre maintained in antebellum life rested on the fact that audiences understood themselves as partly within the frame of performance. This spectatorial habit, perhaps above all others, defined the theatregoing in the era. "Any study of mid-nineteenth-century American theatre," drama critic Marc Robinson argues, "must comes to terms with [spectators'] mixed consciousness—the experience of being both inside and outside the performance. . . . Instead of being passive and anonymous, spectatorship in the nineteenth century is often a form of intervention, as audiences are invited to become witnesses, analysts, historians, and even reformers."[1] Accordingly, the stage functioned as a kind of moral institution that indexed Americans' collective merits and shortcomings, and, in turn, projected ways to maintain or rectify them. While this Aristotelian imperative animated eighteenth- and early nineteenth-century theatrical formations throughout Europe, in the antebellum U.S. it took on a distinctive feature: audiences, more than literary or scholarly elites, dictated the shape of dramaturgical and theatrical practices.[2]

Concern for the role of audiences in theatrical production dates back to at least the classical period. Plato, for example, blasted the control audiences began to wield over the dramaturgy of ancient Greece, scorning their influence as a "base theatocracy." In his *Laws*, speaking as "The Athenian," Plato protests, "Hence the spectators, who were once silent, became noisy, as though they understood what is good and bad in art, and in the place of an aristocracy in the artistic realm there came about a base theatocracy."[3] This criticism built on his earlier condemnation from the *Republic*, in which Plato deems audiences' "great deal of noise and great lack of moderation" as detrimental to the cultivation of philosophic and civic knowledge.[4] Both of these censures of theatocracy emerged forcefully in the antebellum period: the literati blamed the lack of an indigenous national drama on audiences' power over playwriting, such as their insatiable demand for adapted or translated European forms and plots; and social critics argued that the milieu of the theatre engendered dissolute and rowdy collectives, thereby corrupting civic, moral, and religious rectitude.[5] Though critical accounts of the relation of theatre and philosophy nearly always ignore American theatre history before realism, the respective objections of cultural elites and social critics raised against the theatre were essentially Platonic attacks on theatocracy and its ostensibly negative effect on antebellum dramaturgy and society.

It is no surprise, then, that reformers dedicated to social movements such as abolitionism and temperance usually spurned the theatre. Very often steeped in bourgeois and Victorian sensibilities, these men and women argued that the theatrical enterprise, both the entertainment on stage and the antics in the audience, contaminated mind, body, and soul. As the editors of the *Colored American* cheered in 1841, "It must be a matter of rejoicing to the moral and the religious public, and to all the friends of purity, to know that the *Drama* at the north, is getting to be exceedingly out of favor, and that lectures on moral and scientific subjects are taking its place. Nearly all the *theatres* of our city [New York] have been closed during the past winter, for want of patronage. The same has been true, also, with the *theatres* in Boston and other northern cities."[6] At the time, the nation was in the throes of a depression, which was then the most severe economic crisis it had ever suffered; thus, the closing of theatres that winter was far more the result of economic exigencies than moral convictions. Nonetheless, American theatre culture continued to thrive because, in large part, it took new shape. Ironically, the report from *The Colored American* points to those novel formations: namely, the explosion of "lectures on moral and scientific subjects" and the rise of didactic, reformist theatrical entertainments in the late 1840s and 1850s. To be sure, the most fervent antitheatricalists continued to inveigh against the theatre. But others who objected to the improprieties endemic to minstrelsy and other popular performance practices could not ignore the considerable purchase the theatre held on the public consciousness; thus, they adopted a more strategic relation to the stage, using it to promulgate their ideals and project the polity anew in their respective images. In this way, the collective of reformers and "friends of purity" did not eschew American theatocracy but, rather, contributed to its dynamism.

With their theatrical and performance formations, reformers sought to rectify what they recognized as a relentlessly unscrupulous north, and a number of them marked out one so-called social problem that many northerners viewed as an exacerbation of all others: free blackness.[7] Despite never constituting more than 4 percent of the northern population, antebellum African Americans maintained a decisive grip on the white imagination.[8] Their detractors argued that black communities contributed mightily to the economic strain and moral laxity that animated the period's many reform movements, particularly in urban areas. More decisively, African Americans in the north refused to recede into the background but continued to assert themselves as principal contributors to the project of American nation-building. Denied the limited, though at times fruitful economic opportunities extended to free black people in the south, black northerners crafted an aggressive political culture that was both instrumental and self-constitutive. As Ira Berlin argues, "For northern freemen and the elite in particular, politics was more than a means of racial advancement; it was a way of life."[9] The concatenation of politics to black subjectivity throughout the antebellum period redoubled after the late 1830s, when African Americans largely isolated themselves from their erstwhile white benefactors and fully embraced an ethic of black self-determination. Above all, they rejected white patronage because the vast majority of white reformers were paternalistic in their aims and approach. From the increasingly assertive stance of the collective of African Americans, racial paternalism was simply a translation of slavery, albeit without chains and off the plantation.

This chapter considers how proslavery thought undergirded normative expectations of free black subjectivity among white social reformers and the ways African Americans performed refusals of them. In particular, I explore the representational politics of "romantic racialism," the ideology that historian George M. Fredrickson famously described as, in part, the conceptualization of the African (American) as inherently religious, submissive, and virtuous. With their cultural and philosophic expressions of romantic racialism, white reformers extolled the black presence as necessary to the nation's moral constitution, but they (symbolically) curbed black self-determination. While the most well known of these expressions concern slaves, with Harriet Beecher Stowe's *Uncle Tom's Cabin* as the exemplar, there are others that imagine free(d) black people away from the trappings of slavery. In texts such as Harry Seymour's temperance drama *Aunt Dinah's Pledge* (1850, 1853), which I read in this chapter as a response to black performances of racial and self-autonomy, African Americans are lauded for their moral value but denied full political and social inclusion. Instead, they linger comfortably in a kind of purgatory, somewhere between citizenship and slavery, and it is the mode of romantic racialism that articulates this reconciliation, if not integration, of proslavery premises with antislavery ends.

## BLACK PESSIMISM, BLACK PRAGMATISM

In its historical, literary, and pseudoscientific delineations, romantic racialism classifies the African as a benign "stock" naturally endowed with docility, fidelity, and religiosity. These favorable traits, when combined with those of other "stocks" like the Anglo-Saxon's "love of liberty [and his] spirit of individual enterprise and resourcefulness," refine human society and propel it to perfection, romantic racialists argued.[10] Though Fredrickson finds that the ideology was "widely espoused by Northern humanitarians who were more or less antislavery," he establishes it within a surprising intellectual genealogy: "At its most tentative, the romantic racialist view simply endorsed the 'child' stereotype of the most sentimental school of proslavery paternalists and plantation romancers and then rejected slavery itself because it took unfair advantage of the Negro's innocence and good nature."[11] Despite their rejection of chattel slavery, however, white reformers who idealized the African (American) as childlike believed in the propriety and necessity of some form of black captivity.

The case of Frederick Douglass' break from William Lloyd Garrison and his cohort in the late 1840s and early 1850s is perhaps the most familiar illustration of the ways romantic racialism beset antebellum reform movements. While white Garrisonians valued the black struggle against slavery, most of them repudiated black autonomy. They spurned Douglass' popularity on the abolitionist lecture circuit and his increasing desire for leadership roles. This friction reached a crisis point following Douglass' speaking tour of Great Britain from August 1845 to April 1847, during which he acquired a renewed sense of freedom. Cultural historian John Stauffer offers a fine sketch of how the trip prompted Douglass' transformation from Garrisonian devotee to independent leader: "He left for Great Britain as a brilliant author and orator, but subservient to the white paternalism of the American Anti-Slavery Society. He returned as a proud and self-reliant black man determined to strike out on his own and fulfill a dream of becoming an editor."[12] Once back in the U.S., Douglass quickly established his first newspaper, *The North Star*, in late 1847, an act that marked one of the most consequential declarations of black independence in American literary and social history. Douglass' friend and a leading radical abolitionist, James McCune Smith, went so far as to claim the publication of *The North Star* constituted an act of racial birth for Douglass: "You will be surprised to hear me say that only since his Editorial career has [Douglass] seen to become *a colored man!*"[13]

That which McCune Smith recognized as Douglass' gateway into his blackness, most white antislavery reformers blasted as wrongheaded and detrimental to their movement. One of these men termed Douglass' actions "monkeyism," by which he meant Douglass was untamed and violated appropriate norms and expectations.[14] What the white antislavery establishment wanted from Douglass and other African Americans was their tales of black/slave life; loftier matters such as leadership and strategy should remain out of their purview.[15] As John A. Collins, the general agent of the Massachusetts Anti-Slavery Society, ordered Douglass in 1841, "Give us the facts, we will take care of the philosophy."[16] With the "philosophy" of abolitionism left solely to white men and women, the movement would run its proper and most productive course, Garrisonians maintained. Yet by the time of Douglass' striking out on his own in the mid-1840s, it was too late: the collective of black northerners had already begun to shun white-controlled reform movements and social agendas.[17]

Monkeyism, to re-appropriate the term positively, became a feature constitutive of black political performance after the late 1830s; it structured the ways in which African Americans articulated and cultivated their own programs of action in opposition to those of their white antislavery allies. Philosopher of religion Eddie S. Glaude, Jr. argues this "immanent conversation constituted a call of sorts for solidaristic efforts to reject white paternalism and to alleviate the condition of black people in general."[18] In their intra-racial discussions, African Americans gave public voice to aggressive and at times insurrectionary impulses that were largely absent from earlier black political discourses, with the notable exception of David Walker's 1829 *Appeal*. These calls for armed resistance, slave rebellion, or vigilantism very often set the terms of debate among black publics and their white onlookers for the rest of the antebellum period.

The most conspicuous forum for the evolution of this discourse and the broader move away from white patronage was the National Negro Convention movement. Beginning in 1830, black delegates and representatives from across the north and, at times, from border or slave states convened in order to discuss the condition of black America and to hammer out strategies of redress and tactics of survival. In his groundbreaking account of the convention movement, historian Howard H. Bell identifies three primary reasons that motivated African Americans "to feel that they must have their own assemblies if they were to reach the goals desired." He writes:

In the first place, prejudice against people of African descent was on the rapid increase in the North; [second,] a growing demand for self-

expression which had been denied to the man of color for a half
century following the American Revolution; [and third,] the existence of specific problems which affected the Negro alone, or were
intensified in regard to him.[19]

No subject was off-limits for the conventioneers. From confronting northern racism to boycotting slave-produced products to using other forms of
economic empowerment; from emigration to the parameters of black civic
participation; from prescribing "respectable" forms of public behavior to
encouraging slave insurrection: the expansive and omnibus nature of their
deliberations further strengthened the epistemic and material bonds of the
black north, despite regional conflicts (usually between the Philadelphia
and New York factions) and problems of representation for disorganized
or scantly populated localities.[20]

   But the conventions did more than address racial inequities; they were
also pivotal sites of intra-racial negotiations. What are the respective functions of men and women in the making of black families and communities?
Is a liberal arts education necessary for all black children or only the gifted
select few? Should race language such as "African," "Colored," or "Black"
be used in the names of institutions dedicated to black uplift?[21] These questions, among others, were some of the most pressing ones that delegates
tackled and, together with the factors Bell lays out, evidence the ways in
which antebellum African Americans always situated their sociopolitical
discourses upon the inextricable nexus of "outside-inside . . . the State and
Us," to use Glaude's pithy term.[22] Although African Americans tackled
such matters in formal and informal channels before 1830, the national conventions became a space of unprecedented exchange, productivity, and
visibility for antebellum black reform.

   At the first national conventions from 1830 to 1835, delegates were especially concerned with acts of self-improvement and self-empowerment.
They weighed structural options such as emigration and erecting schools
for black children, outlined modes of personal conduct such as participation (or lack thereof) in public celebrations, and prescribed strategic con-
sumer practices. Always with an eye on collective and interpersonal forms
of racial hostility, the delegates centered on black corrective action as an
"awakening [of the] spirit in our people to promote their elevation," as an
1832 conventional address put it.[23] The conventions remained dedicated to
black uplift throughout the antebellum period, but in the mid-1830s many
influential delegates and conventioneers attempted to expand their mis-
sion to raise the entire nation, irrespective of race. Most of these individuals

would comprise the Philadelphia-based American Moral Reform Society (AMRS). The AMRS' greatest charge was its refusal of "either national or complexional distinctions in the prosecution of moral action."[24] These reformers clashed with other delegates who believed the convention movement and the broader complex of black sociopolitical agitation should be devoted exclusively to the emancipation of slaves and the political and personal betterment of African Americans.

Reared politically amid these debates, a new generation of black activists and thinkers emerged in the 1840s that doubted the efficacy of moral suasion, interracial or otherwise. For one, this new cadre believed moral suasion was largely ineffective because of the proliferation of mob violence and racial terror in the 1830s. With the rise of a more aggressive antislavery ethic following Garrison's lead in 1831, anti-abolitionist and race-based violence mushroomed and became a national phenomenon. As historian Leonard L. Richards concludes in his classic study of mobs in the Jacksonian period, "Mob violence not only increased markedly but became a feature of American life—not urban life, or Southern life, or Western life—but American life."[25] Mobbing peaked between 1833 and 1838, in particular, the very years during which African Americans began to separate themselves from white-led reform movements in consequential numbers.[26] Steeped in this ethic of black self-determination and as victims of widespread mob violence, younger black reformers injected an unprecedented degree of militancy in the conventions and the northern public sphere at large.

It was in the 1820s and 1830s when African Americans saw their already limited political rights further curtailed. For example, a few northern districts allowed all black men the right to vote, others upheld prohibitive property qualifications, and still others disenfranchised all African Americans. The racialization of the elective franchise and of other political and social rights across the north meant that racial inequality took different shapes throughout the region; nonetheless, African Americans felt a common bond of oppression.[27] Given the ongoing dominance of legal and extralegal proscriptions against black life in the 1830s, it is no surprise that African Americans increasingly rejected moral suasion agendas and began to espouse more direct forms of political and social action.

While the deepening entrenchment of race-based inequities and violence eventually gave rise to the militant black political discourses of the early 1840s, the intra-black negotiations of the 1830s had provided the conceptual horizons out of which such (rhetorical) militancy might develop in the first place. As Glaude explains, "The pressing pessimism that developed among blacks in the mid-nineteenth century [was] an outgrowth, as it were, of entrenched racism and the pragmatic view of race in the late thirties. For lingering on the borders of the call for an immanent conversation was the specter of violence: the raging swell of despair in the face of repeated indifference and the 'demand to the strike a blow for freedom.'"[28] For Glaude, this *pessimism* (or, the belief that the U.S. was unwilling to end slavery and state-sanctioned racism) and its underlying *pragmatic view of race* (or, "the recognition that social and political conditions make racial solidarity an important social and political strategy") fostered new forms of political ideology and redressive action.[29] Amid the tempest of Jacksonian race relations, a number of these pessimist and pragmatic black reformers concluded that violence would be the most legible and utilitarian of acts with which to foster substantive change in the polity. Of these, the most emphatic was abolitionist and minister Henry Highland Garnet who, in his speech at the National Negro Convention of 1843 in Buffalo, New York, pressed for slave insurrection.

## THE CALL: PERFORMING MONKEYISM

Garnet was born a slave in Maryland and around 1825 escaped with his family to New York City, where he attended the African Free School No. 1. The New York Manumission Society created the African Free Schools in the late 1780s to "prepare blacks, especially ex-slaves, for citizenship," stressing "intellectual and moral education."[30] During his years at the African Free School, Garnet was a classmate of several boys who would become cultural, intellectual, and political leaders in the U.S. and abroad, including world-renowned tragedian Ira Aldridge, radical abolitionist and physician James McCune Smith, and international activist Samuel Ringgold Ward.[31]

In 1835, Garnet moved to Canaan, New Hampshire, where abolitionists, "disgusted with the negro-hatred of the schools," established a high school for "youth of any and all races, and of both sexes."[32] His stay at the Canaan Academy was short-lived, however, because a number of local white citizens deemed the school a blight on their community and therefore dedicated themselves to its removal. As one of Garnet's classmates recalled, "Fourteen black boys with books in their hands set the entire Granite State Crazy!" Consequently, a mob "from the neighboring town, seized the building, and with ninety yoke of oxen carried it off into a swamp about a half mile from its site."[33] He goes on to report that since the boys expected the mob to lead an attack on their residence, they molded bullets and banded under Garnet's leadership. When one member of the mob fired at their boarding house, "Garnet quickly replied by a discharge from a double-barrelled shotgun which blazed away through the window."[34] The shot saved the boys from the mob, but state officials ordered them to leave New Hampshire within two weeks because their presence disrupted civil society.[35] Eventually Garnet (and a few of his classmates from Canaan Academy) enrolled at Oneida Institute in New York, a "radical, interracial, abolitionist college dedicated to revolutionizing American society," and he graduated in 1839.[36]

This crucible of profound vulnerability, radical education, and violent resistance molded the young Garnet into the fiery man who would publically call for slave insurrection. His pessimism and pragmatism were deeply grounded in, and emerged from, a vagarious life that ranged from fugitive slave to free man, from precocious adolescent to armed protector of his classmates—all before the age of twenty-one. This experiential and epistemological charge seemed to have propelled Garnet to public life, despite the fact that he initially committed himself to the ministry. (His first professional position was pastor to a small Presbyterian congregation in Troy, New York.) Garnet's classmate at Canaan Academy, black nationalist and pastor Alexander Crummell, explained the seeming ineluctability of Garnet's rise to prominence: "He began life with the expectation of exclusive devotion to the ministerial calling. But such splendid abilities could not be confined to such an obscure corner. Soon his fame spread around the city and county where he lived. At that time the colored people were holding their annual conventions for the purpose of securing the right of suffrage. Garnet at once became one of its leading spirits."[37] That spirit never moved audiences as much as it did in his performance of "An Address to the Slaves of the United States" at the black national convention in Buffalo in 1843.

Garnet was one of the leaders of that new crop of fervent, action-minded reformers who changed the tenor of the national conventions in the early 1840s. These pessimistic and pragmatic young delegates subsumed the concerns of behavioral and moral reform, such as the appropriateness of race language and public respectability, for direct political agitation, such as acquiring the vote.[38] Reflecting on this cohort in 1861, a "Caleb" wrote in the *Weekly Anglo-African* newspaper that they were not the "psalm-singing and Bible-quoting saints" of the 1830s moral reform campaigns but "hard-working and clear-headed men" who advocated practical action.[39] Slave rebellion was the action Garnet proposed, and shrewdly so: he couched it in the language and logic of Christian philosophy.

In the speech, Garnet exhorted slaves to rebel because bondage keeps them away from God, who wants His black children free. Garnet charged, "Your condition does not absolve you from your moral obligation [to God]. The diabolical injustice by which your liberties are cloven down, neither God nor angels, nor just men command you to suffer for a single moment. Therefore it is your solemn and imperative duty to use every means, both moral, intellectual and physical, that promises success."[40] Rather than alienate those "psalm-singing and Bible quoting saints" in attendance, to borrow Caleb's designation, Garnet framed his appeal to insurrection as a Christian necessity. As Glaude explains, "Garnet turned religious benevolence on its head: the focus was not on the demand for proponents of slavery to forsake sin and believe in the mercy of Christ but, rather, on the duties of black Christian slaves to forsake the obstacles to obtaining the grace of God. Thus, moral reform for the slave, according to Garnet, might require general insurrection because the slave was still obligated, in spite of his condition, to obey the laws of God."[41] In this way, Garnet melded Christian persuasion with violent action to create a liberation theology that is explicitly embodied and temporal.

Garnet also grounded his call for bloody action within a grand trajectory of world history. At the end of the "Address," he offered a catalog of famous insurrectionaries alongside whom the rebellious slave would stand in the historical imagination. These were Denmark Vesey, Moses, John Hampden, William Tell, Robert the Bruce and William Wallace, Toussaint L'Ouverture, Marquis de Lafayette, George Washington, Nat Turner, Joseph Cinque, and Madison Washington. To be among these men is to be counted as an agent of world change, Garnet argued: "Noble men! Those who have fallen in freedom's conflict, their memories will be cherished by the true-hearted and the God-fearing in all future generations; those who are living, their names are surrounded by a halo of glory."[42] But there was more than personal veneration at stake. Garnet also maintained that the slave must revolt because he has a filial obligation to his forebears who, from their graves, enjoin him to overthrow his masters: "Where is the blood of your fathers? Has it all run out of your veins? Awake, awake, millions of voices are calling you! Your dead fathers speak to you from their graves. Heaven, as with a voice of thunder, calls on you to arise from the dust. Let your motto be, Resistance! *Resistance!* RESISTANCE!"[43] This peroration, like the entirety of the "Address," strove for an immediacy of action that suasion efforts lacked. Rather than wait for moral behaviors to erode dominant perceptions of blackness, Garnet urged direct confrontation as the way to end slavery and racism. White racist minds were of little concern to

Garnet; he wanted slaves to attack the system itself, and he maintained it was their duty to do so.

But Garnet's entreaties were also intended for another constituency: African Americans in the north. Although Garnet addressed his speech to the "slaves of the United States," he delivered it in Buffalo, New York, far from the fields and factories of the south and west where slaves toiled. The black conventioneers were his immediate audience, and in the speech he quickly equated their plight with that of the slave. At the beginning of the "Address" he observes, "While you have been oppressed, we have also been partakers with you; nor can we be free while you are enslaved. We, therefore, write to you as being bound with you."[44] Thus, *all* black people in the U.S. were slaves according to Garnet, and his pleadings were for *national* insurrection. Like the enslaved, free African Americans throughout the nation were under the same Christian, historical, and moral imperatives to resist systems of racial oppression with direct force. Those in attendance were not proxies, then, but actual subjects of address whom Garnet called to actualize his apocalyptic vision. Simply put, he charged them to prepare to kill and be killed: "However much you and all of us may desire it, there is not much hope of redemption without the shedding of blood. If you must bleed, let it all come at once—rather *die freemen than live to be slaves*."[45] If northern African Americans were bound to their captive brethren and therefore could not be fully free, then his "call for general slave insurrection in the South and mass 'black' political action in the North" were principally one and the same.[46]

The printed minutes and proceedings of the convention do not show that delegates made as explicit an equivalence between the southern slave and northern black freeman as Garnet did, but they did admit that the reverberations of slave insurrections would traverse state and regional borders. They rightly understood that mass slave uprisings in the south and west would affect free black life in those regions as well as in the northern states.[47] A. M. Sumner, a delegate from Cincinnati, "remarked that the adoption of [Garnet's] address by the Convention would be fatal to the safety of the free people of color of the slave States, but especially so to those who lived on the borders of the free States."[48] Sumner was especially attuned to the social precariousness that African Americans endured because Cincinnati had some of the nation's harshest racial laws and, in the 1830s, witnessed some of the bloodiest riots against black interests.[49]

Garnet's resolution deeply distressed Frederick Douglass, too, who argued there "was too much physical force" in Garnet's words and suggested they should keep "trying the moral means a little longer." Garnet replied that his resolution was a bargain of sorts: it "advised the slaves to go to their masters and tell them they wanted their liberty, and had come to ask for it; and if the master refused it, to tell [him], then we shall take it, let the consequence be what it may." Douglass countered that this scheme "would lead to an insurrection, and we [the delegates and other black leaders] were called upon to avoid such a catastrophy." The minutes go on to show that Douglass "wanted emancipation in a better way, as he expected to have it."[50] For him, the "better way" was the "moral means," and he and Sumner did sway the delegates, barely: Garnet's resolution was defeated by one vote, 19 to 18.

That Garnet nearly persuaded these men to encourage and sanction slave insurrection betrays the efficacy of his performance of the "Address." The minutes note that his performance "was a masterly effort, and the whole Convention, full as it was, was literally infused with tears. Mr. Garnit concluded amidst great applause."[51] Thus, the power of the event of Garnet's address rested on affect, presence, and theatricality, all of which were central to the black convention movement and, more broadly, black activism in the period. "Techniques of performance" were especially critical to the "production and contestation of racialized national discourses" among black Atlantic populations, performance historian Jill Lane writes, because "the historically unprecedented social circumstances that [slavery produced] required complex cultural processes of public memory, surrogation (in [Joseph] Roach's term), and self-invention that performance made possible."[52] Indeed, the sociality of performance was essential to the fashioning of the antebellum black public sphere because it engendered modes of deliberation and protest among present bodies that an imagined community of readers could not. Garnet's performance, for example, fostered an immediacy and multiplicity of responses because of the actuality of collective presence; he bore the potency of his "Address" equally, if not more, in the *enactment* of the speech. When Douglass declared, "There was too much physical force" in the "Address," he characterized Garnet's performance of the text even more than the words themselves, I argue.

Douglass, of course, knew how important oratorical performance was in the shaping of public opinion, as the spoken word was what launched him to international influence. His career as a public figure began in 1841 at an antislavery convention in Nantucket, when he addressed an interracial audience for only the second time. He recalled, "The truth was, I felt myself a slave, and the idea of speaking to white people weighed me down. I spoke but a few moments, when I felt a degree of freedom, and said what I desired with considerable ease. From that time until now, I have been engaged in pleading the cause of my brethren."[53] William Lloyd Garrison participated in the Nantucket meeting and spoke immediately after Douglass. As Garrison remembered it, "As soon as [Douglass] had taken his seat, filled with hope and admiration, I rose, and declared that Patrick Henry, of revolutionary fame, never made a speech more eloquent in the cause of liberty, than the one we had just listened to from the lips of that hunted fugitive."[54] Following the convention, Garrison and John A. Collins eventually convinced Douglass to serve as a lecturing agent for the Massachusetts Anti-Slavery Society. Garrison extolled Douglass' performances in that capacity: "As a public speaker, he excels in pathos, wit, comparison, imitation, strength of reasoning, and fluency of language. There is in him that union of head and heart, which is indispensible to an enlightenment of the heads and winning of the hearts of others."[55] Garrison's assessment of Douglass points to the ways in which the material of performance—affect, liveness, and presence— prevailed upon antebellum publics, material that largely accounted for Douglass' popularity throughout the nineteenth century.

Black reformers were particularly attentive to the ways oratory, spectatorship, and theatricality powered their sociopolitical efforts. For example, Crummell remembered how the audience of Garnet's "Appeal to the Slaves of the United States" was "uplifted by his passionate appeals, and convulsed by his harrowing statements," so much so that "the whole multitude of people were ready at the moment to run any risks, to do any deeds for the freedom of man, and for the destruction of slavery."[56] Fortunately for those delegates who opposed violent action, the convention waited two days to vote on the resolution. That interval between the "Address" and the vote most likely cooled the immediacy that his performance produced. Nonetheless, Garnet's ability to move the leaders of a severely marginalized population to come within one vote of resolving to support collective violence against an immeasurably more powerful population affirms Crummell's characterization of Garnet as a singular performer and "a master of great [oratorical] style." Crummell argued that the "large gift of speech [was] bestowed upon Garnet," who as an adolescent subdued his audiences "by the tenderest of passages" and aroused "them to fiery ardor by the fervency of his own excited feelings."[57] The older Garnet relied on these same identificatory attachments to sway members of his audience at the Buffalo convention.

But there were some in that audience who had no tolerance for Garnet's performance or his call for slave insurrection: the Garrisonians. They believed that by appealing to Americans' moral and religious sense they would expose the evils of slavery and convert the slaveholding nation to a free one. Violence, they argued, was never the answer; thus, the organ of the Garrisonian movement, *The Liberator*, condemned Garnet's address. Maria Weston Chapman, assistant editor of *The Liberator* and stalwart of the Boston abolitionist community, wrote in her review of the convention that anyone who advocates violence "knows nothing of nature, human or Divine, — of character, — good or evil [if he] imagines that a civil and servile war would ultimately promote freedom." Chapman went on to question Garnet's Christian commitments: "Does he find that gospel in harmony with his address?"[58] Garnet responded to Chapman's charges in a letter to another newspaper, the antislavery *Emancipator* (Boston), but *The Liberator* reprinted it shortly thereafter. In his response, Garnet defended his character, reasserted his intellectual and political autonomy, and made clear that it was his right—indeed, his obligation—to articulate what he thought was the best course of action for his people: in this case, slave insurrection.[59]

For Chapman and the Garrisonians, violence was an act of spiritual weakness that would neither bring about nor sustain real freedom; physical force had no place in their crusades for abolition and moral perfection. In 1838, Garrison founded a pacifist association, the New England Non-Resistance Society, and Chapman served as one of the editors of its official newspaper, the *Non-Resistant* (Boston, 1838–42).[60] For all of their commitments to non-violence, however, Garrison and his cohort did not condemn or even minimize the violent acts of liberation that Douglass performed and subsequently described in his 1845 slave narrative. In fact, Garrison supplied the text's imprimatur, and in his "Preface" he assured the reader that Douglass' *Narrative* "was true in all its statements; that nothing has been set down in malice, nothing exaggerated, nothing drawn from the imagination; that it comes short of the reality, rather than overstates a single fact in regard to SLAVERY AS IT IS."[61] Garrison especially lamented the moments in Douglass' enslaved life when "the longings after freedom took possession of his breast, and how his misery augmented, in proportion as he grew reflective and intelligent." It was Douglass' two-hour fight with one of his masters, Edward Covey, that had re-fueled those "longings" and, once and for all, induced him to make his escape from slavery.[62] As Douglass described it, "This battle with Mr. Covey was the turning-point in my career as a slave . . . [and] recalled the departed self-confidence, and inspired me again with a determination to be free."[63] After this clash, Douglass resolved that he would always fight back whenever a white man attempted to attack or whip him, as he did a few years later while working as a caulker on the docks of Baltimore.[64] In some sense, Garnet urged slaves to do the same thing: to answer the inherently violently regime of chattel slavery with violence of their own. Why, then, the discrepancy between the Garrisonians' acceptance of Douglass' code of violence and their rejection of Garnet's proposed slave insurrection?

In my view, this contradiction in reception stemmed mostly from the difference in medium: Garnet's embodied performance in contrast to Douglass' disembodied text. The Garrisonians spurned Garnet's "Address" because it was thoroughly *performative*—"There was too much physical force" in it, Douglass said.[65] With his performance, Garnet sought to transfer that very "force" of resistance and black self-determination onto the (black) listener. The performative strives for some sort of change by way of its very enactment or utterance, and in Garnet's case that was the transformation of his listening audience into the insurrectionary body that would begin the work of eradicating slavery with physical might. In fact, Garnet crafted the "Address" in such a way that it always took place in the "now," within the enclosure of the performance setting. As the existential equivalence Garnet made between free African Americans in the north and slaves in the south produced a uniform black subjecthood ("We . . . being bound with you"), the accretion of directives throughout the speech fostered its immediacy and expectation of direct re-action. The phrases "Look around you and behold," "Hear the cries," "Remember the stripes," "Think of the torture," "Appeal to their sense," "Promise them," "Do this, and forever after cease to toil," among several others, culminate in the command "Brethren, arise, arise! Strike for your lives and liberties. Now is the day and the hour."[66] These directives were first and foremost for the conventioneers in attendance, not slaves.

In large measure, the Garrisonians opposed the bloody future articulated in the "Address" because they had no control over Garnet's performance and could not regulate its immediate effect. By contrast, they tolerated the representation of Douglass' violence in his *Narrative* because they calibrated its production and circulation. Since Garrison's words open the *Narrative*, what follows in the text is mediated through his subjectivity. Moreover, the representations of Douglass' violent acts in the *Narrative* are not intended to arouse insurrectionary energies in the reader, as there are no entreaties for the slave or African American to follow Douglass' example; instead, they simply explain how violence shaped Douglass' resolve in the midst of his enslavement.[67] In this way, they function as constatives. The constative reports on the world; unlike the performative, it does not strive for instantaneous change by means of its very utterance. The description of Douglass' fight with Covey, for instance, explains how past action produced a subsequent state, which at the time was a (public) devotion to

Garrisonian principles. In other words, the retelling of violent acts in the *Narrative* is a constative move that explains a past performative one.

Because it is more passive than the performative, the constative is in some sense safer. The representations of violence in Douglass' *Narrative* are more restricted than Garnet's insurrectionary appeals because Douglass and his intermediaries embedded those representations within an explanatory frame. The violence in Garnet's "Address," however, extended well beyond explanation and even beyond the words themselves: it spread into what Peggy Phelan calls "the oversound," that is, "the thing not in the words, not in the melody, not in the dance, not in the meter."[68] The oversound of Garnet's performance resonated in his sweeping body and enrapturing voice, and in his listeners' convulsing bodies and tearful voices.[69] This *collective* oversound endowed Garnet's insurrectionary call with an insurrectionary presence that the disembodied text alone cannot create; it was what the Garrisonians feared most, because they could not govern its influence and movement. As active lecturers themselves, they understood the power of performance and of the voice in particular. "Voice leaves the body so that it might arrive in us," Phelan contends.[70] Garnet's voice certainly arrived in the delegates and conventioneers to the Buffalo convention, who came within one vote of advocating what was essentially race war; it arrived in the white Garrisonians who rejected it as one of the convention's greatest "mistakes and wrong-doing."[71] His voice also arrived in Douglass that day, despite his objection to the resolution of slave insurrection: in the midst of his break with the Garrisonians a few years later, Douglass' voice became strikingly similar to Garnet's.[72]

Douglass' shift in register turned on his recognition of the ways white paternalism circumscribed black autonomy and amounted to another form of black captivity. Furthermore, Douglass began to liken the plight of free African Americans with that of the slaves, just as Garnet had. In his "Address to the Colored People of the United States," which he delivered at the National Negro Convention of 1848 in Cleveland, Ohio, Douglass proclaimed:

> In the Northern states, we are not slaves to individuals, not personal slaves, yet in many respects we are the slaves of the community. We are, however, far enough removed from the actual condition of the slave to make us largely responsible. It is more than a figure of speech to say, that we are as a people chained together. We are one people—one in general complexion, one in common degradation, one in popular estimation.—As one rises, all must rise, and as one

falls all must fall. Having now, our feet on the rock of freedom, we must drag our brethren from the slimy depths of slavery, ignorance, and rum. Every one of us should be ashamed to consider himself free, while his brother is a slave.[73]

In this stirring assessment of the condition and possibility of African Americans in the antebellum north, Douglass deftly combined the pessimistic with the pragmatic in an attempt to compel African Americans to accept that they were, at once, slaves and slavers. That is, he asked them to recognize how, despite its relative achievements post-emancipation, the free black population remained the social and political captives of the northern polity *and* helped perpetuate the institution of chattel slavery elsewhere throughout the U.S.

The rhetorical tenor of Garnet's voice from his 1843 "Appeal" was present in Douglass' 1848 "Address." Black pessimism and black pragmatism opened up to both men a new set of options—such as slave insurrection, expressly all-black associations, and political activism—that would infuse the movements for abolition and black citizenship with an energy and urgency they otherwise lacked. Historian Wilson Jeremiah Moses notes that such a "position may seem contradictory" because Douglass and Garnet "sought to use nationalistic means for integrationist and assimilationist ends."[74] Indeed, the aim of their calling on the ideological and practical tools of black nationalism was not racial separatism, just as it was not the goal of their early national forebears. Rather, they looked forward to a free polity that did not exclude white people but made sure to fully include African Americans in the practices of their shared democracy. The social circumstances of the 1848 National Negro Convention in Cleveland bear this out: whites attended in large numbers. Their presence pleased Douglass a great deal, as he related to the readers of *The North Star*: "There was no feature of the Convention more gratifying, than the spirit with which it was regarded by the white citizens of Cleveland. On these, the Convention exerted a most cheering influence. Our day meetings were all largely attended by white persons, while our evening meetings were literally thronged, many being compelled to leave the Court House and the Tabernacle (large rooms where the Convention was alternately held) unable to gain admission."[75] Like their counterparts at all the black national conventions until that point, the delegates of the 1848 convention proudly performed their (black) nation with whites watching because they aimed to bring about a future of full democratic inclusivity and social equity.

## THE RESPONSE: IMAGINING (THE) FREEMAN

After one of those white witnesses, Maria Chapman, castigated Garnet for the physical and political aggression he performed in his "Appeal" at the Buffalo convention, Garnet charged that Chapman "desire[d] to sink me again to the condition of a *slave*, by forcing me to think just as [she and her ilk] do."[76] Garnet's concise, trenchant response was synoptic of the way an ever-growing number of black northerners from the early 1840s onward understood the ethic of racial paternalism that coursed throughout antebellum reform movements: namely, an effort to re-enslave free black people. White paternalists doubted the African American's ability to govern himself, arguing he was in need of their guidance and protection. As the antislavery, northern Unitarian minister Orville Dewey put it in 1844, "Grant that in his inferiority, the African is singular, that he has not brought within the pale of civilization the rough, fierce Northern energies to rend and tear in pieces, that his nature is singularly childlike, affectionate, docile and patient."[77] Such beliefs in racial inherence, both black and white (i.e., "rough, fierce Northern energies") proved to Dewey and similar-minded thinkers the necessity of race-based paternalism, while sentimentalist proslavery ideologues used similar constitutional arguments to legitimate chattel slavery.[78]

Thus, both groups "scientifically" legitimated their socio-racial arguments, claiming the childlike essence of the African (American) as nature's or God's doing; consequently, the forces of the environment, history, or sociality could not counteract racial inherence. "The racial dialogue of 1840s and 1850s tended increasingly to start from a common assumption that the races differed fundamentally," Fredrickson explains, "but those who ascribed to the priority of feelings over intellect sanctioned both by romanticism and evangelical religion could come up with a strikingly different concept of Negro 'differences.' [They] discovered redeeming virtues and even evidences of black superiority."[79] It was that class of northern reformers who most forcefully defended those "redeeming virtues" of blackness (e.g., benevolence, docility, and religiosity) that fashioned romantic racialism. Despite its seemingly positive affirmations and conceptualizations of certain forms of "black superiority," then, romantic racialism was born of proslavery ideology insofar as it rendered the black subject as inherently lacking that which is necessary for a self-determined individual to survive and progress in a hostile, modern world.

Of course, African Americans repudiated these arguments in their formal protests and quotidian practices. From the public performances of Garnet and Douglass to the less theatrical everyday acts of self-sustaining black communities, African Americans exemplified the way in which they were not infantile but fully capable of governing themselves, even in the face of slavery and white supremacy. These performances, however, did not stop white paternalists from imagining the African American as deficient in social and political competence. Indeed, romantic racialism proliferated precisely because it countered the very public stagings of black self-determination. As noted, one of those stagings was the convention movement, which whites attended and whose proceedings they documented in antislavery newspapers such as *The Genius of Universal Emancipation, The Liberator,* and *The North Star.* In short, they were well aware of the growing ethic of black pessimism and black pragmatism. As a cultural response to the growing indignation of black publics, romantic racialist reformers fashioned casts of free black subjectivity that conceded African Americans had distinguished themselves as more than chattel, but still undeserving of full inclusion. Harry Seymour's temperance drama, *Aunt Dinah's Pledge,* is a particularly illustrative example that not only deploys romantic racialism as its primary mode of racial representation; the play also imagines black violence and the black voice in ways that expressly counter what Garnet and Douglass articulated.

*Aunt Dinah's Pledge* depicts black people as the central figures in the fight for national temperance, the social crusade to curb if not fully abolish the production and consumption of alcohol. *Aunt Dinah's Pledge* was first a novel by Mary Dwinell Chellis, who was one of the most popular women temperance writers of the nineteenth century and whose works were frequently adapted for family and Sunday-school reading.[80] Although originally published in the early 1850s, the National Temperance Society and Publication House (NTSPH) re-released Chellis' *Aunt Dinah's Pledge* after the Civil War in their effort to inject temperance ideals into the sociocultural reconstruction of the nation. Their summary of the novel indicates the kind of moral work the NTSPH hoped it might perform: "Aunt Dinah was an eminent Christian woman. Her pledge included swearing and smoking, as well as drinking. It saved her boys, who lived useful lives, and died happy; and by quiet, yet loving and persistent work, names of many others were added who seemed almost beyond hope of salvation."[81] For the NTSPH, *Aunt Dinah's Pledge* might provide the postbellum U.S. a model of collective and personal restitution based in the exercise of voluntary total abstention.

But in the antebellum period, more people most likely encountered the dramatic adaptation of Chellis' work rather than the novel itself.[82] Playwright Harry Seymour first adapted *Aunt Dinah's Pledge* for the stage in 1850 and published the script of the 1853 production at Boston's Howard Athenaeum, one of the city's leading professional playhouses.[83] The site of this production signals the primary audience whom Seymour sought to attract with the play as theatre and as a published text: reformist, middle-class whites. The *Boston Courier*'s description of the Howard Athenaeum at the time of its 1845 opening neatly summarizes the cultural tastes of the playhouse and its patrons: "We trust that . . . the new effort will receive that support for which it asks; and that in the midst of that city, which are proud to have styled the Literary Emporium, we can support a dramatic establishment, in which good taste will never receive a shock, while a refined and cultivated mind can receive the highest gratification."[84] Indeed, over the next two decades the Howard Athenaeum catered to the more learned in and around Boston, offering a steady stream of ballet, legitimate drama, opera, and orchestral concerts.

The cultural and social politics articulated in Seymour's *Aunt Dinah's Pledge* fully accorded with the Howard Athenaeum's Victorian ethic. The play's black characters, despite their linguistic and physical antics, guide their white counterparts to temperance and thus personal redemption by impassioned reasoning and personal example. Aunt Dinah leads this effort, and all others in the play follow her; she is the moral compass of their world. As one character describes her, "Poor old Aunt Dinah; she is a good and conscientious christian, and does, in her humble station in life, all the good it is possible to accomplish, educating her children to the best of her ability, in paths of religion and temperance."[85] Clearly, Aunt Dinah is a product of the romantic racialist imagination, and eventually all of the play's characters, white and black, become her "children" whom she ushers down the "paths of religion and temperance."

Aunt Dinah's biological offspring, Edgar and Rufus, work with her in the employ of the wealthy Dempster family. The Dempsters' prosperity and social status attracts Edgar in particular, whom Seymour describes as "an aspiring young negro."[86] Aunt Dinah recognizes her son's potential and asks the Dempsters' family tutor, Miss Marvin, to educate her son, too. After Miss Marvin agrees ("I have no prejudice on account of color"), she interviews Edgar to find out what he has learned thus far. Edgar recites his "poetry" for her:

(*Assuming a serio-comic attitude.*) Yes, mum.
Adam was de fust man, an' Eve he was the toder,
And Cain he was a wicked cus, 'cos he killed his broder.

De worl' was made in six days, an' finished on de sebenth,
But 'cordin' to de contract, it ought to bin de elebenth;
But de carpenters got drunk, an' de mason's wouldn't work;
So de quickest way to end it was to fill it up wid dirt.[87]

The maladroit and minstrelized language of this speech was certainly a source of comedy for Seymour's audiences. But these spectators, especially those in major cities like Boston, were aware of black oratorical mastery because they saw African Americans speak at antislavery meetings, black conventions, lyceum tours, and temperance meetings. Thus, the minstrel-speak of Edgar's "poetry" served a purpose larger than comic relief: it delegitimated the respectable black voice and its rhetorical appeals.

In his decision to deride African Americans' speech, Seymour committed a political act. By appropriating minstrelsy and even earlier print-performance practices like "Bobalition" to fashion his "aspiring young negro," Seymour (symbolically) derogated and infantilized African Americans and black political culture. Edgar's "poetry" and his language throughout the play detracted from the politicized respectability that African Americans embodied and performed daily. Respectability, here, "was not based in a defense of extent social relations," as cultural historian Tavia Nyong'o argues, "but enacted through a mimetic performative intervention into those relations, upon terms . . . that claimed respect in the face of its quotidian denial."[88] Seymour's play enacted that very denial in the frame of an ostensibly benign representation of an "aspiring" African American.

Further, Seymour's derision was a matter of authorial and spectatorial choice, because in Chellis' novel Edgar speaks more like his white counterparts. This change, in both form and content, was one of the most significant that Seymour made in his text. As theatre historian Heather Nathans notes, "Throughout the play, Edgar refers to himself as a 'nigga' — a marked contrast to his refusal to tolerate even the mild label, 'darkey,' in the novel."[89] Had his audiences objected to the play's minstrelization, Seymour might have reverted back to Chellis' rendering of the more well-spoken and self-determined Edgar when he published the script; but he did not do so. Instead, Seymour's audiences delighted in the minstrelized Edgar, and it remained a feature constitutive of the text he offered them for purchase.[90]

The commercial and political ends that Edgar's language served derived from the wild popularity of Zip Coon, the urban, fast-talking dandy figure of the minstrel stage. Zip Coon, like Jim Crow, is an archetype of American blackface minstrelsy. He lampooned black ambition, culture, and intelligence. In one of the earliest versions of a "Zip Coon" chorus from the early 1830s, minstrels sang: "Old Zip Coon is a very larned scholar, Old Zip Coon is a very larned scholar, Old Zip Coon is a very larned scholar, He plays on the Banjo and Cooney in de hollar."[91] As signifiers of black working-class life, both the banjo and the tune "Cooney in the Holler," which was popular in urban dives, clashed with the idea of the scholarly. For the dominant northern imagination, this narrative and symbolic incongruity enacted the ridiculousness of black aspiration. Furthermore, the iconographies of the effeminate, over-dressed Zip Coon disparaged African Americans' material gains and subverted their performances of respectability. These images not only played on stage; they also circulated in political cartoons, public broadsides, and as front-pieces to sheet music and songsters.[92]

In pre-1843 performances of Zip Coon, actors like George Washington Dixon and Bob Farrell attracted working-class audiences because their acts drew on racial and class hostilities.[93] "The animus toward [Zip Coon] was not only racial but also class-fueled" because, as Eric Lott explains, the figure "literally embodied the amalgamationist threat of abolitionism, and allegorically represented the class threat of those who were advocating it."[94] But in their effort to defer and disdain the sexual menace they believed the black dandy posed, working-class minstrels provided the frame of derision by which white middle-class performers and publics might also scorn black achievement and aspiration. When stripped of his sexual threat, Zip Coon remained an inarticulate, ridiculous, and, ultimately, childlike representation of free black subjectivity that whites across classes could uphold. Edgar in Seymour's *Aunt Dinah Pledge* is a product of this negotiation.

To be sure, when *Aunt Dinah's Pledge* played in the first half of the 1850s, derisive performances and images of the "edjumkated" African American were ubiquitous in northern culture.[95] These literary, theatrical, visual representations often centered on the black voice. For example, in his 1855 minstrel songster, *Charley White's Ethiopian Joke Book,* Charles White offered his version of an African American expounding on transcendentalism: "Transcendentalism is dat spiritual cognoscence ob psychological irrefragibility, connected wid conscientient ademption ob incolumbient spirituality and etheralized connection."[96] By publishing this and similar speeches in his pocket-sized *Joke Book,* White allowed his audiences and the general public to perform as "larned" black scholars, too. Indeed, minstrelsy was often an amateur effort, taking place outside the theatre, in the home, in parlors, and on the street.[97]

Minstrel joke books and songsters, which are collected lyrics without musical notation, were material carryovers from, and carriers-on of, perfor-

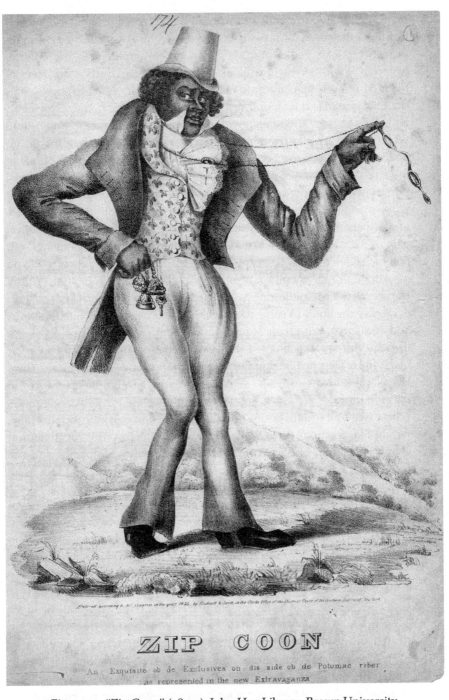

Figure 10: "Zip Coon" (1830s). John Hay Library, Brown University.

mance. Without burnt-cork and without their favored performers, antebellum audiences used these easily portable collections to stage their own performances. Joke books and songsters are examples of what cultural historian Robin Bernstein calls a "scriptive thing," which is an "item of material culture that prompts meaningful behaviors."[98] Scriptive things flout the spatial and temporal strictures of the theatrical frame, allowing its audiences to enter and remain within the fold of performance. Antebellum white northerners crafted their own performances of "mindless black simpletons" like Zip Coon because such figures "added further emphasis to minstrels' portrayals of Northern Negroes as lazy, pretentious, frivolous, improvident, irresponsible, and immature—the very antithesis of what white men liked to believe about themselves."[99] In addition to its psychological benefit, the Zip Coon figure also offered them a kind of political gain in the ways it counteracted African Americans' performances of self- and racial determination.

Although not as bombastic and tortuous as the discourse of White's transcendentalist "philosopher," Edgar's language in *Aunt Dinah's Pledge* evidences the political value minstrelsy offered bourgeois white reformers and audiences. With their appropriations and recasts of minstrelsy's figures and forms, they blunted the effect of the pessimistic and pragmatic black voice. Despite his aspirations for education and economic gain, then, Edgar was both amusing and safe for normative consumption: amusing in his evocations of Zip Coon, safe in his unthreatening childlike ignorance. (These two traits might be one and the same.) For a romantic racialist playwright like Seymour these limitations were not necessarily negatives, but simply reflections of black people's essential docility, simplicity, and virtue. In fact, Edgar's full name suggests that Seymour imagined him as an ideal of free black subjectivity: Edgar Freeman.

An essential part of Seymour's model of (the) Freeman was the devotion to total abstinence, which Edgar threatens to use violence to protect. Early in the play, Edgar pledges himself fully to temperance ideals. When one of the white characters attempts to cajole him to drink, Edgar warns:

> Yes, Massa Albert; I can take a joke, an' gib one back again, too; and if you gibs dis chile de lie any more, I'll just butt dis yar woolly head ag'in your os *frontis*, and I'll make you see more stars than you can in the hebbens, on a clear frosty night. Nigga, eh? a lyin' nigga! I'se just a good mind to get mad, but jus' you keep a-drinkin' that 'ere hell-fire and destruction p'ison stuff, an' I'll have revenge enough! shoo! go along, white man: your breff's too strong for dis nigga; de

smell of the rum'll kill all God-A'mighty's pretty flowers if you stays around here much; yes, sir.[100]

Edgar's fiery rebuke is ostensibly out of place in this otherwise seemly domestic temperance drama. But his drive, like that of the other black characters in *Aunt Dinah's Pledge*, is the achievement of collective abstention from alcohol. As such, even the specter of alcohol is worth repelling with physical force, the play suggests.

Yet there is more to Edgar's threat, particularly in light of the ways Seymour and other romantic racialists imagined the moral and social functionality of free blackness. By the time *Aunt Dinah's Pledge* first premiered in 1850, a vibrant black temperance movement was well under way. In the late 1830s and early 1840s, black temperance reformers began to leave white-controlled temperance organizations. They, too, were part of Garnet's generation, that group of young reformers who successfully pressed for the "adoption of political action as a reform measure and generally of greater militancy among blacks."[101] As a result, temperance became inseparable from African Americans' general struggle for full inclusion and "virtually synonymous" with abolitionism.[102] In his Garnet-inflected "Address" at the 1848 National Negro Convention, for example, Douglass succinctly captured this political calculus. As he put it in a directive to the convention, "We must drag our brethren from the slimy depths of slavery, ignorance, and rum."[103] Abolition, education, and temperance were the three main pillars of antebellum black activism; in fact, black reformers, particularly after the early 1840s, believed one cause could not be accomplished without the others. Douglass forcefully expressed this sentiment at a temperance convention in London in 1846. After a group of white American speakers lauded the U.S. for its role in the international temperance movement, Douglass followed and, forgoing his prepared text, proclaimed that he could not "fully unite with . . . their patriotic eulogies" because there were "three millions of the American population, by slavery and by prejudice, placed entirely beyond the pale of American temperance Societies."[104] The crowd jeered Douglass' proclamations but he withstood their heckling for the rest of his speech.[105]

The reaction to Douglass' improvisation exemplified the strain that black participation caused the antebellum temperance movement. African Americans' involvement proved problematic for organizations like the American Temperance Society, the leading association in the crusade for national abstention, because they wanted to appeal to southerners as well as northerners who did not oppose slavery. Renderings of black freemen like those in *Aunt Dinah's Pledge* functioned as a symbolic compromise, enacting temperance ideals but refusing racial equality and black autonomy. Edgar, in particular, articulated a different kind of violence and voice than that African Americans performed in the public sphere; that is, he proclaimed temperance was worth fighting for, but full black inclusion was not.

Thus, the black subjectivities imagined in *Aunt Dinah's Pledge* appealed to white audiences because, above all else and despite their freedom, they remain servants to white society. Aunt Dinah, for instance, is an exemplar of virtue for her white counterparts and, by extension, Seymour's audiences. She is essentially a mammy figure, a black matriarch with a "natural constitution" of "light-heartedness" and "the willingness to *serve*, the most beautiful trait of humanity," to use the terms of one racial philosopher in the period.[106] Aunt Dinah's service is not simply a matter of physical labor; she also fulfills the moral needs of the whites around her by allowing her inherent religiosity and virtue to shine forth as a model for those around her. As Fredrickson explains, "The idealized Negro was a convenient symbol to point up the deficiencies, not so much of the white race itself as of the racial self-image it seemed in danger of accepting. . . . Many [whites] could be consoled by contemplating a people supposedly free of a lust for wealth and power and therefore immune to desires that led Anglo-Saxons to expand their domain by enslaving or exterminating other peoples."[107] In short, characters like Aunt Dinah served as a kind of perfecting mirror for a deteriorating white society.[108]

But before Aunt Dinah improved the white characters in the play, she first ensured her own black children's moral rectitude. After Edgar learns his mother has secured tutoring lessons for him, he cheers, "Yes, an' when I knows dem rudimans I'se gwine to Boston; maybe Mr. Dempster will have work for me there."[109] To this reverie, Aunt Dinah explodes, "Stop dat, stop dat, chile. I'd bury you, an' dig de grave wid dese old hands, 'fore I'd let you work for Hiram Dempster."[110] Dempster, it turns out, keeps a drinking and gambling house in the city, and Aunt Dinah would rather her children were dead than to consort with such company. Immediately following this exchange, Aunt Dinah instructs Edgar to bring his brother Rufus and the Bible. When they return, she tells Rufus "to take dat are pen, ink, and paper, and you write down just what I'm gwine to tole you." Her dictation becomes the play's titular pledge. It reads:

> This is for everybody and all de world to distinctly and sartin sure to know dat the undersigned individooals, whose names is writ unto, and added, and signed to this pledge, at the bottom of this paper,

dat we do promise and vow, and swear and testify and proclaim, to de ole world, that we never will drink nor taste sperrits, wine, beer, ale, cider, or cordials, nor use tobacoo, either for snuffing chewing, or smoking, so long as we live. And moreover and accordin', we will not encourage any other persons to use the same, but will prevent them, if within our power—and to this pledge we sign our names, which we will sacredly keep. So God help and keep us![111]

Both Rufus and Edgar sign the pledge (Edgar with an "X" because he does not yet know how to write), and from that moment on they serve as warriors in Aunt Dinah's crusade for temperance. Moreover, as Aunt Dinah and her sons are signing the pledge, Mira, Dempster's daughter, enters. After they explain the solemn vow they just have made, Mira exclaims, "Oh, Aunt Dinah, I am so happy that you should have done this. Now, give me the pen. (*Writes her name.*) There is my name added to Aunt Dinah's Pledge."[112]

The rest of the play follows the efforts of these four signatories to the pledge as they work to convert the rest of their social circle, especially Mira's father, Dempster, and her cousin, Albert. Both of these men profit from the distribution of alcohol in their own particular way: Dempster owns a tavern but does not drink, whereas Albert tipples heavily to drown his personal sorrows. Orphaned at a young age, Albert turned to alcohol to cope with the loss of his parents, a loss that is doubly responsible for his alcoholism because they were not around to keep him away from the bottle. As he tells his uncle Dempster, "I suppose my father loved me as well as you love [your son]. If he had lived, I might have been better. But I shall get through the world soon—a short life and a merry one for me."[113] The play steadily emphasizes the importance of parental protection to the campaign for abstinence because, according to antebellum temperance principles, the evils of alcohol tempt children at a very young age. Historian Holly Berkley Fletcher argues that women were particularly important in this work because, "besides simply attending temperance meetings, [their] primary role . . . in the cause was as mothers."[114] The home became the central site where parents, especially mothers, set the child on the path for a life free of alcohol by their instruction and personal example. A temperance reformer in 1849 called this relation "*the transmission of organism from parent to child*" because "it is well known that organization, good or bad, is transmissible."[115]

In Seymour's play, Aunt Dinah attempts to bring about a "good organization," a family rooted in sobriety and personal restraint. She assumes a parental role and attempts to fill the ethical void that devastated the young Albert. Her pledge, therefore, functions as a kind of adoptive contract between her and her white "children." Once signed, it becomes a material trace of transmitted virtue from the pure black "parent" to the sullied white "child." (Albert, Mr. Dempster, and their neighbors sign the pledge by the play's end.) But as she secures the signatures and therefore the souls of the whites around her, Aunt Dinah's relationship to her own black children, Rufus and Edgar, is belittled. Once Mira signs the pledge, Aunt Dinah exults, "Thank the blessed Lord; it's the proudest day of ole Dinah Freeman's life, to see your name on that ere Temperance pledge."[116] It is Mira's commitment to temperance, rather than Rufus's and Edgar's, that gives Aunt Dinah the greatest joy. Furthermore, after Aunt Dinah learns that the tutor, Miss Marvin, is going to sign the pledge, she admits, "'Pears like dey's all my own chil'en; I hardly knows which I loves best—dese yere woolly-headed boys, or dem gals, what's only white folks."[117] Ultimately, Aunt Dinah devalues the biological relation between black parent and black child in favor of the morally restitutive relation between herself and her white charges. In the play, as in romantic racialism generally, the primary function of the African (American) and her inherent benevolence is to fix the problems of white society; that is, she is to serve white interests, even to the detriment of her own black family.

Aunt Dinah's children, too, recognize and value the esteem white people bestow upon her. When Edgar promises he will always remember his mother after he has finished "l'arnin' scholarship," he does so with reference to the affection and love that Aunt Dinah has earned from the white community. He proclaims, "Here's one thing I'll never learn . . . to forget to be good to the dear old mother who's been so good to me an Rufus, here, whose looked upon with more respect by her good white friends than if she was a queen; 'cas she's kind, true, and good to all."[118] He takes special note of the reverence that Aunt Dinah's "good white friends" grant her because he, too, craves their respect and society. Not only does he imagine himself as Dempster's potential business associate, but also he minimizes Aunt Dinah's temperance efforts and champions his white superiors as the true exemplars of generosity and virtue. As he tells his tutor Miss Marvin, "That's nothing to be proud of [i.e., Aunt Dinah's pledge]. If she's done good, you and Miss Mira and Mr. Dempster's been good to all of us; we shouldn't have had a comfortable home if it hadn't been for them. Anybody can do good, no matter how poor they are, but the merit is, in being good to those who are poor and humble."[119] Like his mother, Edgar reserves his highest admiration for the whites around him, even though, collectively, they are far more dissolute than he and his black family. According to the logic of the play and of dominant antebellum racial discourses generally, whites remain ontologically superior to blacks, despite any acts of depravity the former might commit.

Notwithstanding the Freemans' self-degradation, the broader significance of romantic racialist cultural productions like *Aunt Dinah's Pledge* was that the African (American) offered whites a paradigm of humility and righteousness. At the same time, black people needed white protection because they lacked the necessary constitution to withstand an unforgiving world. In this way, romantic racialism was doubly aspirational: its producers not only hoped the figure of the submissive and virtuous African (American) would help rectify the villainies of white society; they also wished that figure might serve as a model of free black subjectivity, a model that countered monkeyism. This is not necessarily to claim that Garnet's (proposed) violence and Douglass' voice directly caused someone like Seymour to imagine black subjectivity the way he did in *Aunt Dinah's Pledge*. Rather, it is to suggest performances of black self-determination in the 1840s and 1850s and contemporaneous cultural expressions of romantic racialism were relationally linked, and continuously refused each other. Thus, an actual aspiring young negro could turn to the theatocracy of antebellum social reform and make a choice: he could follow the example of Garnet and Douglass, and craft his own performances of monkeyism; or, he could embrace the example of Seymour's Edgar and use those lessons to serve white society at the expense of black society. From the perspective of the black public sphere, this was a choice between freedom and slavery because Edgar and other figurations of the romantic racialist imagination were, at bottom, proslavery designs.

# FIVE

Melodrama and the Performance of
Slave Testimony; or, William Wells
Brown's Inability to Escape

In the decade and a half before the Civil War, the explosion of firmly defined theatrical entertainments spurred the development of spatial and formal sacrosanctity in American performance culture. To be sure, before this
period there were playhouses that catered to particular groups, such as
New York City's Park Theatre and its tony audiences, and performers who
became virtuosos of specific roles, such as Thomas "Daddy" Rice and his
Jim Crow. But these places and persons were part of a more comprehensive
and fluid cultural landscape within which theatrical practices, including
opera and Shakespeare, were not "sacred" but, rather, "performed by artists who felt free to embellish and alter, add and subtract."[1] (In the late
1820s, for example, the Park Theatre offered blackface entertainments in
order to compete with its rivals.) Beginning in the mid-1840s, however, socially and financially enterprising theatre producers began to cater to patrons' increasingly doctrinal aesthetic sensibilities with far more regularity.[2] This proliferation of highly delimited performance spaces and
entertainments marks the rise of what Lawrence Levine calls the ideal of
the "sacralization of culture" in the United States, when the eclecticism and
elasticity that defined American cultural production in its first half century
would give way to more rigid and hierarchical (i.e., highbrow, middle-
brow, lowbrow) approaches to culture.[3]

In the theatrical context, performer specialization is essential to the project of sacralizing culture. The sacred strives for a "truth," that which is beyond contestation or debate; thus, who better to reveal the affective and
analytical "truth" of a phenomenon or practice than the expert in that particular phenomenon or practice? In large measure, it was this demand for
the "truth" and the "authentic"—a demand that also reflected the collective turn to empiricism in the West—that led to the steady inclusion of
black performers in the nineteenth-century theatrical mainstream, from P.
T. Barnum's exhibitions of purported racial oddities to all-black minstrel

troupes from the late 1850s through the *fin de siècle* who were billed as "genuine," "real," "bona-fide," and "real nigs," among other epithets.[4] This desire for "real" blackness also shaped what cultural theorist Dwight McBride calls "the staging of abolitionism," or "the carting out of black bodies onto the stage to bear witness to their authentic experiences of slavery [because] this black body that testified was somehow more truthful than the word of white abolitionists."[5] Whether it was the so-called abolitionist lecture circuit or blackface minstrelsy, the growing presence of African Americans on mid- to late nineteenth-century stages was the result of the same spectatorial expectations that sustained other bounded, specialized live entertainments of the era.

These black theatrical practices contributed to the ever-more-regimented theatre culture of the nineteenth century and, more tellingly, instantiated the deeply ambivalent relationship with cultural performance that African Americans cultivated in the period.[6] On the one hand, the stage allowed black performers to achieve economic and social capital as well as intervene in the cultural and racial politics of the period.[7] As cultural historian Daphne Brooks has shown, these performers "engineered and experimented with diverse cultural innovations and, in doing so, crafted new forms of narrative agency and corporeal representation in theatricalized spaces."[8] On the other hand, their efforts were not without serious complications. Ex-slave Henry "Box" Brown, for example, achieved transatlantic fame with his theatrical and visual representations of his escape from slavery.[9] His audiences craved the details of his journey, which he happily related and often embellished for effect.[10] But critics like Frederick Douglass censured "Box" Brown, noting the problematics of his divulgence: "The practice of publishing every new invention by which a slave is known to have escaped from slavery, has neither wisdom nor necessity to sustain it. Had not Henry Box Brown and his friends attracted slaveholding attention to the manner of his escape, we might have had a thousand *Box Browns* per annum."[11] In a similarly fraught case, songstress Elizabeth Greenfield, popularly known as the "Black Swan," gained national acclaim for her renditions of operatic standards and songs of Americana. In 1853, she performed at a number of the nation's most refined concert venues, from New York City's Metropolitan Hall to Cincinnati's Smith and Nixon's Hall. Both Metropolitan Hall and Smith and Nixon's Hall prohibited African American audience members, and critics ranging from black nationalist Martin Delany to the white editors of Pittsburgh's most popular daily, the *Dispatch*, blasted Greenfield for such performances. "If she consents that her own people shall, on account of their color, be shut out from a room where she sings, the glorious gifts of Genius and of Song have been bestowed on one most unworthy their possession," the editors railed.[12] As these examples from the careers of Greenfield and "Box" Brown suggest, black performance practices sometimes stressed the movements for abolition and black inclusion, especially when satisfying the demands of white spectatorship.

This chapter delves further into the vexed cultural politics of African Americans' theatrical efforts in the decade leading up to the Civil War, turning to the autobiographical and dramatic work of fugitive slave–turned–leading man of nineteenth-century American letters, William Wells Brown. A central figure in the staging of abolitionism, Wells Brown strove for legibility and legitimacy among his white audiences. To that end, he used representational forms and modalities fashioned in the dominant racial imagination of the antebellum north, which took shape outside the purview of the slave and, as I have argued throughout this book, derived greatly from proslavery thought. In this way, the formal bounds within which he worked regulated the signifying potential of his output. Terry Eagleton argues that this regulation is the work of a form's Aesthetic Ideology, what he defines as the "signification of the function, meaning, and value of the aesthetic itself within a particular social formation."[13] In other words, a form has a system of ideals and principles independent of those of its content, and that system is further bound by the historical context within which it is situated. Given the contorted and grotesque ways in which blackness signified within normative sociocultural practices, Wells Brown's reliance on mainstream forms such as blackface minstrelsy and melodrama yielded representations whose significations were perhaps more overdetermined than he might have intended or his abolitionist allies might have wished.

As an ex-slave and highly sought-after lecturer, Wells Brown's decision to blend minstrelsy and melodrama as means to (re-)stage certain remembrances of slavery did make great strategic sense. As he put it, "People will pay to hear the Drama that would not give a cent in an anti-slavery meeting."[14] But he could not overcome the forms' limitations, even if he was an "expert" or, to use a mid-nineteenth-century epithet, a "genewine artekil" of slavery. Wells Brown's various retellings of his enslavement, particularly *The Escape; or, A Leap for Freedom* (1858), evidence many of the problematics of slave testimony enacted within the frames, and upon the stages, of (white) abolitionism. As I argue in an extended reading of *The Escape*, the play manipulates but ultimately upholds the national status quo, a slaveholding polity unwilling and unable to incorporate free(d) African Americans; as a result, Wells Brown not so implicitly suggests that the campaigns for black citizenship and full inclusion are essentially nugatory. Before turning to the play, however, I first want to sketch the field of slave testimony in the 1850s in order to establish the discursive bounds that Wells Brown both embraced and breached leading up to and with *The Escape*.

## SLAVE TESTIMONY AND THE MELODRAMATIC

In a deeply lyrical rumination on redress, tourism, and the legacy of slavery, Saidiya Hartman pursues a line of inquiry that, although proposed in a vastly different historical context, bears a particular relevance to the practice of slave testimony in the antebellum north. She asks:

> I wonder to what degree the backward glance can provide us with the vision to build a new life? To what extent need we rely on the past in transforming the present or, as Marx warned, can we only draw our poetry from the future and not the past? . . . If the goal is something more than assimilating the terror of the past into our storehouse of memory, the pressing question is, Why need we remember? . . . Can remembering potentially enable an escape from the regularity of terror and the routine of violence constitutive of black life in the United States? Or is it that remembering has become the only conceivable or viable form of political agency?[15]

To be sure, fugitive and former slaves remembered their lives as chattel in an array of cultural forms because they and their patrons believed bearing witness to those lives was a political act that could transform their slaveholding present. They surmised that if they made the brutalities of slavery and the hypocrisies of American democracy sensate, then the nation would surely rally to abolish the institution. But as Hartman suggests, this was a vexatious sort of cultural work. Indeed, in what ways did such remembrances help routinize black suffering and anesthetize the spectator or reader from the terror and violence constitutive of slave life? In what ways did they help convert the politicized figure of the black *body* into the eroticized pornotrope of black *flesh*, the "primary narrative" of "total objectification" by which the slave lacks personhood, and his wounding serves the economic, psycho-sexual, and social needs of the free?[16]

As scholars such as Houston Baker, Jr., Frances Smith Foster, Carla Peterson, and Robert Stepto have shown in their foundational analyses of embodied and literary forms of slave testimony, the production of these acts of memory was fraught with coercion, desire, and expectation from white amanuenses, benefactors, and readers.[17] Dwight McBride is perhaps most unswerving in this regard, stressing how white abolitionist "discourse is what allowed the slave to come and speak in the first place. . . . It produced the occasion for bearing witness, but to an experience that had already been theorized and prophesized. . . . Before the slave ever speaks, we know the slave; we know what his or her experience is, and we know how to read that experience."[18] These assumptions and expectations established the discursive bounds within which the ex-slave had to articulate her life as chattel, if she were to achieve legibility. If the slave did not adhere to these bounds, her testimony was invalid among white and abolitionist publics; it became "black noise," or "the kinds of political aspirations that are inaudible and illegible within the prevailing formulas of political rationality."[19]

My point is not to disparage the sociopolitical integrity of those who performed on the abolitionist lecture circuit or wrote slave narratives; nor do I mean to trivialize their very real impact on American cultural and literary production. Rather, I am suggesting that *any* act of memory is vulnerable to the possibility of undermining itself because of *how* and *where* it is performed. To remember for others is a process of assembling a history of one's own subjectivity that is subject to instructions that emerged outside that subjective experience. For ex-slaves that contributed to the staging of abolitionism, for example, these were instructions that often had very little, if anything, to do with their particular experiences. As literary historian Christopher Castiglia notes, slave "suffering [was] shaped to correlate with texts whites audiences had previously encountered: other slave narratives, white reports of slavery such as Theodore Weld's *Slavery as It Is*, or popular works of fiction such as *Uncle Tom's Cabin*."[20] Because these texts supplied the testifying slave with narrative frames and logics that upheld dominant spectatorial expectations, they worked to cultivate (white) empathy for the testifying ex-slave, one of the most pressing demands she had to fulfill with her performance. In an age when sentimentality obtained in literary and performance culture, black pain had to "be brought close" to white bodies; that is, abolitionists believed empathetic attachments would clarify the crimes of slaveholding and induce antislavery sensibilities in readers and spectators not yet convinced of the institution's depravity or fully dedicated to its eradication.[21]

Yet (white) empathy for the black slave was not without complications, or what Hartman calls its "slipperiness," in that the (white) empathizer's feelings for the suffering slave often served his own affective, corporeal, and political needs more than those of the slave herself. As Hartman explains, "By exploiting the vulnerability of the captive body as a vessel for the uses, thoughts, and feelings of others, the humanity extended to the slave inadvertently confirms the expectations and desires definitive of the relations of chattel slavery. In other words, the ease of . . . empathetic identification is as much due to [one's] good intentions and heartfelt opposition to slavery as the fungibility of the captive body."[22] Empathy, then, too readily occludes the inimitability of the captive's suffering as means to confirm the onlooker's freedom; as a result, it promotes stasis and erases the magnitude of the nation's originary sin.

William Wells Brown, it seems, sensed these risks. In his *Narrative of William W. Brown, an American Slave. Written by Himself* (1847), he often refuses to foster empathetic bonds with his white readers. The most illustrative instance of this refusal occurs when Wells Brown details the mental agony he endured the night before what became his successful escape north. That night, he reflected on the fact that he would never again see his mother and siblings, who had all been separated and sold to different regions of the south. Eventually his imagination wanders, and he calls attention to the singularity of his thoughts and of slave life:

> The love of a dear mother, a dear sister, and three dear brothers, yet living, caused me to shed many tears. If I could only have been assured of their being dead, I should have felt satisfied; but I imagined I saw my dear mother in the cotton-field, followed by a merciless task-master, and no one to speak a consoling word to her! I beheld my dear sister in the hands of a slave driver, and compelled to submit to his cruelty! *None but one placed in such a situation can for a moment imagine the intense agony to which these reflections subjected me.*[23]

Wells Brown's divulgence operates on two primary levels. On the one hand, it does unite him with those who were "placed in such a situation" as he. In this way, the passage reaches out toward a community of slave and ex-slave listeners and readers, making the *Narrative*, for that moment at least, a black thing. On the other hand, Wells Brown forecloses empathy with his primary audience by refusing to open an affective and imaginative space within which to position themselves *as* him: whites—and never-enslaved African Americans, for that matter—cannot displace their conceptual, readerly injuries over his real, evidential ones. In this scene the text remains about the slave and his emotional claims.

Although the *Narrative* rejects cross-racial empathy in such moments, it frequently relies on the articulation of unrestrained emotionality to appeal to its readers, especially when detailing domestic and familial woes. After Wells Brown and his mother are captured in their attempted escape to Canada, for example, her owner decides to sell her south. Wells Brown finds her on the ship bound for New Orleans, and recounts what would be the last time he would be with his mother: "On seeing me, she immediately dropped her head upon her heaving bosom. She moved not, neither did she weep. Her emotions were too deep for tears. I approached, threw my arms around her neck, kissed her, and fell upon my knees, begging her forgiveness, for I thought myself to blame for her sad condition; for if I had not persuaded her to accompany me, she would not then have been in chains."[24] By means of starkly legible emotional terms, Wells Brown's narration of this final encounter lays bare slavery's immolation of innocence (the mother), and assigns collective (the American polity) and personal (Wells Brown) culpability.

This passage also performs a kind of epistemological work in its unwavering delineations of black emotional life. Proslavery ideologues, following the lead of Thomas Jefferson in his *Notes on the State of Virginia*, regularly argued that the African (American) could not experience, perhaps even lacked, the full range of human emotions; thus, he is singularly fit for enslavement.[25] To counter such arguments, ex-slaves stressed the emotional heights and depths they experienced as bondsmen and bondswomen, thereby claiming their humanity on the very same terms whites claimed theirs. Even when they could not find the words, they knew the importance of affirming black affect. "I wish I could commit to paper the feelings with which I beheld it," Frederick Douglass remarked in response to the brutal beating of his Aunt Hester he witnessed.[26]

As central, organizing constituents of slave testimony, narrations of black emotional outpourings bespoke the crimes of slavery and, often more implicitly, the propriety of full black inclusion. In the mid–nineteenth century, the expression and subsequent recognition of pain became another way to claim citizenship. This "second model of citizenship," which supplemented the abstractionism of the prevailing "liberal, Constitutional model," theorist Linda Williams writes, "emerged around the visible emotions of suffering bodies that, in the very activity of suffering, demonstrate worth as citizens. In this model, pioneered by abolitionists and feminists of the nineteenth century[,] . . . citizenship is paradoxically established not through reason, nor the acquisition of wealth and power, but through 'the trumping power of suffering.'"[27] With suffering as a legitimating currency of American citizenship, African Americans were well equipped: for them, pain and hardship were not in short supply.

No literary or performance genre enacted the claims of suffering sub-jects with greater clarity and moral legibility than did melodrama. Melo-drama's animating drive, Peter Brooks notes, "strives toward making of life the scene of dramatic conflict and clash, of grandiose struggle represented in hyperbolic gestures."[28] Given their objectives, black cultural producers used melodrama (and the melodramatic mode) because it offered them a set of aesthetic and dramaturgical resources that approached, if not exactly equaled, the "conflict and clash" and "hyperbolic gestures" of chattel slav-ery and its legacies of racial inequality. At the same time, the social and personal vagaries of chattel slavery gave melodrama a subject that, in the main, readily lent itself to such a framing.

In *Playing the Race Card: Melodramas of Black and White from Uncle Tom to O.J. Simpson*, Williams establishes the ways melodrama continues to func-tion as the chief epistemic frame through which Americans make sense of the social value of racial difference. She writes, "Melodrama will be under-stood not as an aberration, archaism, or excess, but as the fundamental mode by which American mass culture has 'talked to itself' about the en-during moral dilemma of race." Williams goes on to suggest that there is an essential relation between melodrama and racial signification: "Looking back at Uncle Tom from the vantage point of [the 1990s], I began to see that the emotionally charged 'moral legibility' that we see to be so crucial to the mode of melodrama is intrinsically linked to a 'racial legibility' that habitu-ally sees a Manichean good or evil in the visual 'fact' of race itself—whether it is the dark male victim of white abuse or the dark villain with designs upon the innocent white woman."[29] One of the most insightful summations of melodrama and racial meaning in the U.S., Williams' observations are generative in terms of thinking about the formal structure of slave testi-mony: although these texts and practices were not always melodramas proper, they frequently employ the melodramatic mode because its Mani-chean devices render moral claims, political appeals, and social obligations emphatically patent.

As I considered above, Wells Brown employed the melodramatic in his *Narrative* to sketch the psychological and corporeal trauma slavery exacted on his family because the mode precludes (moral) ambiguity.[30] This attri-bute also led him to use the mode to detail his escape north to freedom. He begins with a caveat, which establishes the action's terms of conflict: "I had long since made up my mind that I would not trust myself in the hands of any man, white or colored. The slave is brought up to look upon every white man as an enemy to him and his race; and twenty-one years in slav-ery had taught me that there were traitors, even among colored people."[31]

But as Wells Brown makes his way north, he runs out of food, catches cold, and, as a result, decides to violate this precept. He trusts in an old white Quaker couple; they nurse him back to health and hide him in their home because he was "in a very pro-slavery neighborhood." In a conversation with the couple that is somewhat stilted yet adds to the melodramatic tenor of the scene, he tells them that he "ha[s] no other name besides William." He then gives the patriarch the "privilege of naming" him, and the old man decides to give his fugitive guest his own: Wells Brown. "So be it," the newly dubbed William Wells Brown proclaimed, "I have been known by that name ever since I left the house of my first white friend, Wells Brown."[32]

The naming scene marks an emotional high point in Wells Brown's escape north and, more broadly, functions as a climax in the *Narrative*. Its melodramatic plotting charts the scene's transformations and transitions in Manichean terms. The Quaker patriarch, for instance, passes from "enemy" to "first white friend" to namesake—and it is to him whom the *Narrative* is dedicated.[33] For ex-slaves, the acquisition of a name that was unrelated to their former masters was a crucial marker of freedom and a step toward full self-rule. Wells Brown put it this way: "But I always detested the idea of being called by the name of either of my masters. . . . So I was not only hunting for my liberty, but also hunting for a name."[34] The story of obtaining a new name is one of the defining points in slave testimony, especially in the narratives.

That said, the melodramatic was not the obligatory mode with which to recount that story. Frederick Douglass, by contrast, declined to employ it. Recounting his own renaming, he writes:

> I gave Mr. Johnson [the abolitionist who helped him in New Bedford, Massachusetts] the privilege of choosing me a name, but told him he must not take from me the name of 'Frederick.' I must hold on to that, to preserve a sense of my identity. Mr. Johnson had just been reading from [Walter Scott's] 'The Lady of the Lake,' and at once suggested that my name be Douglass. From that time until now I have been called 'Frederick Douglass,' and as I am more widely known by that name than by either of the others, I shall continue to use it as my own.[35]

Although the scenarios of how Douglass and Wells Brown obtained their new names are similar—both bestow the "privilege" on benefactors, both keep the first name their mothers gave them—the ways in which they narrate those scenarios are markedly different: Douglass' is succinct, analytical, almost matter-of-fact; Wells Brown's is expansive, sentimental, and melodramatic.

What, then, was it about the melodramatic that appealed to Wells Brown so that he used it in his most intimate and meaningful scenes, particularly vis-à-vis Douglass' highly influential *Narrative* that predated his? Wells Brown might have sought to differentiate his *Narrative*, not to mention his literary persona, from that of Douglass. As well, their respective corpora suggest these two men also possessed different representational sensibilities. In his autobiographical writing, newspaper work, and lecturing in the decades before the Civil War, Douglass maintained a level of analytical complexity and subtlety that reflected his own personal oscillations between factions, ideologies, and tactics.[36] Wells Brown, however, was more absolute, preferring the sensational and the theatrical. And although Wells Brown adapted and in some cases plagiarized several of the period's most influential texts as means to subvert and "rearticulate" the period's "strict equations of race and gender," it was his use of the melodramatic, and eventually melodrama, that exteriorized those rearticulations in the most clear and legible of terms.[37]

Peter Brooks' theorization of melodrama's symbolic potency helps account for Wells Brown's attraction to the melodramatic. He explains, "The force of melodrama derives from the very origins of theatricality, of self-dramatization, in the infantile dream world. But it is important that, in talking of affective structure . . . we not be deluded into thinking we are referring to the psychological structures of melodrama's characters. There is no 'psychology' in melodrama in this sense; the characters have no interior depth, there is no psychological conflict."[38] The melodramatic, too, precludes the "traps" and "inconveniences" of moral and psychological nuance; that is, the mode compels its readers and audiences to choose a side because it offers no middle space within which to defer or waver. That middle space is precisely the terrain that Wells Brown sought to avoid in his antebellum cultural work; he did not want to contribute to the moderation of one's antislavery position or support for full black inclusion. As the mode that tells-all-of-what-it-is-telling, the melodramatic allowed Wells Brown to make plain what he viewed as slavery's essential, incontrovertible truths.

The ubiquity of the melodramatic mode in Wells Brown's corpus from the late 1840s through the 1850s—including his *Narrative*, so-called novel *Clotel; or, The President's Daughter* (1853), lectures performed on both sides of the Atlantic, and travelogues (1852, 1855)—culminated in his writing, performing, and publishing a melodrama proper, *The Escape; or, A Leap for*

*Freedom*, in 1858.[39] This decision was a judicious one, as Wells Brown could capitalize on the genre's vast popularity. Beginning in the mid-1840s, abolitionists and other social reformers increasingly used melodrama because, when manipulated in their favor, it offered more than entertainment.[40] As Hartman explains, "Melodrama provided the dramatic frame that made the experience of slavery meaningful in the antinomian terms of the moral imagination. The emotional power of melodrama's essential language of good and evil armed antislavery dissent with the force of moral right and might."[41] Combining melodrama's aesthetic appeal with the genre's moral lucidity that Hartman spells out here, *The Escape* makes Wells Brown's antislavery politics theatrically pleasurable—a politics, I argue, that deemed the American polity as fundamentally iniquitous and unable to eradicate slavery without a complete social and political reconstitution. In his view, the course of American history yielded a nation in 1858 unwilling to undergo such a wholesale reordering; as a result, *The Escape* cannot project a U.S. without chattel slavery, thereby producing a lasting proslavery effect.

## LEAP ON: THE EMERGENCE AND REMOVAL OF THE BLACK SELF IN *THE ESCAPE*

Although scholars consider *The Escape* to be the first play by an African American to be published, we know it was not Wells Brown's first drama. In 1856, he wrote *Experience; or, How to Give the Northern Man a Backbone* and toured the play as a solo act on the abolitionist lecture circuit. Although the script remains lost, reviews in the antislavery press give an idea of its poetics, Wells Brown's performance, and how audiences received it. *Experience* follows the odyssey of a northern white pastor with "Southern partialities" who is mistakenly sold into slavery. As a slave, he "undergoes the frightful 'breaking in' process" and eventually learns that his positive "views of slavery were taken from a wrong stand-point." After friends of the eventually enlightened pastor secure his freedom and return him to the north, he encounters a fugitive slave "seeking aid to escape to Canada." In the closing moments of the play, the "trembling fugitive bursts forth into a peroration, towering and noble in language and sentiment, in favor of freedom as it should be." For Wells Brown's audience in Vergennes, Vermont, the play left "scarcely a dry eye . . . to be seen in the room."[42]

These accounts, which the editors of *The Liberator* made available to a national reading public when they reprinted them in their newspaper, reveal a great deal about Wells Brown's dramaturgical and sociopolitical aims with *Experience*. First, it is clear that *Experience* is a direct, perhaps satirical rejoinder to Massachusetts clergyman Nehemiah Adams' 1854 influential proslavery treatise, *A South-Side View of Slavery; or, Three Months at the South*. Adams writes that after seeing the day-to-day operations of several homes and plantations in Georgia, South Carolina, and Virginia, and interviewing both masters and slaves, he realized that slaveholding was not the brutal and dehumanizing practice that he presumed and that northern abolitionists described. As Adams' "field work" would have it, slavery was indeed the benign institution that many proslavery ideologues claimed it to be. Thus, he concluded, "the South is best qualified to lead the whole country in plans and efforts for the African race."[43] Adams justified this and all other judgments in *A South-Side View of Slavery* by means of the fact that he actually witnessed the institution in practice; his assertions were based on real contact as opposed to northern, abolitionist assumptions.

Adams' proslavery claims share this legitimating premise with ex-slaves' antislavery testimony: both are grounded in an epistemology of experience. For these opposing sets of witnesses, real knowledge of slavery derives from firsthand participation and observation. In some sense, *A South-Side View of Slavery* and its quasi-ethnographies garnered Adams an advantage over northern abolitionists who never witnessed slavery but attacked the institution from the desk and in the terms of an abstracted ethicality or moral law. But Adams' experiential edge could only be levied against these conceptualists, as ex-slaves offered more in their testimony than could Adams in his. That is, their perspective demonstrated how limited Adams' experience was in that all he could do was observe; but the ex-slave was both observer *and* participant. In fact, ex-slaves were also in a more privileged position than the still enslaved. Notwithstanding the circumscribed discursive field within which fugitive and former slaves had to testify, the boundaries of that field were still broader than those of the slaves whom Adams interviewed. The captive interviewee testified under a form of psychological coercion and threat of violence that ex-slaves testifying in the north did not confront.

Further, another set of restrictions circumscribed perspectives such as Adams': the concealment of the actual operation of the institution. As Harriet Jacobs detailed in her 1861 slave narrative *Incidents in the Life of a Slave Girl*, masters and slaves hid the truth of their relations and the privations of slave life from the northern observer, erecting a world of benign paternalism. The result, Jacobs declared, was a blinding and misleading theatricalism:

What does *he* [the white observer] know of the half-starved wretches toiling from dawn till dark on the black plantation? of mothers shrieking for their children, torn from their arms by slave traders? of young girls dragged down into moral filth? of pools of blood around the whipping post? of hounds trained to tear human flesh? of men screwed into cotton gins to die? The slaveholder showed none of these things and the slaves dared not tell of them if he had asked them.[44]

As Jacobs' testimony intimates, Adams' views of the institution and subsequent proslavery arguments were deficient because his very role as observer was deficient.

But with *Experience*, Wells Brown decided to expand Adams' practical knowledge, so to speak. That is, he not only laid bare what was hidden from Adams *qua* observer, but also he tried to reveal what would always be hidden from Adams *qua* white man: life as human chattel. In his dramatization of the pastor's existential vicissitudes and ideological shifts, Wells Brown demonstrates how the constitution of meaning is fundamentally contextual and contingent. Thus, *Experience* counters *A South-Side View of Slavery* with a "slave-side" view of slavery: the play makes plain the ways in which the signification of the slave's relation to family, geography, movement, punishment, or self-making depends on one's positionality. These concerns have no fixed meaning that float above the actuality of experience. What it means to be "broken in," for instance, depends on whom one asks—the onlooker, the breaker, or the broken. Indeed, how the slave understood was always and already different than how the observer and enslaver understood.

For the concerns of this chapter, *Experience* does more than gainsay the proslavery arguments of *A South-Side View of Slavery*. The play also establishes a dramatic through-line that Wells Brown maintained in *The Escape*: namely, the centrality of violence to the formation of new knowledge, specifically an antislavery awakening in a central character. Upholding the formal dictates of melodrama, Wells Brown renders the violent acts in *The Escaped* as, in Peter Brooks' terms, the "clash of grandiose forces" (e.g., north vs. south; antislavery vs. proslavery; black slaves vs. white masters) and "sweeping gestures and spectacular confrontations" (e.g., escapes from dungeons; runaway slaves battling slave catchers; shooting Niagara Falls for freedom in Canada).[45] Like the institution of slavery and its real-world actors, violence is at the core of *The Escape* and the ways in which its characters understand their relation to the world and each other.

The play's focus on the grandiose, sweeping, and spectacular was not without its representational problems, however. *The Escape* is like the classic Pixérécourt melodrama whose "possibilities . . . must necessarily be limited" in the theatre because the stage is a space "whose register of signs is so highly codified, where the restrictions of real space, real color and contour are so evident" that often it cannot adequately frame the enormity of the genre.[46] Brooks argues that because of these limitations "the stage may not have been the place to unfurl the melodramatic imagination," as melodramas "tend to stretch the physical stage to its limits, and to look toward the novelistic. . . . In the novel, the struggle of ethical imperatives will open up convincing recesses in a world that no longer needs to be realized through visual simulacra, but in words alone."[47] With the finitude of the theatre in mind, Wells Brown's decision to "read" or "recite" *The Escape* (reviewers in the period never settled on which term to use) was logical, especially in light of the ease with which he could tour the play on the abolitionist lecture circuit. In fact, many of the events of the play were simply unstageable given theatre technology of the period. More important, if the ever-more-literate audiences of the mid-nineteenth century needed "words alone" to realize melodrama's "struggle of ethical imperatives," as Brooks suggests, then Wells Brown's solo performance of *The Escape* using only his body and voice offered the most efficient and, perhaps, most effective staging possible.

The sprawling action and multiple characters of *The Escape* that necessitated Wells Brown's acting virtuosity were very familiar to antebellum audiences. As literary historian John Ernest notes, "In itself, the five-act play that Brown wrote and read offered very little material that was new. *The Escape* is, in part, a recontextualization and a significant rearrangement of established literary conventions and familiar antislavery commentary."[48] Indeed, stock characters of antebellum cultural production—hypocritical slaveholders, maladroit black slaves, northerners ignorant of the norms of southern slavery, so-called tragic mulattoes—make up the dramatis personae of *The Escape*. The play's central narrative thread follows three slaves, Glen, Melinda, and Cato, who run away from their duplicitous masters and seek freedom in Canada. Forbidden to marry, Glen and Melinda are strikingly reminiscent of Stowe's mixed-race heroes of *Uncle Tom's Cabin*, George and Eliza. They fear that if they do not head north, Melinda's master, Dr. Gaines, will buy Glen and sell him far from the vicinity of the Gaines' plantation, Muddy Creek. Although states prohibited legal marriage between slaves, and masters frequently forbade extralegal slave unions for reasons that had to do with work production and the regulation of childbearing, Dr. Gaines denies the union because he wants Melinda for himself. His desire for Melinda is well-known at Muddy Creek, and his wife, Mrs. Gaines, issues an ultimatum in front of visiting business associates, clergy, and neighbors: "I tell you that Melinda shall leave this house, or I'll go. There, now you have it. I've had my life tormented out of me by the presence of that yellow wench, and I'll stand it no longer. I know you love her more that you do me, and I'll—I'll—write to my father. (Weeps.)"[49] Shortly after this scene, Dr. Gaines tells Mrs. Gaines that he has sold Melinda, but she surmises, "He is trying to deceive me. . . . No man ever fools me."[50]

Of course, Mrs. Gaines' suspicions are accurate. Dr. Gaines has hidden Melinda in a "room in a small cottage" he owns "ten miles from Muddy Creek."[51] In the final scene of the third act, Dr. Gaines visits Melinda and promises her a life of freedom if she agrees to be his paramour: "Come, Melinda, no more reproaches! You know that I love you, and I tell you again, that if you will give up all idea of having Glen for a husband, I will set you free, let you live in this cottage, and be your own mistress, and I'll dress you like a lady. Come, now, be reasonable!"[52] (In his earlier *Clotel*, Wells Brown imagines how such an arrangement might look—and brutally end—if agreed to.[53]) But Melinda spurns Dr. Gaines' proposition and announces that she and Glen are already married: "Old Uncle Joseph married us one night by moonlight."[54] Dr. Gaines vows to punish Glen, whom he has purchased by this point, and leaves in a fury.[55] Shortly after his exit, Mrs. Gaines, who had followed her husband to the cottage, enters, and orders Melinda to drink a vial of poison: "I tell you drink the poison at once. Drink it, or I will thrust this knife to your heart! The poison or the dagger, this instant." Melinda refuses, fights Mrs. Gaines and knocks off her "cap, combs, and curls," and escapes from the cottage. [56]

This battle between the woman to whom Dr. Gaines is married and the woman whom he sexually desires (and perhaps loves) constitutes one of the play's pivotal climaxes. Characteristic of melodrama, the dramatic arc of *The Escape* undulates and contains several climaxes of varying degrees. The dramaturgical model of rising action–climax–falling action such as that outlined in Gustav Freytag's important *Technik des Dramas* (1863) cannot be applied to melodramas because they rely on frequent climatic clashes as means to bring about *continuous* moral clarity and emotionality. In the peak when Melinda overcomes Mrs. Gaines' physical aggressions, for example, Mrs. Gaines represents a dark force rooted in the pernicious rhizome of slavery, while Melinda represents innocence and virtue entangled therein. With Melinda's victory, Wells Brown not only melodramatizes the triumph of good over evil; he also supplies a phenomenal form to the inner thoughts and feelings of the slave. Earlier in the play, Melinda soliloquizes that she wishes "those who think the slave incapable of the finer feelings, could only see our hearts, and learn our thoughts, — thoughts that we dare not utter in the presence of our masters!"[57] In Melinda's *physical* defeat of both Dr. and Mrs. Gaines, then, black innocence and interiority are made material in the realm of tangible, easily interpretable signs.

The mechanistic import of Melinda's triumph accentuates her position as an exile caught between the sexual terror of Dr. Gaines and the death threats of Mrs. Gaines. This position becomes the crucible within which she is forced to act. At the onset of *The Escape*, Melinda is extremely restrained in her bearing; prudence and an oft-misguided trust in negotiation immobilize her. When Glen reports that Dr. Gaines continues to refuse their slave union, Melinda asks, "But did you appeal to his generosity?" The question of Dr. Gaines' "generosity" is somewhat curious given that he "wants [Melinda] himself," as Glen puts it, and had previously denied the union.[58] Despite the fact that Dr. Gaines' desire for her was common knowledge at and around Muddy Creek, Melinda still believed in the ability to appeal rationally to her libidinous master. Her disposition to reason also prompted her to discourage Glen's dream of escaping to Canada. "But we could never succeed in the attempt to escape," she tells him early in the play.[59] But once she is exiled and under the threat of death, Melinda fights her mistress and runs away into the night. To be sure, it makes sense that she would defend her life and refuse to drink the vial of poison. But the scene also constitutes a tipping point for Melinda as her measured approaches are pressed out of the realm of possibilities. Such compressions are essential to melodrama because they charge the Manichean clashes that typify the form. In terms of Melinda's struggle, the exigencies of her existential and geographic loci conditioned that compression and left her no room but to act or be acted upon.

For Wells Brown, this binary was the underlying design of slavery. Throughout his lectures and writings he stressed how slaveholders "keep the [slave] mind forever locked in darkness."[60] Just as essential to the maintenance of slavery as corporeal brutality, such mental shuttering fostered the conditions that made for the passive slave—he who was always acted upon. Frederick Douglass wrote profoundly about how devastating the slave's mind produced an alternate "realization": namely, the slave hating freedom itself. He contended, "I have found that, to make a contented slave, it is necessary to make a thoughtless one. It is necessary to darken his moral and mental vision, and, as far as possible, to annihilate the power of reason."[61] In order to combat this insidious hegemony, Douglass and Wells Brown argued, slaves must counter the slaveholder's actions with equivalent actions of their own; that is, the slave's *physical* resistance serves as a kind of clearing act that opens *cognitive* space where he could forever imagine, and therefore continue to defend, himself as a free man. This effect was the larger function of Melinda's battle with her mistress: spark her fire for freedom and scorch her erstwhile manner of accommodation, capitulation, and circumspection. By choosing to act she chooses the life of the free; it was Melinda's first "leap for freedom," one might say.

This figural, existential leap is critical to the dramaturgy of *The Escape* because it makes possible the literal leap to Canada that she, Glen, and Cato perform in the final tableaux. The play suggests the individual act is prerequisite to grand collective acts, as Glen and Cato also undergo their own metaphorical leaps. Glen's takes place at the same time and in the same forest as Melinda's. The temporal and locational symmetry of their respective leaps is striking, as both suffer in a state of exile that Dr. Gaines devises and his agents compound. Just as Dr. Gaines' sexual desire motivated Mrs. Gaines to murder Melinda, that same desire prompted him to send his overseer, Mr. Scragg, to inflict at least "five hundred lashes upon [Glen's] bare back" as punishment for marrying Melinda.[62] Thus, Wells Brown situates Glen in the same sort of agonistic and compressed scenario as Melinda's, one in which Glen must act or be acted upon.

Although his confrontation with Mr. Scragg does not appear in the play, Glen reports the details to Melinda as they wander under the night sky as fugitives:

> Come, come, Melinda, we must go at once to Canada. I escaped from the overseer, who Dr. Gaines sent to flog me. Yes, I struck him over the head with his own club, and I made the wine flow freely; yes, I pounded his old skillet well for him, and then jumped out the window. *It was a leap for freedom. Yes, Melinda, it was a leap for freedom.* I've said "master" for the last time. I am free; I'm bound for Canada. Come, let's be off, at once for the negro dogs will put upon our track. Let us once get beyond the Ohio river, and all will be right.[63]

Although prior to this scene Glen talked of escaping to Canada so that he and Melinda could live free as husband and wife, it was not until after he vanquished Mr. Scragg and, by extension, Dr. Gaines that he actually set off northward. The performativity of Glen's physical victory, like Melinda's, was essential: it exteriorized his Black Self—that is, the desire for freedom inherent to the black captive. If the originary condition of black people in the New World was enslavement, then the Black Self emerged as the originary core from which all modes of affective, physical, and psychological resistance to bondage flowed. The various leaps performed in *The Escape* stand for this existential relation.

John Ernest, too, reads the play's leaps in terms of the exterior and the interior. He writes, "What Brown terms the leap for freedom is the outward performance on an inner resistance, a performance that immediately places one in a new, differently restrictive relation to one's surroundings, one's cultural role, and one's former self."[64] Of course, there was a certain kind of safety involved in all this symbolic leaping: in *The Escape*, the battle scenes function as climaxes in the highly codified genre of the melodrama. In this way, racialized violence in antebellum melodrama, including the defeat of white antagonists at the hands of non-white protagonists, worked to satisfy aesthetic, dramaturgical, and spectator demands, which were what allowed such representations to circulate regularly in northern theatre culture.[65] The question becomes, then, how, if at all, does the representation of two slaves, Glen and Melinda, overcoming the frightful conditions of their captivity by bloodying an overseer and a mistress, signify beyond the formal ideology of melodrama?

What is clear is that these violent acts in *The Escape* are not models of action for slaves themselves, because they were very unlikely to encounter the play. Instead, Wells Brown intended them for his northern audiences, especially white and abolitionist, as means to enlighten them to the fact that violent resistance would be indispensible to any kind of sustained crusade against slavery. Though Wells Brown espoused major tenets of Garrisonian moral suasion, he never shied away from upholding the utility of violence in the antislavery struggle, either. In the beginning of the appendix to the 1848 edition of his *Narrative*, for example, Wells Brown offers a paean to Nat Turner and defends Turner's 1831 uprising in Southampton, Virginia: "[Turner] commenced the struggle for liberty; he knew his cause was just, and he loved liberty more than he feared death. He did not wish to take the lives of the whites; he only demanded that himself and his brethren might be free."[66] Moreover, in his 1854 lecture "St. Domingo: Its Revolutions and its Patriots," Wells Brown praised slave rebellion, claiming "the God of Justice [was] on the side of the oppressed blacks" whose physical struggle would help realize the "glorious sentiments of the Declaration of Independence."[67] Read in relation to these and other instances of real-world violence that Wells Brown venerated throughout his antebellum career, Glen's and Melinda's leaps memorialize and reiterate the history of black resistance—a history that proved the goals of abolitionism could not be met by words alone. This was Wells Brown's own experiential truth, and he imparted it to audiences and readers of *The Escape* by means of the popular types and stark figurations of antebellum melodrama.

The play's Manichean structure renders Glen's and Melinda's violent acts palatable. Their absolutist and compressed plight—act or be acted upon—amounts to a choice between life and death, thus ranking their physical resistance positively: by striking down Mr. Scragg and Mrs. Gaines, virtue triumphs over vice at the same time as new subject positions are born for Glen and Melinda (and probably for Mr. Scragg and Mrs. Gaines). Here, the personal is inextricably political, as *The Escape* instantiates melodrama's formalist expanse and its coequal concern with the collective and the individual. (Fundamentally, comedy is about the collective whereas tragedy is about the individual.) In mid-nineteenth-century cultural production, mixed-race characters like Glen and Melinda were especially popular for this imaginative work because, paradoxically, their racially ambiguous bodies (i.e., white skin, black blood) were sites on and through which collective anxieties and individual desires regarding race could be mediated. "The mixed-race character represented a testing of boundaries and a quest for knowledge of origins," literary critic Werner Sollors explains. "Since the Mulatto character may deflect from the assumption that race is a matter of 'either/or,' denouncing the figure may have become a new consensus stereotype that helps to stabilize racial boundaries and may be functional in sustaining racial dualism."[68] Thus, mixed-race characters suffered as the limit case with which (antebellum) society could work out its convoluted and entangled racial engagements.

In many of these instances, the mixed-race character falls victim to her own divided sense of self, becoming the so-called tragic mulatta. She suffers from a kind of imposed psychic vertigo resultant to the fact that the privileges she receives because of (the desire for) her white body are always undone by her black bloodlines. Her story is tragic because she can find no place in a world whose social economy can only thrive on absolute racial difference; thus, she is expelled, and often fatally so. Daphne Brooks understands such removals "as means to reconstituting order." She argues that a nineteenth-century racial melodrama like *The Octoroon* (1859), the most popular tragic mulatta drama of the period, "presents and exposes this [mixed-race] body of excess in order to finally purge it from the community."[69] In *The Octoroon*, the racially excessive body is the beautiful Zoe's, and she commits suicide in the closing moments of the play, an act that adds both honor and irony to her purging.

Unlike Zoe, Glen and Melinda live at the end of *The Escape*. And yet they are still purged. They leave the U.S. for, as one character sings,

[That] country far away
I think they call it Canada,
And if we reach Victoria's shore,
They say that we are slaves no more.
Now haste, all bondmen, let us go,
And leave this *Christian* country, Oh;
Haste to the land of the British Queen,
Where whips for Negroes are not seen.[70]

Glen and Melinda's leap to Canada serves the same function as Zoe's death: rather than weaken the structural foundations and racial binds of chattel slavery, their final leap to Canada actually *upholds* them. Their escape expels the play's most objectionable and rebellious characters; it is reinscription by removal, as racial meanings are resettled and the Black Self is purged.

This proslavery effect is redoubled because a fellow slave from Muddy Creek, Cato, joins them in the leap. In the play's penultimate scene, Cato finds Glen and Melinda at the home of a white abolitionist that serves as a stop on the Underground Railroad. Cato says that he came north "wid ole massa to hunt you" but "I am now huntin' for Canada. . . . I is gwine wid you."[71] Cato's transformation from hunter to the hunted marks the emergence of his own Black Self. At the same time, his escape to Canada amounts to another loss in the fight against slavery because he, too, is sacrificed. Brooks places a different emphasis on Cato's journey. She centers on the way this "expedient house servant . . . wages a one-man, slow-burning insurrection of blackface minstrelsy in his solo bid for freedom."[72] For Brooks, this "insurrection," what she describes as his "unlikely conversion from feckless burnt-cork puppet into ruminative and resistant runaway," reflects "the social-political commentary at the heart of *The Escape*."[73] She begins her important study *Bodies in Dissent* with Cato because his conversion typifies how crafty and enterprising black performers from the antebellum period through the *fin de siècle* used the mask of racial alterity to forge liberatory identities, texts, and practices. Without question, Cato's act is clearly a "spectacular performance of race and freedom." But what were the *communal, familial,* and *institutional* consequences of his leap to freedom? That is, how did the attainment of individual freedom hamper the attainment of collective freedom? In what ways did those remaining in bondage have to suffer the consequences of their counterparts' fugitivity?

These uncertainties haunted Wells Brown. In his *Narrative*, he explains how, after first broaching the idea of Canada with his mother and sister, he "pledged [to himself] not to leave them in the hands of the oppressor" and to run for freedom without them.[74] But eventually he would change his mind, and more than once. The first time occurred after his sister's master decided to move to Natchez, and "she advised [him] to take [their] mother, and try to get out of slavery" because "she [i.e., his sister] must live and die a slave."[75] Wells Brown and his mother obeyed her entreaty but were captured in their attempt. His mother was sold to a master in New Orleans, but he remained in Missouri, a state whose relative newness (Missouri was admitted to the union in 1821 and Wells Brown ran away in 1834), proximity to the north, and high port activity due to the Missouri River system offered him another chance to run away. This opportunity would not have been available to him had he been sold to the Lower Mississippi Valley. Just as his sister did before she was shipped southward, his mother implored him to flee slavery to live his love of liberty: "*You have ever said that you would not die a slave; that you would be a freeman. Now try to get your liberty! You will soon have no one to look after but yourself!*"[76]

Heeding her exhortation, Wells Brown ran away on New Year's Day while he was serving as a steward on his master's ship, which was docked in Ohio. Given the agony Wells Brown suffered once he left his family behind and the sociological vexation he intimated therein, it is no surprise that he resurrects these feelings and concerns before the grand finale of leaps that conclude *The Escape*.[77] After harboring Glen and Melinda in his home the night before they make their final move for Canada, the abolitionist Mr. Neal welcomes Cato and tells Glen, "This is pleasant for thee to meet one of thy friends." Glen responds, "Yes, sir, it is; I would be glad if we could meet more of them. I have a mother and sister in slavery, and I would give worlds, if I possessed them, if by so doing I could release them from their bondage."[78] Clearly an allusion to Wells Brown's personal history, Glen's sorrowful admission articulates a fraught but fundamental reality of slave fugitivity: individual success often meant new forms of hardship for the fugitive and those he left behind. Thus, the acquisition of freedom produced more loss, which was precisely the sort of treacherous social logic constitutive of chattel slavery.[79]

Cato, too, mourns the fact that his escape to Canada will sever one of his relationships from the plantation. He laments, "I wish I had Hannah wid me! It makes me feel bad when I tink I ain't a-gwine to see my wife no more."[80] Coupled with Glen's grief-stricken remembrance of his mother and sister, Cato's recall of his "wife" draws further attention to the price of their successful escape: namely, the rupturing of those familial and kinship bonds slaves forged in order to bear the diurnal forms of subjection exacted on their bodies and minds. The recursivity of such scenes in Wells Brown's corpus (or my focus on them) is not meant to suggest that slaves should not have fled but, rather, it is to bring into relief the institution's far-reaching and insidious systematicity; escaping physical captivity did not mean escaping all forms of psychosocial captivity. Slaveholders regularly flaunted the threat of severed slave communities as a way to ensure slaves would not flee, especially while doing their masters' work in free states. Frederick Douglass argued that "thousands would escape from slavery who now remain there, but for the strong cords of affection that bind them to their families, relatives, and friends."[81] Indeed, the appeal to slaves' humanity and their human relations was fundamental to the system of total coercion slaveholders fashioned, a system in which "effective mastery was not achieved through force alone."[82]

Cato's being "carried back" to his "wife" at the end of *The Escape*, to use a favored phrase of Wells Brown when he got "to talking about Slavery as it is," also recalls the brutal forms of compulsion that masters routinely administered.[83] It was Mrs. Gaines who forced Hannah to "jump the broomstick with Cato." She did so as a reward to Cato because he informed his masters that Hannah and her man of choice, Sam, "stole a goose, killed it, cooked it, and . . . had a fine time eating it." For their actions, Sam is sold down river whereas Hannah is whipped and betrothed to Cato, whom Mrs. Gaines calls her "faithful servant." Mrs. Gaines assigns most of the blame to Sam, who in her view is an uncouth field slave: "I never will again let one of my house servants marry a field hand—never!"[84] Consequently, she believes that what Hannah needs is to be with a loyal house slave like Cato.

After initially learning of her mistress' plans, Hannah confronts Cato in a scene Wells Brown titles "Slaves at Work." She begs him, "Oh, Cato, do and tell missis dat you don't want to jump de broomstick wid me,—dat's a good man! Do, Cato, kase I nebber can love you." To this Cato replies, "No, Hannah, I ain't gwine to tell a lie for you ner nobody else . . . I is better lookin' den Sam; an' I is a house servant, an' Sam was only a fiel hand; so you ought to feel proud of a change."[85] Unsurprisingly, Cato takes advantage of the hierarchy of slaves that structured plantation life, and until he decides to quit hunting for Glen and Melinda and instead hunt for Canada, Cato is the Gaines' most reliable and unctuous slave. When Dr. Gaines hides Melinda in the small cottage in the forest, for example, he trusts Cato to guard it and keep the secret of her location. Turning to her fellow slave for help, Melinda tells watchman Cato that she must escape in order to help Glen. But he replies, "No, you ain't a gwine-to 'scape, nudder. Massa tells me to keep dese eyes on you, an I is gwine to do it. . . . No; I tells you massa telled me to keep you safe; an' ef I let you go, massa will whip me."[86] The expedient Cato seeks to navigate his enslavement with as little injury as possible, and what happens to other slaves in the process is of little conse-quence to him; he chooses to sacrifice the interests of the group for his own personal gain. Such scheming was effective because the institution of slav-ery pit slave against slave, and one could derive power from his sycophan-tic attachment to the master. If, as poet Dionne Brand puts it, "captors . . . enter[ed] the captive's body" and "slaves became extensions of slave own-ers," then slaves like Cato took that attachment as literally as possible and exploited it to curry favor with their masters.[87]

In light of this theory of the double possession of slaveholding—that is, the captor possesses (i.e., owns) the captive and the captive is possessed (i.e., haunted) by the captor—Brooks' categorization of Cato as a "burnt-cork puppet" suggests more than a theatrical genealogy. While Cato clearly derives from blackface minstrelsy, his puppet show does more than heighten the play's comedic registers and allow Wells Brown to intervene in the cultural politics of the minstrel stage.[88] It also marks the way Dr. Gaines' control of Cato for the majority of The Escape is an absolute affair: he directs Cato's physical movements from the outside in and his affective and cognitive activity from the inside out. Cato's worldview is a warped version of Dr. Gaines' worldview, and any sense of self that Cato maintains throughout most of the play emerges from his sense of who his masters are.[89] In psychoanalytic terms, this is Cato's introjection of Dr. Gaines.

In his apologia for those "few slaves who have, after making good their escape, turned back to slavery," Douglass explains the psychological toll of slaves' introjection of their masters. He writes, "It is difficult for a freeman to enter into the feelings of such fugitives. He cannot see things in the same light with the slave, because he does not, and cannot, look from the same point which the slave does. . . . A freeman cannot understand why the slave-master's shadow is bigger to the slave, than the might and majesty of a free state. . . . His master is to him a stern and flinty reality, but the state is little more than a dream."[90] The "reality" of the master's "shadow" re-mained operative in these runaways' lives because it promised them a number of assurances in the face of the uncertainties of freedom. As Doug-lass put it, "[They] prefer the actual rule of their masters, to the life of loneliness, apprehension, hunger, and anxiety, which meets them on their first arrival in a free state."[91] In *The Escape*, Cato signifies much of this condition, but unlike those whom Douglass accounted for, Cato will *not* turn back to slavery. His leap to Canada is final, because finality is the way of melodrama.

In addition to melodrama's formal principles, the awakening that Cato undergoes in the midst of his hunt for Glen and Melinda, when he begins to imagine himself outside the shadow of slavery as a free man, suggests Cato won't return to Muddy Creek. Brooks reads this moment as the culminating act of a "fugitive asserting his subjectivity through the tools of performance and using those same tools to mock and destabilize the subjectivity of the ruling class."[92] Those tools were costume, equivocality, and parody. Specifically, Cato dons Dr. Gaines' clothes and contemplates the implications of his costumed, slave-catching self:

> (*Enter* CATO, *in disguise*): I wonder ef dis is me? By golly, I is free as a frog. But maybe I is mistaken; maybe I is mistaken; maybe dis ain't me. Cato, is dis you? Yes, seer. Well, now it is me, an' I em a free man. But, stop! I muss change my name, kase ole massa might foller me, and somebody might tell him dat dey seed Cato; so I'll change my name, and den he won't know me ef he sees me. Now, what shall I call myself? I'm now in a suspectable part of de country, an' I muss have a suspectable name. Ah! I'll call myself Alexander Washington Napoleon Pompey Caesar. Dar, now, dat's a good long, suspectable name, and everybody will suspect me.[93]

As Brooks notes it, in this "encounter with himself" Cato "confronts and transforms slavery's putative 'social death,' turning that estranged condition into a rhetorical and social device and a means to survival."[94] In this transformation, Cato's self-nomination is decisive, notwithstanding its minstrelsy-inflected malapropisms (e.g., a "suspectable name" and "everybody will suspect me"). Unlike Wells Brown and Douglass, Cato retains the power to name himself. Though his choice, "Alexander Washington Napoleon Pompey Caesar," evokes the common slaveholder practice of naming slaves after historical figures, especially those of ancient Rome, Cato's decision to maintain that privilege rather than bestow it upon a white benefactor constitutes perhaps the most propulsive gesture toward his fully embracing fugitivity. Runaway slaves are "not only hunting for [their] liberty," Wells Brown argued, "but also hunting for [their] name."[95]

Immediately after naming himself, Cato decides to steal his sleeping master's clothes. This act completes his transformation from hunter to the hunted. He sings:

> Ole massa lock de door, an' den he went to sleep,
> I dress myself in his bess clothes, an jump into de street. . . .
> Sed I, dis chile's a freeman now, he'll be a slave no more.[96]

Although Cato does not exact violence upon a white captor as Glen and Melinda do, the physical dynamics of his soliloquy completes his figural, existential leap that allows for his literal leap to Canada. His theft of Dr. Gaines' clothes is instrumental in this regard, because melodrama signifies mechanistically. Besides the word, Peter Brooks explains, the "melodramatic message must be formulated through . . . registers of the [physical] sign."[97] By way of melodrama's formal logic, then, Cato must undergo both discursive and phenomenal conversions if he is to become a new man, one dedicated to his and others' freedom. As he speaks, dresses, and sings his Black Self into the world, he seizes control of his own strings and begins the work of becoming his own (puppet) master.

In his self-confrontation and subsequent manipulation of his own alienation, Cato acquired a set of potent tools to wield against the institution of slavery. But he escapes to Canada never to return, taking those tools and the collectivist ethic he obtained with him. Brooks elucidates the dramaturgical trajectory at work, here, and the way in which such conclusiveness is the culminating move of melodrama: "Melodrama regularly rehearses the effects of a menacing 'primal scene,' and the liberation from it, achieved through articulation and a final acting-out of conflicts."[98] These poetics, from the initiating and undulating circumstances of multiple conflicts to the liberating scene of ultimate release, are, in Aristotelian terms, the whole and complete action of melodrama. With *The Escape*, Wells Brown stages a number of slavery's "primal scenes" and a "final acting-out" that produces a double release: freedom in Canada and the removal of the Black Self from the U.S.

For Wells Brown's mainly abolitionist audiences, an explicit pleasure tempers this release. Unlike Metamora, Uncle Tom, or Zoe, the iconic heroes of antebellum racial melodrama, Glen, Melinda, and Cato live.[99] Theirs is a sacrifice with a certain sort of moral satisfaction, as the leap to freedom in Canada is both triumphant and tragic. Typical of its affective twists and turns throughout, *The Escape* precludes emotional clarity at its end. Yet if there is one dominant constituent of this emotional field, it is grief. In the world of chattel slavery, the price of black freedom was always some form of black loss. This was one of the institution's twisted logics that Wells Brown never refused to rehearse, and in *The Escape* he memorializes all that is lost in the protagonists' gain. In this way, the play functions as a text of deep mourning.

## 1858: MOURNING THE NATION AND PERFORMING *THE ESCAPE*

The losses that *The Escape* allowed its audiences to mourn were not only its transformed protagonists and their insurgent energies. For a great deal of those dedicated to abolitionism and full black inclusion, the play also registered the loss of the nation itself: in 1858, the U.S. had become a nation juridically, statutorily, and socially dedicated to the protection of chattel slavery. Wells Brown's inability to imagine Glen, Melinda, and Cato as freepersons in the north was both a dramaturgical verity and an archiving of the harrowing state of socio-racial relations in the U.S.[100] Perhaps no one articulated the miserable prospects African Americans faced in the late 1850s more plainly than leading black Philadelphian and erstwhile racial optimist William Whipper. In a heated epistolary exchange with abolitionist James McCune Smith they made public in *Frederick Douglass' Paper*, Whipper claimed, "Faith in the future ought to be considered an illusion."[101] Wells Brown's *The Escape*, published and first performed the same year (1858) as Whipper's exchange with McCune Smith, proposes one way for African Americans to overcome this fatalism: a leap *out* of the U.S.

For Wells Brown and a growing number of crestfallen African Americans, the logic of black self-removal was clear vis-à-vis the nation's unwavering commitment to slavery and race-based inequities throughout the 1850s.[102] Nothing marked the severity of the defeats in the struggle for black freedom and citizenship more clearly and definitively than did the Fugitive Slave Act of 1850 and the *Dred Scott* decision of 1857. Part of the package of bills known as the Compromise of 1850 that Congress hoped would alleviate sectional tensions following the Mexican-American War and thereby stave off southern secession, the Fugitive Slave Act made it easier for slaveholders to recover the value of their runaway chattel, even if the person they "recaptured" was not their (or anyone's) slave in the first place. Historian Don Fehrenbacher explains the tremendous expanse of the act:

> A pursuing slave owner or his agent could himself seize an alleged fugitive or else obtain a warrant for his arrest by a federal officer. . . . Testimony from the prisoner was expressly barred [and he] was cut

off from the traditional legal resorts of an accused person. . . . Framed by southerners for enforcement among northerners, the law of 1850 . . . was utterly one-side, lending categorical federal protection to slavery while making no concession to the humanity of African Americans or to the humanitarian sensibilities of many white Americans.[103]

Not to be outdone by its legislative counterpart, the Supreme Court decided in the infamous *Dred Scott v. Sanford* case that the nation's framers never intended for *any* black person to receive the protections and promises of the Constitution. Thus, African Americans were not and could never be citizens in the American polity.

Although Wells Brown believed *Dred Scott* might embolden the abolitionist cause, he did not take the decision in a "cheerful spirit," as the more sanguine Frederick Douglass did.[104] As Wells Brown reflected in 1867, "The Constitution, thus interpreted [in *Dred Scott*] became the emblem of the tyrants and the winding sheet of liberty, and gave a boldness to the people of the South, which soon showed itself, while good men at the North felt ashamed of the Government under which they lived."[105] With his touring performances of *The Escape*, he gave these "good men" an occasion and communal space within which to express their shame, reflect on its causes, and grapple with their own shortcomings. Written and performed only a year after *Dred Scott* and eight years into the operation of the Fugitive Slave Act, the play forced its audiences to confront the weaknesses of the antislavery crusade vis-à-vis southern Slave Power, an accommodating Congress, and a reactionary Supreme Court.

*The Escape* is rather stark in its depictions of the defeats of abolitionism and black inclusionary efforts. "Yes, a few miles further, and you'll be safe beyond the reach of the Fugitive-Slave Law," the abolitionist who helps Glen, Melinda, and Cato leap from New York to Canada says.[106] But it was the final verse of Cato's solo after he steals Dr. Gaines' clothes that was the most damning and distressing:

I've not committed any crime, why should I run away?
Oh! Shame upon your laws, dat drive me off to Canada.
You loudly boast of liberty, an' say your State is free,
But ef I tarry in your midst, will you protect me?[107]

The "state" in this song is not only New York; it is the collection of putatively free states whose borders slave owners and their hired agents readily

and legally crossed in their hunt for runaway slaves or adequate replacements. Moreover, the play extends special ridicule for white northerners
because, along with their powerlessness, many of them only spoke ab-
stractly against slavery rather than taking steps toward its demise. As literary critic Glenda Carpio puts it, "Mr. White, the play's representative
northerner . . . is no more enlightened than any of the play's southern characters and is, arguably, worse than any of them."[108] With these sorts of
personal and societal reproaches throughout *The Escape*, Wells Brown never
allowed his audiences and readers to settle comfortably in the play's familiar modalities, narratives, and stock characters.

Because a once-fugitive slave, William Wells Brown, performed the
play, the discomfiture and shame audiences experienced were redoubled.
Reviewers frequently commented upon Wells Brown's skills as a performer, and one went so far as to claim that, in several moments, he "lost
sight of the speaker."[109] But in addition to his considerable talents, Wells
Brown's well-known personal history as a runaway slave also contributed
to the ways in which his performances signified. As this same reviewer
noted, Wells Brown's "flashes of wit and sparkling gems of thought scat-
tered with rapidity and force convince you that *no ordinary man* is swaying
the feelings of the deeply interested and breathless auditory."[110] A fugitive
slave who became a pioneer of American literary and performance culture,
Wells Brown was anything but ordinary. With his own past framing his
performances, questions concerning Wells Brown's future were sure to
arise. For example, if the fictive fugitives of *The Escape* had to escape to
Canada for freedom, how safe was Wells Brown when he traveled the abolitionist circuit? Given the protections the Fugitive Slave Act afforded
slaveholders, could Wells Brown's audiences definitively protect him from
his former masters, or someone simply claiming to be one, despite the fact
his allies bought his freedom in 1854? Indeed, how did audiences wrestle
with the fact that the night they attended *The Escape* could have been Wells
Brown's last as a free man?

At the time of his tour of *The Escape*, there was very little to assure African Americans they would maintain their freedom, let alone procure citizenship. What Wells Brown told the Female Anti-Slavery Society of Salem
in 1847 held doubly true after the Fugitive Act and *Dred Scott*: "If I wish to
stand up and say, 'I am a man,' I must leave the land that gave me birth. If
I wish to ask protection as a man, I must leave the American stars and
stripes. Wherever the stars and stripes are seen flying upon American soil,
I can receive no protection."[111] For a number of despairing critics, the worsening juridical, legal, and social conditions black people endured through-

out the 1850s culminated in a kind of final and compressed crucible, when black people had to act or be acted upon. For Wells Brown and similar-minded thinkers, emigration from the U.S. increasingly became the most sensible act for African Americans to perform. In an 1860 speech before the American Anti-Slavery Society, Wells Brown laid out the animus behind the campaign for voluntary black emigration: "I say we are going backward. This nation is determined not only to keep the colored man in slavery, *but to reduce the free colored people to slavery,* and blot out, so far as they can, everything that tends to show that the colored man is a man, and at all worthy of respect as citizen of this country."[112]

In both its form and content, *The Escape* anticipates Wells Brown's tendentious embrace of emigration in the early 1860s. The play finds little place or promise for free(d) black people in the U.S., thus ceding the nation to slaveholders and their interests. Wells Brown's espousal of black self-removal in *The Escape* and in other contemporaneous works classes him among the collective of dejected black critics and writers who increasingly argued that African Americans should expend their energies somewhere other than in efforts to gain full inclusion in the American polity. These men and women, as literary historian Samuel Otter explains, "all trace, with different tones and consequences, the double-edged progress of freedom from the 1830s to the 1850s, in which African Americans struggled to advance and their status was undermined, in which investments led to the accrual, not of interest, but of enmity."[113] The retrogressive course of race relations that Wells Brown and other African Americans mourned in the late 1850s and early 1860s belied the hope free black publics projected in the early part of the nineteenth century. Instead, with slavery entrenched and racial progress thwarted, they had to contend with a proslavery imagination and its resultant network of policies and perceptions that sought to "reduce" them to slavery, to use Wells Brown's term. For more African Americans than ever before, the time to leave the U.S. had come.

# Epilogue

*No Exit, but a New Stage*

By the end of 1861, William Wells Brown had become one of the most vocal and prominent advocates of black emigration to Haiti. Not only had the complex of structural and quotidian white supremacist rule left African Americans no place in the United States wherein to prosper, but also the Canada that the protagonists of *The Escape* imagined was largely an illusion. In a seven-article series called "The Colored People of Canada" (1861) for *The Pine and Palm*, a short-run, Boston-based paper dedicated to abolitionism and Haitian emigration, Wells Brown chronicled the ways in which the economic, political, and social marginalization of black people in southern Ontario, where the vast majority of the black Canadian population lived, was practically the same as that in the U.S. As he declared in the sixth installment, "The more I see of Canada the more I am convinced of the deep-rooted hatred of the negro here."[1] For Wells Brown and similar-minded emigrationists, Haiti was the most viable destination because "the building of the . . . *great Negro Nation*" of Haiti "alone affords us a foundation near enough to influence Slavery and its brood of prejudices here, broad enough to establish a nationality of the necessary importance and durability there."[2] For proponents of Haitian emigration, then, the combination of the nation's status as a black-led republic and its propinquity to the U.S. was what made it more attractive than Canada as well as Liberia and other proposed destinations in Western Africa. (Liberia was particularly unappealing because it was the contrivance of the American Colonization Society, the white-controlled organization with ties to slaveholding interests that the vast majority of African Americans believed to be dedicated to their expulsion, not their betterment.) Wells Brown traveled around the U.S. north and southern Ontario promulgating the virtues of Haitian emigration, but he faced decisive opposition on both fronts, where African Americans refused to leave the land of their birth, and black emigrants to Canada maintained their new home offered them the best opportunities to thrive as free people.[3]

The most articulate defender of Canadian emigration was Mary Ann Shadd Cary, who, as literary historian Carla Peterson describes her, "remained [throughout the 1850s] the only black woman who took an active part in the debate over emigration." Shadd Cary's "opposition to Haitian and African emigration was both practical and ideological" in that "she saw these lands as fundamentally alien: in them, emigrants would be subjected to disease and malnutrition; their religious freedom would be in jeopardy; they would be forced to adapt to foreign social and political systems. . . . Shadd Cary viewed the inhabitants of these lands as strange (and inferior) Others with whom African Americans could have no relationship."[4] Synoptic of general objections to moving to Haiti or West Africa, Peterson's explanation of Shadd Cary's emigrationist position points to the cultural and interpersonal distance that most mid-nineteenth-century African Americans felt between themselves and other diasporic black peoples; it also intimates the on-the-ground difficulties that several black American emigrants experienced in their new settlements. For example, when James T. Holly, the first black priest ordained in the American Episcopal Church (1856), moved to Haiti with his "New Haven Pioneer Company of Haytian Emigrants" in 1861, over 40 of his 140-member group died within six months of their arrival. (His wife, mother, and two of his children were among the fatalities.) There were also reports of significant strife between Holly's company and native Haitians.[5] Given these accounts, others detailing similar material privations and emigrant-autochthonous discord in western Africa, and reports outlining racial inequities in southern Ontario such as Wells Brown's "The Colored People of Canada," there was seemingly nowhere for African Americans to escape the racist policies and practices they suffered daily. It seemed only a complete reconstitution of the American polity would begin to remedy their collective ills.

For even the most disillusioned of African Americans, the Civil War provided that opportunity to begin again and anew. The war was, as Frederick Douglass termed it at its beginning, that "tremendous revolution pertaining to the possible future of the colored people of the United States."[6] Earlier that year, Douglass' opposition to emigration softened greatly; he organized an exploratory visit to Haiti "in view of the settled fact that many of [our people] are already resolved to look for homes beyond the boundaries of the United States, and that most of their minds are turned towards Hayti," as he explained in an article for his *Douglass' Monthly*.[7] But while preparing the article for publication and having it set in type, the outbreak of the Civil War forced him to cancel the trip. Douglass welcomed this development with the utmost enthusiasm, recognizing in the first rounds of armed conflict the start of what could abolish slavery and propel black citizenship and full inclusion. He was hardly alone in viewing the war this way, as even leaders of the emigration movement renounced leaving the U.S. and worked on behalf of the Union cause.[8] Indeed, the war became the conclusive turning point when the collective of African Americans, including the most despairing of black critics, decided they would make no exit but work to usher in a new stage of economic, political, and social relations by which black people would act as coequal participants in the polity.

As a new horizon of possibilities accompanied the Civil War, much of the antebellum racial and social logics that engendered the horrifying conditions African Americans endured and allowed for the perpetuation of slavery remained operative. Animating these logics was the question that Thomas Jefferson wrestled with in his *Notes on the State of Virginia* and John Murdock negotiated by way of his character, Sambo, in *The Triumphs of Love* and *The Politicians* in the late eighteenth century; the question that blackface minstrels, abolitionists, and other social reformers thought they solved in their respective theatrical formations; the questions that African Americans continuously addressed from the very beginnings of black freedom: "What shall be done with the Negro?" In an 1863 speech delivered at The Church of the Puritans in New York City, Douglass offered his own answer to this perpetual query, which, as he put it, "met us before the *war*; it meets us during the *war*, and will certainly meet us after the *war*." He urged "for the negro his most full and complete adoption into the great national family of America. I shall demand for him the most perfect civil and political equality, and that he shall enjoy all the rights privileges and immunities enjoyed by any other members of the body politic."[9] With the Civil War, full black inclusion in the American polity became viable once again.

Complementing the efforts of white Radical Republicans and African Americans serving in the realm of formal politics who sought to achieve this end, a wide array of black critics, performers, and writers seized the novelty of the postbellum moment and cast their work as instruments of political activism and cultural reparation. Pauline Hopkins' 1879 musical, *Peculiar Sam; or the Underground Railroad* is an exemplar of this effort. *Peculiar Sam* follows a band of fugitive slaves who, over the course of four acts, escape their Mississippi plantation and settle in Canada. After their master marries the widely admired "young mulatto" slave, Virginia, to his expedient black overseer, Jim, Virginia readies herself to run away before she has to consummate the marriage. When she announces her plan to the collective of field slaves, Sam, who is in love with her, responds that she "needn't bid any on us good-bye, kase dis night I 'tends to tote you and Mammy [his mother] and Juno [his sister] 'way from hyar. Yas, an' I'll neber drop ye till Ise toted you safe inter Canidy."[10] Typifying the titular firebrand, who is deemed "pecoolar" because of his ever-present rebellious disposition, this declaration propels the soon-to-be fugitives on their flight from slavery to freedom. Their journey, as Daphne Brooks notes, is "akin to Cato's odyssey" in Wells Brown's *The Escape* in that Hopkins' characters "inhabit and utilize shifting forms of disguise in their quest to be free."[11]

The narrative and formal similarities between *The Escape* and *Peculiar Sam* are manifold.[12] Both texts emphasize the constitutive apprehensions and instabilities of mid-nineteenth-century black subjectivity. "In spite of its optimistic ending," Brooks writes, "*Peculiar Sam* is a text that articulates, as did *The Escape* before it[,] . . . the profound anxieties and questions attending strategies of performing black identity."[13] In *Peculiar Sam*, though, it is in that very "optimistic ending" that Hopkins proposes African Americans might begin to attend to, if not settle, those "questions and anxieties": though the Civil War has ended and the clan of former slaves is living happily and comfortably in Canada (probably southern Ontario), they will return to the U.S. because Sam has won a seat in the House of Representatives, serving Cincinnati where his "friends have stood by [him] nobly."[14] This anticipated homecoming and the circumstances that occasioned it constitute the signal difference between *Peculiar Sam* and *The Escape*.

The profound social and political reformations that came about as a result of the Civil War and its aftermath engendered the contrasts in the plays' visions and horizons of possibility. It is critical to account for these historical changes' effect on the form and content of (African) American performance culture. That Hopkins could imagine Sam as a Representative-elect of the U.S. Congress in the late 1870s whereas Wells Brown could not imagine African Americans thriving in the U.S. in the late 1850s is simply a historical verity. (Hopkins' character Sam, a former slave from Mississippi elected to Congress, surely reminded audiences of Blanche Bruce, a former slave who represented Mississippi in the Senate at the time of *Peculiar Sam*'s premiere.) In other words, the plays enact a kind of self-periodization that demands we recognize the substantial reordering of the American polity and, as a consequence, black literary and performance praxis. The optimism that defines Hopkins' ending is just as historically and practically legitimate as the pessimism that defines Wells Brown's. Her *Peculiar Sam* archives the emergence of a new stage of black American life, a stage with so much possibility that Hopkins suggests even those emigrants living comfortably abroad should relinquish their adopted homelands, return to the U.S., and get to the work of fixing the problems that continued to beset black America.

This daunting task invigorated Hopkins and other black cultural producers of the era. They knew that the legal, political, and social achievements of Reconstruction could not wholly abrogate the attitudes, convictions, and sensibilities that plagued abolitionism and African Americans' inclusionary efforts in the antebellum period. Particularly attuned to what Saidiya Hartman defines as the "tragic continuities in the antebellum and postbellum constitutions of blackness," these men and women wrestled in the cultural arena to re-condition the perception and place of black people; that is, they sought to negate the ongoing effects of the proslavery assumptions, figures, narratives, and practices that I charted throughout *The Captive Stage*.[15]

A turn to *Peculiar Sam* is, again, illustrative. Sam's mother, Mammy, is not an instantiation of the romantic racialist figuration of the mammy that became the "most visible character in the myth of the faithful slave"; rather, she is an insurgent figure in her own right: not only does she favor her own black children over her white charges, she also runs away from the plantation and prophesies bloody retribution upon slaveholders.[16] As she steadies her crestfallen son after he learns of Virginia's marriage to the plantation's overseer, Mammy declares, "Don't yer gib up nor lose your spirits, for de Lord am comin' on his mighty chariot, drawn by his big white horse, an' de white folks hyar, am a gwine to tremble. Son Ise been waitin' dese twenty-five year, an' I aint guv up yet."[17] Thus, Hopkins' Mammy is both the "first female figure in [*Peculiar Sam*] which charts the heroic efforts of plantation slaves" and, extra-theatrically, a radical inversion of normative figurations of the mammy such as P. T. Barnum's Joice Heth, Aunt Dinah in Harry Seymour's *Aunt Dinah's Pledge*, and, eventually, the iconic Mammy of *Gone With the Wind*.[18]

Hopkins rightly sensed the perceptual and political damage that the mammy figure would exact on black women, and her Mammy in *Peculiar Sam* was an attempt to deaden some of the figure's ongoing harm. That said, such efforts turned out to be largely ineffective vis-à-vis dominant representational sensibilities and spectatorial expectations, as the mammy became a constant in twentieth-century cultural production, from the beloved black domestics and wet nurses of early cinema to the assassin-maids of 1970s blaxploitation movies.[19] In fact, much of the recent backlash surrounding Kathryn Stockett's novel *The Help* and its subsequent film adaptation (2009, 2011) is a reaction against the critical and popular esteem that the story's romantic racialist black domestics garnered.[20]

The varying and often opposing renderings of the mammy figure from the early nineteenth century to the present day tell a tale of continuity across time. An important case in that narrative, Hopkins' Mammy from *Peculiar Sam* also reflected a period of profound change. The archive and rough historicist shape of *The Captive Stage* help explain that dynamic: with the onset of universal emancipation and the extension of constitutional protections to African Americans, the nation looked back to the proslavery imagination northerners forged in their performance cultures for guidance on solving that ever-present, ever-persistent question, "What shall be done with the Negro?" In other words, as the stage of racial, social, and political relations changed in the 1860s and 1870s, much of the *mise-en-scène* from the antebellum period remained.[21]

# Notes

## INTRODUCTION

1. Frederick Douglass, "An Address to the Colored People of the United States" (1848), in *Frederick Douglass: Selected Speeches and Writings*, ed. Philip S. Foner (Chicago: Lawrence Hill Books, 1999), 119. A general note on spelling: I have maintained several original spellings and acceptable British variants, thus rendering a succession of sics unnecessary.

2. Louisiana Civil Code of 1847, Article 173.

3. Erich Fromm, *The Fear of Freedom* (London: Routledge, 2001), 26.

4. Northern states enacted gradual emancipation statutes between 1777 and 1804. Only Vermont banned slavery completely, which it did in its first state constitution of 1777.

5. "Peculiar" was one of antebellum African Americans' favored terms to describe their condition. See Samuel Otter, *Philadelphia Stories: America's Literature of Race and Freedom* (Oxford: Oxford University Press, 2010), 107–30.

6. With the rise of radical abolitionism in 1831, there was an explosion of published and performed defenses of black captivity throughout the decade. In the north, these efforts were more rejections of the political and social aims and implications of abolitionism than they were defenses of chattel slavery as an institution. See Larry E. Tise, *Proslavery: A History of the Defense of Slavery in America, 1701–1840* (Athens: University of Georgia, 1987), 261–85.

7. Benjamin Martin, quoted in *Commonwealth of Pennsylvania, Constitutional Convention 1838*, vol. IX, 321.

8. Antonio Gramsci, *Selections from the Prison Notebooks*, ed. and trans. Quintin Hoare and Geoffrey Nowell Smith (New York: International Publishers, 1971, 2005), 421.

9. One notable exception to this claim is the work of historian Joanne Pope Melish, who argues, "The process of gradual abolition in New England actually inscribed the practices of slavery itself in what was quite arbitrarily defined as a 'free society' to which it gave birth." Joanne Pope Melish, *Disowning Slavery: Gradual Emancipation and "Race" in New England, 1780–1860* (Ithaca: Cornell University Press, 1998), 87. In terms of the literature on free black life in the antebellum north, the foundational work remains Leon Litwack, *North of Slavery: The Negro in the Free States* (Chicago: University of Chicago Press, 1961). Since the late 1990s, there has been an explosion of interest in the topic. One of the most thorough and insightful of these studies is Patrick Rael, *Black Identity*

*and Black Protest in the Antebellum North* (Chapel Hill: University of North Carolina Press, 2002).

10. Stuart Hall, "Gramsci's Relevance for the Study of Race and Ethnicity," in *Stuart Hall: Critical Dialogues in Cultural Studies*, ed. David Morley and Kuan-Hsing Chen (London: Routledge, 1997), 431.

11. *Scenes of Subjection: Terror, Slavery, and Self-Making in the Nineteenth Century* (New York: Oxford University Press, 1997), 7.

12. Gramsci, 419–20.

13. Melish, 76–80.

14. Joseph Jefferson, *The Autobiography of Joseph Jefferson* (1889), reprinted in *The Century Illustrated Monthly Magazine* (New York: Century Company, 1890), 709.

15. James Gilbert Burnett, *Blanche of Brandywine: An American Patriotic Spectacle* (New York, 1858), 14.

16. George Odell, *Annals of the New York Stage*, Vol. VII (New York: Columbia University Press, 1927–49), 37–38.

17. Burnett, 40.

18. See Sylvia R. Frey, *Water from the Rock: Black Resistance in a Revolutionary Age* (Princeton: Princeton University Press, 1993).

19. Abraham Lincoln, "First Inaugural Address" (1861), in *Selected Speeches and Writings* (New York: Library of America), 284. Lincoln was quoting himself from his 1858 debates with Stephen Douglas.

20. Lincoln, it bears noting, never fully rejected black colonization. See Phillip W. Magness and Sebastian N. Page, *Colonization after Emancipation: Lincoln and the Movement for Black Resettlement* (Columbia: University of Missouri Press, 2011).

21. Robert Finley, "Dialogues on the African Colony," in Isaac V. Brown, *Memoirs of the Rev. Robert Finley, D.D., Late Pastor of the Presbyterian Congregation at Basking Ridge New Jersey and President of Franklin College, Located at Athens Georgia, with Brief Sketches of Some of his Contemporaries and Numerous Notes* (New Brunswick: Terhune and Letson, 1819), 341–42. In "Dialogues," Finley imagines a series of three dialogues between William Penn, founder of the Pennsylvania province, Paul Cuffe, the black emigrationist and shipping magnate who urged African Americans to relocate to Western Africa, and Absalom Jones, the famed black minister and abolitionist who fervently opposed colonization. Their conversations take place in heaven, where the recently deceased Cuffe and Jones join Penn. As expected, Penn and Cuffe ultimately convince Jones of the necessity of colonization. See also Rev. Robert Finley, Letter to John P. Mumford, quoted in *African Repository and Colonial Journal*, Vol. 1 (1815, 1825; reprint, Washington, DC: Way and Gideon, 1826), 2.

22. Robert Finley, *Thoughts on the Colonization of Free Blacks*, in Brown, *Memoirs*, 142.

23. Although African colonization was a voluntary effort in that the only people who left were free African Americans who chose to, the long-term vision of colonizationists was the removal of all blacks from the U.S. As George Fredrickson writes, "[Colonizationists] meant that their own program—transporting free people of color to Africa—did not constitute a challenge to the

'right' of slaveholders to control their human chattels and dispose of them as they saw fit; but they generally made it clear that their real aim was to increase voluntary manumissions as part of a movement toward the total elimination of black servitude in the United States." *The Black Image in the White Mind: The Debate on Afro-American Character and Destiny, 1817–1914* (1971; reprint, Hanover, NH: Wesleyan University Press, 1987), 10. For more on Finley, see Christopher Castiglia, *Interior States: Institutional Consciousness and the Inner Life of Democracy in the Antebellum United States* (Durham: Duke University Press, 2008), 102–22.

24. Ira Berlin, "The Structure of the Free Negro Caste in the Antebellum United States," *Journal of Social History* 9.3 (Spring 1976): 300.

25. See ibid.; Shane White, *Somewhat More Independent: The End of Slavery in New York City, 1770–1810* (Athens: University of Georgia Press, 1991); Leslie Harris, *In the Shadow of Slavery: African Americans in New York City, 1626–1863* (Chicago: University of Chicago Press, 2003).

26. Jay Fliegelman, *Declaring Independence: Jefferson, Natural Language, and the Culture of Performance* (Stanford: Stanford University Press, 1993), 3. See also Christopher Looby, *Voicing America: Language, Literary Form, and the Origins of the United States* (Chicago: University of Chicago Press, 1996).

27. Lawrence W. Levine, *Highbrow/Lowbrow: The Emergence of Cultural Hierarchy in America* (Cambridge: Harvard University Press, 1988), 9.

28. Alexis de Tocqueville, *Democracy in America*, trans. Henry Reeve (New York: Random House, 2000), 596–97.

29. Larry E. Tise, for instance, in his *Proslavery: A History of the Defense of Slavery in America, 1701–1840*, centers on the work of northern clerical elites who published "either a book, a pamphlet, or a periodical defense of slavery which argued in favor of the indefinite perpetuation of servitude" (362). Furthermore, a review of collected selections of pre–Civil War defenses of slavery, such as those edited by Drew Gilpin Faust and Paul Finkelman, also reveals the scholarly tendency to spotlight the words of elites and well-known figures such as Thomas Jefferson, Thomas R. Dew, George Fitzhugh, and Alexander H. Stephens. See Drew Gilpin Faust, ed., *The Ideology of Slavery: Proslavery Thought in the Antebellum South, 1830–1860* (Baton Rouge: Louisiana State University Press, 1981); Paul Finkelman, ed., *Defending Slavery, Proslavery Thought in the Old South: A Brief History with Documents* (Boston: Bedford/St. Martin's, 2003).

30. Harry J. Elam, Jr., "The Device of Race: An Introduction," in *African American Performance and Theater History: A Critical Reader*, eds. Harry J. Elam, Jr., and David Krasner (Oxford: Oxford University Press, 2001), 4.

31. Both "fact" and "case" are allusions to the existential and phenomenological considerations of racial life in Frantz Fanon, *Black Skin, White Masks*, trans. Richard Philcox (New York: Grove Press, 2008), especially 89–119; and Fred Moten, "The Case of Blackness," *Criticism* 50.2 (Spring 2008): 177–218.

32. *The Baltimore Sun*, November 9, 1837.

33. *Daily True Democrat* (Cleveland), September 7, 1848; *Daily True Democrat* (Cleveland), September 11, 1848.

34. Frederick Douglass, "The Unholy Alliance of Negro Hate and Abolitionism," *Frederick Douglass' Paper*, April 5, 1856.

35. Ivy G. Wilson, *Specters of Democracy: Blackness and the Aesthetics of Politics in the Antebellum U.S.* (Oxford: Oxford University Press, 2011), 7. Throughout this book, I use the term "full inclusion" to denote what legal scholar Mark Weiner calls "full citizenship in the cultural sense," or the recognition of the "civic majority" that another "group 'belongs,' that it shares certain basic characteristics with the community." Mark Stuart Weiner, *Black Trials: Citizenship from the Beginnings of Slavery to the End of Caste* (New York: A. A. Knopf, 2004), 8.

36. Joanna Brooks, "The Early American Public Sphere and the Emergence of a Black Print Counterpublic," *The William and Mary Quarterly* 62.1 (January 2005): 77.

37. Russell Parrott, "An Oration on the Abolition of the Slave Trade," in *Pamphlets of Protest: An Anthology of Early African-American Protest Literature, 1790–1860*, ed. Richard Newman et al. (New York: Routledge, 2001), 79.

38. Heather S. Nathans, *Slavery and Sentiment on the American Stage, 1787–1861: Lifting the Veil of Black* (Cambridge: Cambridge University Press, 2009), 40.

39. Gary B. Nash, *Forging Freedom: The Formation of Philadelphia's Black Community, 1720–1840* (Cambridge: Harvard University Press, 1988), 143.

40. Ibid., 125–33.

41. The classic study of black nationalism in the U.S. from the mid-nineteenth through the early twentieth century remains Wilson Jeremiah Moses, *The Golden Age of Black Nationalism, 1850–1925* (1978; reprint, Oxford: Oxford University Press, 1988).

42. Michael Warner, *The Letters of the Republic: Publication and the Public Sphere in Eighteenth-Century America* (Cambridge: Harvard University Press, 1990), 21.

43. Corey Capers, "Black Voices, White Print: Racial Practice, Print Publicity, and Order in the Early American Republic," in *Early African American Print Culture*, ed. Lara Langer Cohen and Jordan Alexander Stein (Philadelphia: University of Pennsylvania Press, 2012), 111, 126.

44. Daphne Brooks defines black opacity as "dark points of possibility that create figurative sites for the reconfiguration of black and female bodies on display. A kind of shrouding, this trope of darkness paradoxically allows for corporeal unveiling to yoke with the (re)covering and re-historicizing of the flesh. Dense and spectacular, the opaque performances of marginalized cultural figures . . . [are] able to confound and disrupt conventional constructions of the racialized and gendered body." Daphne Brooks, *Bodies in Dissent: Spectacular Performances of Race and Freedom, 1850–1910* (Durham: Duke University Press, 2006), 8.

45. See Dale Cockrell, *Demons of Disorder: Early Blackface Minstrels and Their World* (Cambridge: Cambridge University Press, 1997); W. T. Lhamon, *Raising Cain: Blackface Performance from Jim Crow to Hip Hop* (Cambridge: Harvard University Press, 1998); and Lhamon, "Introduction," to *Jump Jim Crow: Lost Plays, Lyrics, and Street Prose of the First Atlantic Popular Culture* (Cambridge: Harvard University Press, 2003).

46. William Wells Brown, *The Anti-Slavery Harp: A Collection of Songs for Anti-Slavery Meetings* (Boston: Bela Marsh, 1848), 37.

47. Russ Castronovo, *Fathering the Nation: American Genealogies of Slavery and Freedom* (Berkeley: University of California Press, 1995), 190. See also Carroll Smith-Rosenberg, "Dis-Covering the Subject of the 'Great Constitutional Discussion,' 1786–1789," *Journal of American History* 79 (1992): 841–73.

48. Bruce A. McConachie, *Melodramatic Formations: American Theatre and Society, 1820–1870* (Iowa City: University of Iowa Press, 1992), 158. Both Kimball and Barnum censored the plays they produced. As Kimball alerted the Boston public in an advertisement for his museum theatre: "It is respectfully submitted that in all Pieces produced at this Establishment, all profane expletives and indecent allusions will be totally expunged" ("Boston Museum," *Boston Evening Transcript*, September 2, 1843). As far as matinees were concerned, Barnum's were so popular that he "found it expedient and profitable to open the great Lecture Room every afternoon, as well as every evening on every week-day of the year," but the "day exhibitions were always more thronged than those of the evening" (P. T. Barnum, *Struggles and Triumphs: Or, Forty Years' Recollections* [New York: American News Company, 1871], 120).

49. One recent example that explores the relationship between the theatre and the movements for temperance, abolitionism, and women's suffrage is Amy E. Hughes, *Spectacles of Reform: Theater and Activism in Nineteenth-Century America* (Ann Arbor: University of Michigan Press, 2012).

50. John Stauffer, *The Black Hearts of Men: Radical Abolitionists and the Transformation of Race* (Cambridge: Harvard University Press, 2004), 159.

51. Frederick Douglass, "Intemperance and Slavery: An Address Delivered in Cork, Ireland, on 20 October 1845," in *The Frederick Douglass Papers*, series 1, *Speeches, Debates, and Interviews*, ed. John Blassingame et al. (New Haven: Yale University Press, 1979), vol. 1, 56.

52. George M. Fredrickson, *The Black Image in the White Mind: The Debate on Afro-American Character and Destiny, 1817–1914* (1971; reprint, Hanover, NH: Wesleyan University Press, 1987), 97–129.

53. Dwight A. McBride, *Impossible Witnesses: Truth, Abolitionism, and Slave Testimony* (New York: New York University Press, 2001), 4. I should note that I have decided to forgo extended analyses of *Uncle Tom's Cabin* in light of the vast scholarly literature that traces its enormous impact on American sociocultural life; that is, I hope *The Captive Stage* serves as a supplement to that literature by adding some texture, which does not involve *Uncle Tom's Cabin*, to our understanding of antebellum performance culture. For a brilliant, paradigm-shifting study of *Uncle Tom's Cabin*'s effect on mid-nineteenth-century material and theatrical cultures, see Robin Bernstein, *Racial Innocence: Performing American Childhood from Slavery to Civil Rights* (New York: New York University Press, 2011).

54. Martin Robinson Delany, *The Condition, Elevation, Emigration, and Destiny of the Colored People of the United States, Politically Considered* (Philadelphia, 1852), 203.

55. Ibid., 139.

56. Avery F. Gordon, *Ghostly Matters: Haunting and the Sociological Imagination* (Minneapolis: University of Minnesota Press, 1997), xvi.

57. On April 16, 2013, Lambda Theta Delta of the University of California, Irvine, an Asian and Asian-American fraternity, released a video on YouTube of

one of its members wearing blackface and performing as rapper Jay-Z. http://www.youtube.com/watch?v=4bEz9RTsie8&feature=youtu.be.

58. Eddie Holloway, quoted in Jamelle Bouie, "College Students, Blackface and How to Talk About Race," *The Nation Online*, November 18, 2011.

59. Gordon, xvi.

## CHAPTER 1

1. Sylvia R. Frey, *Water from the Rock: Black Resistance in a Revolutionary Age* (Princeton: Princeton University Press, 1993), 3.

2. There is an extensive literature that details the economic and political exigencies of the post-Revolutionary period. For a thorough and finely wrought survey, see Gordon S. Wood, *Empire of Liberty: A History of the Early Republic, 1789–1815* (Oxford: Oxford University Press, 2009).

3. Carroll Smith-Rosenberg, "Dis-Covering the Subject of the 'Great Constitutional Discussion,' 1786–1789," *Journal of American History* 79 (1992): 844. See Frye, especially 45–242.

4. See Ira Berlin, "The Structure of the Free Negro Caste in the Antebellum United States," *Journal of Social History* 9.3 (Spring 1976): 297–318; Joanne Pope Melish, *Disowning Slavery: Gradual Emancipation and "Race" in New England, 1780–1860* (Ithaca: Cornell University Press, 1998), 50–118. Berlin defines the Upper South as Delaware, Kentucky, Maryland, Missouri, North Carolina, Tennessee, Virginia, and the District of Columbia.

5. For example, in 1780 a group of seven free "poor Negroes & molattoes" petitioned the Massachusetts revolutionary legislature for voting rights because the state taxed them, explicitly equating their demand with the colonial charge of taxation without representation. "Many of our Colour (as is well known) have cheerfully Entered the field of Battle in the defense of the Common Cause and that (as we conceive) against a similar Exertion of Power." In another case in 1784, a North Carolina slave called Ned Griffin appealed to the state's General Assembly asserting that by way of his "Contract [i.e., serving in the war in his master's place] and merit he is Intitled to his Freedom." Both of these petitions are reprinted in Herbert Aptheker, ed., *A Documentary History of the Negro People of the United States* (New York: Citadel Press), 14–15.

6. As Paul Gilroy writes, "The intellectual and cultural achievements of the black Atlantic populations exist partly inside and not always against the grand narratives of the Enlightenment and its operational principles." Gilroy, *The Black Atlantic: Modernity and Double Consciousness* (Cambridge: Harvard University Press, 1993), 48. See also Craig Steven Wilder, *In the Company of Black Men: The African Influence on African American Culture in New York City* (New York: New York University Press, 2005).

7. John Ernest, *Liberation Historiography: African American Writers and the Challenge of History, 1794–1861* (Chapel Hill: University of North Carolina Press, 2004), 80.

8. For a striking pre–Civil War black-authored analysis of Attucks' death and black participation in the American War of Independence, see William

Cooper Nell, *The Colored Patriots of the American Revolution* (Boston: Walcutt, 1855). I explore the form and function of this text in chapter 3.

9. Tavia Nyong'o, *The Amalgamation Waltz: Race, Performance, and the Ruses of Memory* (Minneapolis: University of Minnesota Press, 2009), 7, 33–68.

10. Marcus Rediker, "The Revenge of Crispus Attucks; or, The Atlantic Challenge to American Labor History," *Labor Studies in Working-Class History of the Americas* 1 (2004): 36, 38.

11. Ibid., 43.

12. Ibid., 47.

13. This term is clearly indebted to political theorist Georgio Agamben's notion of the state of exception in *Homo Sacer: Sovereign Power and Bare Life* (Stanford: Stanford University Press, 1998), and *State of Exception* (Chicago: University of Chicago Press, 2005).

14. See Jared Sexton, "People-of-Color-Blindness: Notes on the Afterlife of Slavery," *Social Text* 28.2 (2010): 31–56.

15. Lindon Barrett, *Blackness and Value: Seeing Double* (Cambridge: Cambridge University Press, 1999), 95.

16. Mary Ryan, "The American Parade: Representations of the Nineteenth-Century Social Order," in *The New Cultural History*, ed. Lynn Avery Hunt (Berkeley: University of California Press, 1989), 132; Shane White, "'It was a Proud Day': African Americans, Festivals, and Parades in the North, 1741–1834," *Journal of American History* 81 (1994): 39.

17. Melish, 76–80.

18. For how this unfolded in New England, see Melish, *Disowning Slavery*. For how it took place in New York, which had the largest slave population of any northern state at the turn of the nineteenth century, see Leslie Harris, *In the Shadow of Slavery: African Americans in New York City, 1626–1863* (Chicago: University of Chicago Press, 2003), 72–288; and Shane White, *Somewhat More Independent: The End of Slavery in New York City, 1770–1810* (Athens: University of Georgia Press, 1991), 79–184.

19. Thomas Jefferson, *Notes on the State of Virginia* (1781–82; London: Stockdale, 1787), 229.

20. Heather S. Nathans, *Early American Theatre from the Revolution to Thomas Jefferson: Into the Hands of the People* (Cambridge: University of Cambridge Press, 2003), 93. For more on Murdock, see Heather S. Nathans, "Trampling the Native Genius: John Murdock versus the Chestnut Street Theatre," *Journal of American Drama and Theatre* 14 (2002): 29–43.

21. Richard S. Newman, *The Transformation of American Abolitionism: Fighting Slavery in the Early Republic* (Chapel Hill: University of North Carolina Press, 2002), 1–23.

22. John Murdock, *The Triumphs of Love; Or, Happy Reconciliation* (Philadelphia, 1794), 14.

23. Ibid., 52.

24. Ibid.

25. Ibid., 51–52.

26. Ibid., 52.

27. Ibid., 53.

28. Murdock, 68.

29. Ibid., 69.

30. According to Nathans' research on the play, theatre managers avoided staging *The Politicians* right away because they considered it "too controversial for audiences already on edge from the difficult party politics of the late 1790s." (Nathans, *Slavery and Sentiment*, 48 n. 98).

31. John Murdock, *The Politicians* (Philadelphia, 1798), 20.

32. George Washington, "Farewell Address" (1796), in *George Washington: Writings* (New York: Library of America, 1997), 974.

33. Murdock, *The Politicians*, 20–21.

34. Alice Rayner, *Comic Persuasion: Moral Structure in British Comedy from Shakespeare to Stoppard* (Berkeley: University of California Press, 1987), 7–11.

35. Patrick Rael, *Black Identity and Black Protest in the Antebellum North* (Chapel Hill: University of North Carolina Press, 2002), 21–27.

36. Gary B. Nash, *Forging Freedom: The Formation of Philadelphia's Black Community, 1720–1840* (Cambridge: Harvard University Press, 1988), 70.

37. Melish, 84–162; Nash, 66–211.

38. See Edmund S. Morgan, *American Slavery, American Freedom: The Ordeal of Colonial Virginia* (1975; New York: W.W. Norton, 2003).

39. Nahum Chandler, "Of Exorbitance: The Problem of the Negro as a Problem for Thought," *Criticism* 50 (2008): 345–410.

40. Eddie S. Glaude, Jr., *Exodus!: Religion, Race, and Nation in Early Nineteenth-century Black America* (Chicago: University of Chicago Press, 2000), 164.

41. See Wilson Jeremiah Moses, *The Golden Age of Black Nationalism, 1850–1925* (1978; reprint, Oxford: Oxford University Press, 1988), 15–58.

42. See Mitch Kachun, *Festivals of Freedom: Meaning and Memory in African American Emancipation Celebrations, 1808–1915* (Amherst: University of Massachusetts Press, 2003), 16–53.

43. Jane de Forest Shelton, "The New England Negro: A Remnant," *Harper's Magazine* 88 (New York: Harper and Brothers, 1893), 535.

44. Monica L. Miller, *Slaves to Fashion: Black Dandyism and the Styling of Black Diasporic Identity* (Durham: Duke University Press, 2009), 84.

45. James Fenimore Cooper, *Satanstoe: or, The Little Page Manuscripts; a Tale of the Colony* (New York: D. Appleton, 1873), 69.

46. Frederick Douglass, *Autobiographies* (New York: Library of America, 1994), 66.

47. White, "It was a Proud Day," 31.

48. Glaude, 82–104; White, 31–50.

49. Saidiya Hartman, *Scenes of Subjections: Terror, Slavery, and Self-Making* (New York: Oxford University Press, 1997), 48.

50. *Salem Gazette*, March 18, 1806.

51. *Salem Gazette*, March 21, 1806.

52. *Salem Gazette*, March 18, 1806.

53. James McCune Smith, "Introduction" to Henry Highland Garnet, *A Memorial Discourse* (Philadelphia: Joseph M. Wilson, 1865), 20–21.

54. White, 49–50.

55. Henry Sipkins, "An Oration on the Anniversary of the Slave Trade; De-

livered in the African Church of New York City, January 2, 1809," (New York, 1809), in Dorothy Porter Wesley, *Early Negro Writing, 1760–1837* (Boston: Beacon Press, 1971), 365..

56. Ibid., 371.

57. Ibid., 373 (emphasis added).

58. Glaude, 44–104; David Waldstreicher, *In the Midst of Perpetual Fetes: The Making of American Nationalism, 1776–1820* (Chapel Hill: University of North Carolina Press, 1997), 323–48.

59. Peter Williams, "An Oration on the Abolition of the Slave Trade; Delivered in the African Church in the City of New York, January 1, 1808" (New York, 1808), in Wesley, 350.

60. Glaude, 15–16.

61. Benedict Anderson, *Imagined Communities: Reflections on the Origin and Spread of Nationalism* (1983; reprint, London: Verso, 1991), 24.

62. Ibid., 33.

63. Ibid., 24–39.

64. Slavoj Žižek, *Tarrying with the Negative: Kant, Hegel, and the Critique of Ideology* (1993; reprint, Durham: Duke University Press, 2003), 202.

65. Ibid.

66. Geneviève Fabre, "African-American Commemorative Celebrations in the Nineteenth Century," in *History and Memory in African American Culture*, ed. Geneviève Fabre and Robert G. O'Meally (New York: Oxford University Press, 1994), 73.

67. Jones reprinted in Porter, 335–42; Sidney reprinted in ibid., 356–64; Williams reprinted in ibid., 344–54.

68. Edward Griffin Parker, *The Golden Age of American Oratory* (Boston: Whittemore, Niles, and Hall, 1857).

69. Sandra Gustafson, *Eloquence Is Power: Oratory & Performance in Early America* (Chapel Hill: University of North Carolina Press, 2000), 246, 257.

70. In *Eloquence Is Power*, Gustafson explores black sacred orality, but not African Americans' secular rhetoric.

71. Jay Flielgelman, *Declaring Independence: Jefferson, Natural Language, and the Culture of Performance* (Stanford: Stanford University Press, 1993), 3–4.

72. Ibid., 191.

73. Jefferson, 233 (emphasis added).

74. Absalom Jones, "A Thanksgiving Sermon, Preached January 1, 1808, In St. Thomas's, or the African Episcopal, Church, Philadelphia: On Account of the Abolition of the African Slave Trade, On that Day, By the Congress of the United States" (Philadelphia, 1808), in Porter, 337.

75. Glaude, 94.

76. Porter, 335.

77. Newman, 79.

78. Wilder, 81; *passim*.

79. On these tensions among white listening and reading publics, see Trish Loughran, *The Republic in Print: Print Culture in the Age of U.S. Nation Building, 1770–1870* (New York: Columbia University Press, 2007), 1–29; 161–222.

80. On the political importance of black literary subjectivity in the antebellum period, see Elizabeth McHenry, *Forgotten Readers: Recovering the Lost History of African American Literary Societies* (Durham: Duke University Press, 2002), 1–140; Joanna Brooks, "The Early American Public Sphere and the Emergence of a Black Print Counterpublic," *The William and Mary Quarterly* 62.1 (January 2005): 67–92.

81. See Joanna Brooks; Joseph Rezek, "The Orations of the Abolition of the Slave Trade and the Uses of Print in the Early Black Atlantic," *Early American Literature* 45.3 (2010): 655–82.

82. Michael Warner, *The Letters of the Republic: Publication and the Public Sphere in Eighteenth-Century America* (Cambridge: Harvard University Press, 1990), 38.

83. See Henry Louis Gates, Jr., "Writing 'Race' and the Difference It Makes," *Critical Inquiry* 12.1 (Autumn 1985): 1–20.

84. Williams reprinted in Porter, 353. The signers of Williams' manuscript were Benjamin Moore, bishop of the Episcopal Church of New York; Ezekiel Cooper, minister and historian of the Methodist Church; and John Murray and William T. Slocum. All were powerful members of the New York Manumission Society. Ibid., 353–54.

85. See Robert Stepto, "I Rose and Found My Voice: Narration, Authentication, and Authorial Control in Four Slave Narratives," in *The Slave's Narrative*, eds. Charles T. Davis and Henry Louis Gates, Jr. (Oxford: Oxford University Press, 1985), 225–41.

86. Jacques Derrida, "Signature Event Context," in *Limited Inc.* (Evanston: Northwestern University Press, 1988), 20.

87. Porter, 363–64.

88. Eve Kosofsky Sedgwick, *Touching Feeling: Affect, Pedagogy, Performativity* (Durham: Duke University Press, 2003), 115.

89. The earliest surviving of these broadsides is *Invitation, Addressed to the Marshals of the "Africum Schocietee," at the Commemoration of the "Abolition of the Slave Trade"* (Boston, 1816). The Boston Public Library holds a copy of it. Besides Bobalition, there were also "Reply to Bobalition" broadsides, which "censure both the unknown authors of the initial broadsides and the rowdy white celebrants of the annual celebrations of artillery election and Squantum," and "Riot" broadsides, which "simultaneously define black gender relations as disorderly and dramatize the tyranny of white mobs that attack black households with excessive force." In this chapter, I confine myself to Bobalition but my readings therein apply generally to Reply and Riot. As historian Corey Capers argues, all three forms of the broadsides "were part of a dialogic series; their producers intended them to be read in conversation with one another." Corey Capers, "Black Voices, White Print: Racial Practice, Print Publicity, and Order in the Early American Republic," in *Early African American Print Culture*, ed. Lara Langer Cohen and Jordan Alexander Stein (Philadelphia: University of Pennsylvania Press, 2012), 113.

90. *Grand Celebrashun ob de Bobalition ob African Slabery!!!* (Boston, 1825), Library of Congress.

91. *Grand Bobalition, or 'Great Annibersary Fussible'* (Boston, 1821), Library of Congress.

92. Writing about colonial New England, Michael Warner explains the inseparable bond between orality and textual production in the period. He writes, "New Englanders . . . used [letters] with an intensity equaled by very few other cultures in the world at the time. Yet in an important ideological way it was an oral society. New Englanders accorded a disciplinary privilege to speech and in most contexts insisted on seeing writing as a form of speaking." This "disciplinary privilege," I argue, remained operative in the early nineteenth century. Michael Warner, *The Letters of the Republic: Publication and the Public Sphere in Eighteenth-century America* (Cambridge: Harvard University Press, 1990), 21.

93. Gustafson, 267; see also Fliegelman, 193–95.

94. From the hugely popular Mungo of Isaac Bickerstaffe's transatlantic hit *The Padlock* (1768), to Murdock's Sambo of the post-Revolutionary stage, madcap slave characters delighted audiences with their maladroit and (often unintentionally) punning speech. On Bickerstaffe's Mungo, see Miller, 27–76.

95. Thomas F. Gossett, *Race: The History of an Idea in America* (1963; reprint, New York: Oxford University Press, 1997), 32–53; George M. Fredrickson, *The Black Image in the White Mind: The Debate on Afro-American Character and Destiny, 1817–1914* (Middletown: Wesleyan University Press, 1987), 43–129.

96. Jefferson, 264–66.

97. William Stanton, *The Leopard's Spots: Scientific Attitudes toward Race in America, 1815–59* (Chicago: University of Chicago Press, 1960), 24–196.

98. John Quincy Adams, *Lectures on Rhetoric and Oratory, Delivered to the Classes of Senior and Junior Sophisters in Harvard University*, Vol. 1 (Cambridge: Hilliard and Metcalf, 1810), 13–14.

99. Ibid., 15.

100. Ibid., 15–16.

101. See Fliegelman, *Declaring Independence*.

102. Adams, 16.

103. Henry Home of Kames, *Elements of Criticism*, vol. 2, 8th ed. (1762; reprint, Edinburgh: Neill and Company, 1807), 351.

104. Fliegelman, 16.

105. *Grand Celebrashun ob de Bobalition ob African Slabery!!!* (Boston, 1825), Library of Congress.

106. *The Grand Celebration! Of the Abolition of the Slave Trade* (Boston, 1817), Boston Public Library.

107. *Grand Bobalition, or 'Great Annibersary Fussible'* (Boston, 1821), Library of Congress.

108. *Bobalition of Slavery!!!!!* (Boston, 1818), Boston Public Library.

109. Shane White and Graham J. White. *Stylin': African American Expressive Culture from Its Beginnings to the Zoot Suit* (Ithaca: Cornell University Press, 1998), 108. For a highly original reading of Clay's work, see Nyong'o, 77–83.

110. Hosea Easton, *A Treatise on the Intellectual Character and Civil and Political Condition of the Colored People of the U. States: and the Prejudice Exercised towards Them* (Boston: Knapp, 1837), 41–42.

111. Capers, 111.

112. Ibid., 109–10.

CHAPTER 2

1. Lewis Tappan, *The Life of Arthur Tappan* (New York: Hurd and Houghton, 1870), 172.

2. Ibid., 170–71.

3. Quoted in Tappan, 171–72.

4. Ibid., 172.

5. See Robert Toll, *Blacking Up: The Minstrel Show in Nineteenth Century America* (New York: Oxford University Press, 1974), 3–103; Eric Lott, *Love and Theft: Blackface Minstrelsy and the American Working Class* (1993; New York: Oxford University Press, 1995), 111–67.

6. Nyong'o, 8. See Lott, *Love and Theft*; Dale Cockrell, *Demons of Disorder: Early Blackface Minstrels and Their World* (New York: Cambridge University Press, 1997); W. T. Lhamon, Jr., *Raising Cain: Blackface Performance from Jim Crow to Hip Hop* (Cambridge: Harvard University Press, 1998); Lhamon, "Introduction," to *Jump Jim Crow: Lost Plays, Lyrics, and Street Prose of the First Atlantic Popular Culture* (Cambridge: Harvard University Press, 2003), 1–92. The respective studies of Lott, Cockrell, and Lhamon are the most influential treatments of early minstrelsy.

7. Lhamon, "Introduction," 28.

8. Nyong'o, 8.

9. See David Grimsted, *American Mobbing, 1828–1861: Toward Civil War* (New York: Oxford University Press, 1998); Leon F. Litwack, *North of Slavery: The Negro in the Free States, 1790–1860* (Chicago: University of Chicago Press, 1961); Leslie M. Harris, *In the Shadow of Slavery: African Americans in New York City, 1616–1863* (Chicago: University of Chicago Press, 2003). Multiple versions of Jim Crow songs and plays extol Jackson and the policies of the Democrat party. Also, black violence figures prominently in Jim Crow "street prose" and plays such as *Virginia Mummy*. See Lhamon, *Jump Jim Crow*, 95–135, 159–77, 386–98.

10. African Americans did attend early minstrel acts as spectators. As I explore later in this chapter, black leaders frequently lamented this fact. Before 1843, the black dancer, Master Juba, performed in the haunts of Five Points and in other spaces of Lower Manhattan that scholars often associate with early minstrelsy. Charles Dickens extended high praise for Juba in his popular travelogue of North America, *American Notes* (1842). Between 1843 and the Civil War, there were hardly any all-black minstrel troupes. One of them, Gavitt's Original Ethiopian Serenaders, was reviewed by Frederick Douglass in his newspaper, *The North Star*, on June 28, 1849.

11. Cockrell, 161.

12. Lhamon, 3–4.

13. Shane White, *Somewhat More Independent: The End of Slavery in New York City, 1770–1810* (Athens: University of Georgia Press, 1991); Harris, *passim*.

14. On black seamen and port culture, see W. Jeffrey Bolster, *Black Jacks: African American Seamen and the Age of the Sail* (Cambridge: Harvard University Press, 1997); on the use of slave, indentured, and free black and white labor in

canal construction, see Peter Way, *Common Labor: Workers and the Digging of North American Canals, 1780–1860* (New York: Cambridge University Press, 1993), especially 1–75, for his discussion of pre-1840 canal assembly.

15. Thomas C. Buchanan, "Rascals on the Antebellum Mississippi: African American Steamboat Workers and the St. Louis Hanging of 1841," *Journal of Social History* 34 (2001): 797–98.

16. Ibid., 798.

17. Observations of Catherine Market are some of the earliest and clearest writing extant on secular black expressive culture in the early U.S.

18. Thomas F. De Voe, *The Market Book, containing a historical account of the public markets in the cities of New York, Boston, Philadelphia and Brooklyn, with a brief description of every article of human food sold therein, the introduction of cattle in America, and notices of many remarkable specimens* (New York, 1862), 344.

19. Ibid., 344–45.

20. On radical black (performance) aesthetics as the resistance to enslavement, see Fred Moten, *In the Break: The Aesthetics of the Black Radical Tradition* (Minneapolis: University of Minnesota, 2003), especially 1–84.

21. Lhamon, 2–3.

22. De Voe notes there were some "excellent 'dancers'" and that a competition among them "raised a sort of strife for the highest honors, i.e. the most cheering and the most collected in the 'hat.'" De Voe, 344.

23. Moten, 18, 41.

24. George Odell, *Annals of the New York Stage,* Vol. III (New York: Columbia University Press, 1927–49), 400, 413, 421.

25. Cockrell, 96–97. Cockrell's account of Dixon's life is thorough, and, as such, it deserves attention. See ibid., 96–139. Yet I take issue with what Cockrell does with that story, namely, the overlay of Dixon's biography onto the texts of early minstrelsy, particularly "Zip Coon," as a way to elucidate the politics that the form and the character enact. He writes, "Dixon, in all the complex contradictory ways by which meaning follows the song, actually lived out its themes. His life, thus, becomes the glass by which we can magnify 'Zip Coon'" (96). This methodology is limiting because Dixon was hardly the only composer and performer of Zip Coon narratives. Indeed, the discourse and derision of Zip Coon and black dandyism on the whole censured black uplift, the "dangers" of amalgamation, and the communal aspirations of free African Americans. Thus, Dixon's life insufficiently "magnifies" the significations of Zip Coon as a *public* figuration. (What Zip Coon might have meant to Dixon is something else.) To find parallels between a character and an actor who played that role is to reduce significantly, and therefore neglect, the extent to which that character signified—a reduction that, in Cockrell's case, fails to account for the importance of Zip Coon within broader political and social formations.

26. In the preface to an 1829 version of "Jim Crow" reprinted in his indispensible compilation, *Series of Old American Songs* (Providence, 1936), S. Foster Damon writes that all three cities laid claim as the birthplace of Jim Crow. Indeed, since the 1830s, there has been little consensus as to how and where Rice began

his act. In my view, this is how it should be because it most reflects the character's functionality: the narratives and meanings of Jim Crow are in many ways just as ambiguous as the contemporaneous "west" from where he hails.

27. Lott, 38.

28. On the differences between slavery in the north, south, and west before 1830, see Ira Berlin, *Many Thousands Gone: The First Two Centuries of Slavery in North America* (Cambridge: Harvard University Press, 1998).

29. Lott, 39.

30. Nyong'o, 8–9, 103–34. Lhamon and Cockrell use few, if any, black responses to the form. When they do attempt to understand northern black life, they turn most to police blotters or marriage records to establish intimate sociality—and therefore shared racial and political beliefs—between whites and African Americans. Yet these isolated criminal and erotic relations between individuals are too limited in terms of their evidentiary worth toward broader ideological structures of race. For example, Cockrell writes, "Any reading of the daily newspapers of [Jacksonian] New York, Boston, or Philadelphia, especially the 'Police Court' column, will reveal a common world in which black and whites lived by, worked with, drank among, fought with (to be sure and not to be understated), and loved each other" (85). But "common worlds" are not, *ipso facto*, upheld by common (racial) politics. As I argue in this chapter, the cultural, political, and social history of the Jacksonian north tells a far less utopian story than that Cockrell believes interracial criminality and sex in the period signified.

31. See Rael, *passim*; David Walker, *Appeal, in Four Articles, Together with a Preamble to the Coloured Citizens of the World, but in particular, and very expressly, to Those of the United States of America* (Boston, 1829).

32. Wilentz, 172.

33. See Rael, *passim*.

34. Antonio Gramsci, *Selections from the Prison Notebooks*, ed. and trans. Quintin Hoare and Geoffrey Nowell Smith (New York: International Publishers, 1971, 2005), 419–21.

35. Lott, 92.

36. Former artisan and fervent opponent of private property Thomas Skidmore most forcefully articulated this sentiment in his treatise *The Rights of Property to Man!* (1829), which Sean Wilentz calls "the most thoroughgoing 'agrarian' tract every produced by an American" in its argument that "at all times, property rightfully belonged to the entire community." Wilentz, 184–85.

37. For a classic discussion of the dynamics of working-class politics and the Democracy, see ibid., 190–296.

38. See David R. Roediger, *The Wages of Whiteness: Race and the Making of the American Working Class* (London: Verso, 1992), 66–77. Roediger traces a history of what he calls "the winding road to *white slavery.*" He finds that because "white slavery" was "far more common" than "wage slavery," it "immediately undercut" the ways in which the latter term "called all slavery into question." He goes on to say that "much of the discourse on *white slavery. . .* at times strongly supported the slavery of Blacks" (74). Lott takes issues with Roediger's "skepticism" (Lott's term), arguing that Roediger's analysis suffers from a "fail-

ure to historicize" the terms. He maintains that white labor's alliance with pro-slavery interests grew "as much out of common enmities as proslavery principles" (Lott, 261, n. 24). As true as this might have been, I suggest that it is not necessarily the case that one of white labor's primary concerns was the black slave. Indeed, one of those "common enmities" between white labor and pro-slavery ideologues were African Americans and their economic and sociopolitical interests.

39. The term "white slave" also came to signify prostitution and sexual exploitation, thus "genteel factory women rejected the term" (Roediger, 85). For an account of the relation between the term "white slavery" and sexual exploitation in the antebellum period, see Linda Frost, *Never One Nation: Freaks, Savages, and Whiteness in U.S. Popular Culture, 1850–1877* (Minneapolis: University of Minnesota Press, 2005), 56–87.

40. Wilentz, 62–103.

41. Edmund S. Morgan, *American Slavery, American Freedom: The Ordeal of Colonial Virginia* (New York: Norton, 1975), 376.

42. Lhamon, *Jump Jim Crow*, 4; Lott, 129.

43. Eric Foner, "Abolitionism and the Labor Movement in Antebellum America," in *Politics and Ideology in the Age of the Civil War* (Oxford: Oxford University Press, 1980), 60–61.

44. Roediger, 71–72.

45. Ibid., 73.

46. Ibid., 76–77.

47. Cockrell, 146–54.

48. Thomas Jefferson, *Notes on the State of Virginia* (1781–82; reprint, London: Stockdale, 1787), 229.

49. In 1838, one Pennsylvania Democrat state official put it this way: "[T]he divisionary line between the races, is so strongly marked by the Creator, that it is unwise and cruelly unjust, in any way, to amalgamate them, for it must be apparent to every well judging person, that the elevation of the black is the degradation of the white man; and by endeavoring to alter the order of nature, we would, in all probability, bring about a war between the races" (Benjamin Martin, quoted in *Commonwealth of Pennsylvania, Constitutional Convention 1838*, vol. IX, 321). Influential colonizationist Edward Everett frequently argued that free African Americans should be expatriated outside the United States because their "ignorance" and "want" predispose them to crime. Away from the U.S., he claimed, they might remedy their sociological problems and therefore become productive, law-abiding subjects. See Edward Everett, *Orations and Speeches on Various Occasions* (Boston: American Stationers' Company, 1836), especially 309–22.

50. Charles M. Wiltse, "Introduction" to *David Walker's Appeal, In Four Articles: Together with a Preamble, to the Coloured Citizens of the World, but In Particular, and Very Expressly, to Those of the United States of America* (New York: Hill and Wang, 1965), ix.

51. David Walker, "Preamble" to the *Appeal*, ed. Peter Hinks (University Park: Pennsylvania State University Press, 2000), 5; see ibid., 47–82.

52. Ibid., 27.

53. Peter P. Hinks, *To Awaken My Afflicted Brethren: David Walker and the Problem of Antebellum Slave Resistance* (University Park: Pennsylvania State University Press, 1997), 167–72.

54. Ibid., 152. See *To Awaken*, 116–72, for Hinks' important discussion of the circulation of the *Appeal*.

55. Ibid., 172.

56. Elizabeth McHenry, *Forgotten Readers: Recovering the Lost History of African American Literary Societies* (Durham: Duke University Press, 2002), 36–37.

57. *Richmond Enquirer*, February 18, 1830.

58. Walker, 27.

59. Lhamon, *Jump Jim Crow*, 4.

60. Mikhail Bakhtin, *Rabelais and His World*, trans. Hélène Iswolsky (Bloomington: Indiana University Press, 1984), 305–6.

61. Fanny Kemble, *Journal of a Residence on a Georgian Plantation in 1838–1839, Volume 2* (New York: Harper & Brothers, 1863), 96.

62. Lott, 119.

63. "Jim Crow Still Alive!!!" (Philadelphia 1835). The Library Company of Philadelphia holds a copy of this score.

64. *The Baltimore Sun*, November 9, 1837. The review for *The Baltimore Sun* admits that although these were not Rice's exact words, they capture "the substance of his address."

65. Cockrell, 88.

66. Lhamon, *Jump Jim Crow*, 23.

67. *The Colored American*, December 9, 1837.

68. In early 1841, an "informant" for the *Colored American* sent an account detailing his experience at a minstrel performance. "But what crowned the whole," he reported, was that "he never saw so many *colored persons* at the theatre in his life." According to this informant, the "play was no 'Jim Crow,' nor 'Zip Coon,' but a burlesque upon the colored people" in which the actor "was lost to all self respect, and sunken in the lowest depths of degradation and vice, with his face painted to represent a colored man." Despite this offering of standard minstrel fare, "hundreds [of black spectators] were there, and among whom were many very respectable looking persons." Part of what might also have drawn so many African Americans to the theatre that night was that management, "as a temptation to the poorer and lower classes," lowered ticket prices for the gallery to "twelve and a half cents" from the customary fifty cents. Caught in the middle of the economic crisis that followed the Panic of 1837, theatres throughout the north struggled to remain open. This strategy of cutting prices helped this particular theatre to "survive a short time" longer, according to the paper. *Colored American*, March 6, 1841.

69. The March 6, 1841, account in the *Colored American* notes there were "very respectable looking" African Americans in the audience. Most likely, many of these spectators were simply well dressed workingmen and workingwomen, given how small the black middle class there was and the necessity for that class to follow certain personal and collective standards of behavior, including antitheatricalism, for survival. More to the point, respectability and

"middle-class" appearance were often performative strategies of resistance. These "very respectable looking persons" in the gallery were, in a sense, enacting their own counter-performances of blackness that undermined the "blackness" performed onstage.

70. Harris, *In the Shadow of Slavery*, 170–216.

71. "Steward's and Cook's Marine Benevolent Society," *The Colored American*, May 2, 1840.

72. Harris, 202.

73. Ibid., 170–216.

74. Ibid.

75. Cockrell, 169.

76. As social historians have shown, white and black workers lived near and frequently with each other. See Harris, *In the Shadow of Slavery*, especially 72–133; White, *Somewhat More Independent*, especially 150–216.

77. See George M. Fredrickson, *The Black Image in the White Mind: The Debate on Afro-American Character and Destiny, 1817–1914* (Middletown: Wesleyan University Press, 1987), 43–129.

78. Stanley Aronowitz, "Writing Labor's History," *Social Text* 25/26 (1990): 175.

79. Peter Paul Simons, "Address," reprinted in "A Wicked Conspiracy," *The Colored American*, December 30, 1837.

80. Peter Paul Simons, "Speech" Delivered Before the African Clarkson Association (1839), in *Black Abolitionist Papers*, Volume 3, ed. C. Peter Riley et al. (Chapel Hill: University of North Carolina Press, 1991), 289 (emphasis added).

81. Ibid., 289.

82. Ibid., 291.

83. Ibid., 292.

84. Harris, 216, 170–246.

85. Cockrell, 161.

86. Lott, Cockrell, and Lhamon all find that bourgeois abolitionism was significantly, perhaps wholly, responsible for the failure of the working class to realize interracial solidarity.


CHAPTER 3

1. On race and the franchise in pre-twentieth-century Pennsylvania, see Edward Price, "The Black Voting Rights Issue in Pennsylvania, 1780–1900," *The Pennsylvania Magazine of History and Biography*, 100.3 (July 1976): 356–73.

2. See Alexander Saxton, *The Rise and Fall of the White Republic: Class Politics and Mass Culture in Nineteenth-Century America* (London: Verso, 1990), 53–164.

3. *Reports of the Proceedings and Debates of the Convention of 1821 Assembled for the Purpose of Amending the Constitution of the State of New York: Containing all the Official Documents Relating to the Subject, and other Valuable Matter* (Albany, 1821), 357–78.

4. Robert Purvis, "Appeal of Forty Thousand Citizens, Threatened with Disenfranchisement, to the People of Pennsylvania" (Philadelphia, 1837), re-

printed in Richard Newman et al., eds., *Pamphlets of Protest: An Anthology of Early African-American Protest Literature, 1790–1860* (New York: Routledge, 2001), 133–43.

5. *Public Ledger* (Philadelphia), April 16, 1838.

6. To see how this vast trail of reports on "negro suffrage" played out in Philadelphia, for instance, see *Public Ledger*, January 20, 1838; *Public Ledger*, January 22, 1838; *Public Ledger*, February 6, 1838; and *National Gazette and Literary Register*, February 11, 1838.

7. As political historians often point out, however, Jacksonians protested the centralization and concentration of power in institutions such as Congress or national banks all the while cheering the formidable and overweening power of the Jackson administration and other executive offices. See Sean Wilentz, "On Class and Politics in Jacksonian America," *Reviews in American History* 10.4 (1982): 45–63.

8. Ivy G. Wilson, *Specters of Democracy: Blackness and the Aesthetics of Politics in the Antebellum U.S.* (Oxford: Oxford University Press, 2011), 10.

9. Purvis, 140.

10. Ralph Waldo Emerson, "Nature" (Boston, 1836), in *The Collected Works of Ralph Waldo Emerson*, Alfred R. Ferguson, general editor (Cambridge: The Belknap Press of Harvard University Press, 1971–2008), 7.

11. Russ Castronovo's work is particularly important in this regard. See his *Fathering the Nation: American Genealogies of Slavery and Freedom* (Berkeley: University of California Press, 1995), and *Necro Citizenship: Death, Eroticism, and the Public Sphere in the Nineteenth-Century United States* (Durham: Duke University Press, 2001).

12. I have not been able to find in the writings of southern proslavery ideologues an emphasis on the role of slaves in the world-historical events of the American War of Independence as justification for race-based chattel slavery.

13. Robert S. Cox, "Vox Populi: Spiritualism and George Washington's Postmortem Career," *Early American Studies* 1.1 (Spring 2003): 232.

14. See Alice Rayner, *Ghosts: Death's Double and the Phenomena of Theatre* (Minneapolis: University of Minnesota Press, 2006).

15. Paul Finkelman, *Defending Slavery, Proslavery Thought in the Old South: A Brief History with Documents* (Boston: Bedford/St. Martin's, 2003), 29. For a mordant take on the historical and representational shortcomings of Washington vis-à-vis black freedom and inclusion from the period, see cultural critic and sketch writer William J. "Ethiop" Wilson's ekphrastic renderings of Mount Vernon in "Picture IX" of his 1858 "Afric-American Picture Gallery" in *The Anglo-African Magazine*, January 1859, reprinted in William Loren Katz, ed., *The Anglo-African Magazine* Volume 1 (New York: Arno Press, 1968). See also Wilson, *Specters of Democracy*, 145–68.

16. Castronovo, *Fathering the Nation*, 39.

17. Frederick Douglass, *Autobiographies* (New York: Library of America, 1994), 354; Castronovo, 190.

18. For one of the most thorough accounts of the emergence of the antebellum black public sphere, see Patrick Rael, *Black Identity & Black Protest in the Antebellum North* (Chapel Hill: University of North Carolina Press, 2002).

19. Ibid., 12–53.

20. Ibid., 45.

21. Henry Highland Garnet, "Address to the Slaves of the United States" (1843, 1848), in *Pamphlets of Protest*, 163.

22. Mitch Kachun, "Antebellum African Americans, Public Commemoration, and the Haitian Revolution: A Problem of Historical Mythmaking," *Journal of the Early Republic* 26.2 (Summer 2006): 249–73.

23. William Wells Brown, *St. Domingo: Its Revolutions and its Patriots. A Lecture* (Boston: Bela Marsh, 1855).

24. Ibid., 37.

25. Ibid., 38 (emphasis added).

26. William Cooper Nell, *The Colored Patriots of the American Revolution: with Sketches of Several Distinguished Colored Persons: to which is added a Brief Survey of the Condition and Prospects of Colored Americans* (Boston: Walcutt, 1855), 13–14.

27. For a brilliant reading of Crispus Attucks Day, see Tavia Nyong'o, *The Amalgamation Waltz: Race, Performance, and the Ruses of Memory* (Minneapolis: University of Minnesota Press, 2009), 54–68. On Nell's relationship to drama and theatrical production, see Heather S. Nathans, *Slavery and Sentiment of the American Stage, 1781–1861: Lifting the Veil of Black* (Cambridge: Cambridge University Press, 2009), 238–46.

28. Nell, 18.

29. Nell, 231–32, 233–35, 211–13, 156.

30. Ibid., 231–35.

31. Walter Benjamin and Hannah Arendt, ed., *Illuminations* (New York: Harcourt, Brace, and World, 1968; reprint, New York: Schocken Books, 2007), 225.

32. See Robert S. Cox, *Body and Soul: A Sympathetic History of American Spiritualism* (Charlottesville: University of Virginia Press, 2003).

33. Castronovo, *Necro Citizenship*, 4.

34. Ibid., 6.

35. Castronovo, *Fathering the Nation*, 9.

36. Abraham Lincoln, "Address Before the Young Men's Lyceum of Springfield, Illinois" (1838), in *Complete Works of Abraham Lincoln*, vol. 1, ed. John Nicolay and John Hay (New York: Francis D. Tandy Company, 1905), 47–48.

37. Samuel Woodworth, *The Poetical Works of Samuel Woodworth*, vol. 1, ed. Frederick Woodworth (New York: Scribner, 1861), 11–30.

38. Bruce McConachie, "American Theatre in Context, from the Beginnings to 1870," in Don B. Wilmeth and C. W. E. Bigsby, eds., *The Cambridge History of American Theatre: Beginnings to 1870* (Cambridge: Cambridge University Press, 1998), 154.

39. George Odell, *Annals of the New York Stage*, Vol. III (New York: Columbia University Press, 1927–49), 648.

40. See Hosea Easton, *A Treatise on the Intellectual Character and Civil and Political Condition of the Colored People of the U. States: and the Prejudice Exercised towards Them* (Boston: Knapp, 1837), 35–46.

41. Samuel Woodworth, *King's Bridge Cottage* (New York, 1826).

42. Hartman, 52–53.

43. Two prominent examples are the songs "My Old Kentucky Home" (1853)

by Stephen Foster and "Carry Me Back to Old Virginny" (1878) by James A. Bland.

44. Woodworth, *King's Bridge Cottage* (New York, 1826).

45. See Benjamin Quarles, *The Negro in the American Revolution* (1961; reprint, Chapel Hill: University of North Carolina Press, 1996); Sylvia R. Frey, *Water from the Rock: Black Resistance in a Revolutionary Age* (Princeton: Princeton University Press, 1993).

46. Eugene D. Genovese, *The World the Slaveholders Made: Two Essays in Interpretation* (New York: Pantheon Books, 1969), 187.

47. Fredrickson, 101.

48. Anonymous, *The Life of Joice Heth, the Nurse of Gen. George Washington* (New York: Printed for the Publisher, 1835). This text, as Barnum eventually admitted, was written by his co-manager of the Heth exhibit, Levi Lyman.

49. *New York Evening Star*, August 22, 1835.

50. Benjamin Reiss, *The Showman and the Slave: Race, Death, and Memory in Barnum's America* (Cambridge: Harvard University Press, 2001), 90–105.

51. Ibid., 2.

52. Uri McMillan, "Mammy-Memory: Staging Joice Heth, or the Curious Phenomenon of the 'Ancient Negress,'" *Women and Performance: A Journal of Feminist Theory* 22.1 (2012): 36.

53. Reiss, 100–105.

54. De Tocqueville put it this way: "The position of the Americans is therefore quite exceptional, and it may be believed that no democratic people will ever be placed in a similar one. Their strictly Puritanical origin—their exclusively commercial habits—even the country they inhabit, which seems to divert their minds from the pursuit of science, literature, and the arts—the proximity of Europe, which allows them to neglect these pursuits without relapsing into barbarism—a thousand special causes, of which I have only been able to point out the more important—have singularly concurred to fix the mind of the American upon purely practical objects." Alexis de Tocqueville, *Democracy in America*, trans. Henry Reeve (New York: Bantam Books, 2000, 2004), 548.

55. Reiss, 69.

56. Ibid., 134–40.

57. Ibid., 7.

58. *New York Sun*, August 20, 1835.

59. See Rosemarie Garland Thompson, "Introduction: From Wonder to Error—A Genealogy of Freak Discourse in Modernity," in *Freakery: Cultural Spectacles of the Extraordinary Body*, ed. Rosemarie Garland Thompson (New York: New York University Press, 1996), 1–22.

60. *New York Sun*, August 20, 1835.

61. Ibid.

62. See Paul Finkelman, *An Imperfect Union: Slavery, Federalism, and Comity* (Chapel Hill: University of North Carolina Press, 1981), especially 3–19, 46–69, 126–45; Edlie L. Wong, *Neither Fugitive Nor Free: Atlantic Slavery, Freedom Suits, and the Legal Culture of Travel* (New York: New York University Press, 2009), especially 1–18, 77–126.

63. Reiss, 26. Barnum did upset antislavery clergy in Providence, Rhode Island, but he used their fervor against them, claiming that the proceeds of the Heth exhibition there would go to antislavery causes, including the purchase of her great-grandchildren still enslaved in Kentucky. His ruse worked: the clergy urged the public to patronize the exhibit and thus helped increase Barnum's profits. See ibid., 74–78.

64. See Rael, 82–117.

65. Anonymous, *The Life of Joice Heth, the Nurse of Gen. George Washington*, 3–5.

66. Robert Stepto, "I Rose and Found My Voice: Narration, Authentication, and Authorial Control in Four Slave Narratives," in Charles T. Davis and Henry Louis Gates, Jr., eds., *The Slave's Narrative* (Oxford: Oxford University Press, 1985), 226–27.

67. *New York Atlas*, April 20, 1845, reprinted in Phineas T. Barnum and James W. Cook, ed., *The Colossal P.T. Barnum Reader: Nothing Else Like It in the Universe* (Urbana: University of Illinois Press, 2005), 114.

68. Phineas T. Barnum, *The Adventures of an Adventurer: Being some Passages in the Life of Barnaby Diddleum* (1841), reprint in ibid., 21–22 (emphasis added).

69. Phineas Taylor Barnum, *The Autobiography of P.T. Barnum: Clerk, Merchant, Editor, and Showman* (London: Ward and Lock, 1855), 54–55.

70. Walter Johnson, *Soul by Soul: Life inside the Antebellum Slave Market* (Cambridge: Harvard University Press, 1999), 188. Johnson cautions that it is necessary to recognize that these aesthetics and the "phantasmic dreams" they limn "must be made material if they are to come true," and the less powerful frequently shape and direct those materializations.

71. For more on the "What Is It?" exhibition, see James W. Cook, *The Arts of Deception: Playing with Fraud in the Age of Barnum* (Cambridge: Harvard University Press, 2001), 119–62.

72. A. H. Saxon, *P.T. Barnum: The Legend and the Man* (New York: Columbia University Press, 1989), 84–85.

73. Another example is James Gilbert Burnett's 1858 *Blanche of Brandywine*, which I discuss in the Introduction.

74. Charles Peirce, "The Categories Defended Lecture" (1903), in *The Essential Charles Peirce: Selected Philosophical Writings, Volume 2 (1893–1913)*, ed. The Peirce Edition Project (Bloomington: University of Indiana Press, 1998), 163.

75. George Jaimson, *The Revolutionary Soldier* (Boston: William V. Spencer, 1850). The Federal Street Theatre was the leading theatre in Boston from its opening in 1798 through at least the 1830s.

76. Ibid., 3–4.

77. Ibid., 4.

78. Ibid., 9.

79. Ibid., 9–10.

80. Ibid., 13.

81. Ibid., 19.

82. Ibid.

83. Ibid.

84. Richard S. Newman, *Freedom's Prophet: Bishop Richard Allen, The A.M.E. Church, and the Black Founding Fathers* (New York: New York University Press, 2008), 137.

85. George Lionel Stevens, *The Patriot* (Boston, 1834).

86. Ibid., 36. *The Patriot* also borrowed directly from the contemporary minstrel stage. Throughout the play, Sambo sings and dances his own version of "Jim Crow": "'Weel about—turn about—do just so—ebery time weel about jump Sambo.'"

87. Hartman, 53.

88. Caroline Winterer, *The Culture of Classicism: Ancient Greece and Rome in American Intellectual Life, 1780–1910* (Baltimore: Johns Hopkins University Press, 2002), 1.

89. See Eric Thomas Slauter, "Neoclassical Culture in a Society with Slaves: Race and Rights in the Age of Wheatley," *Early American Studies: An Interdisciplinary Journal* 2 (2004): 81–122. In late 1775, Wheatley sent Washington a letter of support and a poem, "To His Excellency George Washington." In a February 1776 letter, he thanked her and proposed a possible meeting in Cambridge, Massachusetts. Literary historian and biographer Vincent Carretta doubts the two met in Cambridge that winter because it would have been too dangerous, but suggests the two might have visited each other in Providence that April. Vincent Carretta, *Phillis Wheatley: Biography of a Genius in Bondage* (Athens: University of Georgia Press, 2011), 154–57. For more on Powers and the relation between antebellum sculpture and slavery, see Kirk Savage, *Standing Soldiers, Kneeling Slaves: Race, War, and Monument in Nineteenth-Century America* (Princeton: Princeton University Press, 1997), 21–51.

90. John Trumbull, *Autobiography, Reminiscences and Letters of John Trumbull, from 1756–1841* (New Haven: B. L. Hamlen, 1841), 17–38.

91. Ibid., 93.

92. George Washington Parke Curtis, Mary Randolph Custis Lee, and Benson John Lossing, *Recollections and Private Memoirs of Washington* (New York: Derby and Jackson, 1860), 521 (original emphasis).

93. Trumbull, 75.

94. Ibid., 90–98.

95. George Washington, *George Washington Papers at the Library of Congress, 1741–1799: Series 5 Financial Papers, 1750–72*, Ledger Book 1, 261.

96. Thomas Jefferson to Dr. Walter Jones, Monticello, January 2, 1814, in Thomas Jefferson and Merrill D. Peterson, ed., *Writings* (New York: Library Company of America, 1984), 1319.

97. George Washington, *The Diaries of George Washington*, ed. Donald Jackson and Dorothy Twohig (Charlottesville: University Press of Virginia, 1976), vol. 2, 238n, 278, vol. 3, 276n.

98. George Washington Parke Curtis et al., 157, 488.

99. Ibid., 157. Washington's will only stipulates thirty dollars a year for Lee "during his natural life," not one hundred and fifty. George Washington, "Last Will and Testament" (1799), in *George Washington: Writings* (New York: Library of America, 1997), 1024.

100. Ibid. There were more than 124 slaves at Washington's service at the time

of his death, but he did not have legal jurisdiction over the rest, who were either dower slaves from Martha Washington's first marriage or leased from other masters.

101. Michael A. Gomez, "Muslims in Early America," *The Journal of Southern History* 60.4 (November 1994): 683. See also Sylviane A. Diouf, *Servants of Allah: African Muslims Enslaved in the Americas* (New York: New York University Press, 1998).

102. Gomez, 684–87.

103. Ibid., 687.

104. George Washington to Tench Tilghman, Mount Vernon, March 24, 1784, in *Writings*, 555–56.

105. Carrie Rebora Barratt, "Faces of a New Nation: American Portraits of the 18th and Early 19th Centuries," *The Metropolitan Museum of Art Bulletin* 61.1 (Summer 2003): 25.

106. Charles Henry Hart, *Edward Savage, Painter and Engraver: And His Unfinished Copper-Plate of "The Congress Voting Independence"* (Boston, 1905), 6–14; Wendy Wick Reaves, *George Washington, an American Icon: The Eighteenth-century Graphic Portraits* (Washington, DC: Smithsonian Institution Traveling Exhibition Service, 1982), 43.

107. Slauter, 121.

108. See ibid., 81–122.

## CHAPTER 4

1. Marc Robinson, *The American Play: 1787–2000* (New Haven: Yale University Press, 2009), 28.

2. In 1890, reflecting on authorial agency and the compositional dynamics of mid-nineteenth-century American drama, playwright Dion Boucicault noted: "Public opinion [was] the highest and sole court of jurisdiction in literary and artistic matters . . . and the drama is, therefore, made by the collaboration of the people and poet." Dion Boucicault, quoted in Jeffrey H. Richards, ed., *Early American Drama* (New York: Penguin Books, 1997), 444.

3. Plato, *Laws*, quoted in Andrea Wilson Nightingale, *Genres in Dialogue: Plato and the Construct of Philosophy* (Cambridge: Cambridge University Press, 1996), 53.

4. Plato frets, "When they crowd into the seats in the assembly or law courts or theatre, or get together in camp or any other popular meeting place, and, with a great deal of noise and a great lack of moderation, shout and clap their approval or disapproval of what is proposed or done, till the rocks and the whole place re-echo, and redouble the noise of their boos and applause. Can a young man's heart remain unmoved by all this? How can his individual training stand the strain? Won't he be swamped by the flood of popular praise and blame, and be carried away with all the stream till he finds himself agreeing with popular ideas of what is admirable or disgraceful, behaving like the crowd and becoming one of them (492b-c)." H. D. P. Lee, trans., *The Republic*, 4th ed. (London: Penguin, 2003), 214.

5. In 1824, the *North American Review* lamented that American playwrights

could not produce a "literature of the people" because audiences' tastes were not "peculiar." This view, of course, prefigures the respective calls of Ralph Waldo Emerson and Walt Whitman to abandon European literary and cultural models. *North American Review*, October 19, 1824; Ralph Emerson, "The American Scholar" (1837); and Walt Whitman, "Preface" to *Leaves of Grass* (1855).

6. *The Colored American*, March 6, 1841.

7. For a good sketch of antebellum reform, see Steven Mintz, *Moralists and Modernizers: America's Pre–Civil War Reformers* (Baltimore: Johns Hopkins University Press, 1995).

8. Patrick Rael, *Black Identity & Black Protest in the Antebellum North* (Chapel Hill: University of North Carolina Press, 2002), 20.

9. Ira Berlin, "The Structure of the Free Negro Caste in the Antebellum United States," *Journal of Social History* 9.3 (Spring 1976): 303.

10. George M. Fredrickson, *The Black Image in the White Mind: The Debate on Afro-American Character and Destiny, 1817–1914* (1971; reprint, Hanover, NH: Wesleyan University Press, 1987), 97–102.

11. Ibid., 101–2.

12. John Stauffer, *The Black Hearts of Men: Radical Abolitionists and the Transformation of Race* (Cambridge: Harvard University Press, 2002), 158. For a detailed biographic account of Douglass' break with the Garrisonians, see William S. McFeely, *Frederick Douglass* (1991; reprint, New York: Norton, 1995), 104–62.

13. James McCune Smith, Letter to Gerrit Smith, July 20, 1848, in James McCune Smith and John Stauffer, ed., *The Works of James McCune Smith: Black Intellectual and Abolitionist* (Oxford: Oxford University Press, 2006), 312.

14. Stauffer, 158–60.

15. Radical Abolitionists differed from most abolitionists and antislavery organizations in this regard. See ibid., 8–26.

16. Frederick Douglass, *Autobiographies* (New York: Library of America, 1994), 367.

17. See Yacovone, "The Transformation of the Black Temperance Movement, 1827–1854: An Interpretation," *Journal of the Early Republic* 8 (1988): 281–97; and Leslie Harris, *In the Shadow of Slavery: African Americans in New York City, 1626–1863* (Chicago: University of Chicago Press, 2004), 134–246.

18. Eddie S. Glaude, Jr., *Exodus!: Religion, Race, and Nation in Early American Nineteenth-Century Black America* (Chicago: University of Chicago Press, 2000), 119.

19. Howard H. Bell, *A Survey of the Negro Convention Movement, 1830–1861* (New York: Arno Press, 1969), 6–8.

20. Rael, 29–35.

21. See the proceedings of the conventions in Howard H. Bell, *Minutes of the Proceedings of the National Negro Conventions, 1830–1864* (New York: Arno Press, 1969); see also Julie Winch, *Philadelphia's Black Elite: Activism, Accommodation, and the Struggle for Autonomy, 1787–1848* (Philadelphia: Temple University Press, 1988), 91–169, and Glaude, *Exodus!*, 107–59.

22. Glaude, 114.

23. *1832 Minutes*, in Bell, 35.

24. William Whipper, "American Reform Moral Society," in *The Liberator*, July 2, 1836.

25. Leonard L. Richards, *"Gentleman of Property and Standing": Anti-Abolition Mobs in Jacksonian America* (London: Oxford University Press, 1970), 14.

26. Ibid., 10–81. See also David Grimsted, *American Mobbing, 1828–1861* (Oxford: Oxford University Press, 1998).

27. Rael, 12–13.

28. Glaude, 144.

29. Ibid., 147.

30. Harris, 64.

31. Alexander Crummell, "Eulogium on Henry Highland Garnet, D.D." in *Africa and America: Addresses and Discourses* (Springfield, MA: Wiley, 1891), 275.

32. Ibid., 278.

33. Ibid., 280.

34. Ibid.

35. Ibid., 278–81.

36. Milton C. Sernett, *Abolition's Axe: Beriah Green, Oneida Institute, and the Black Freedom Struggle* (Syracuse: Syracuse University Press, 1986), xxi.

37. Ibid., 280.

38. See *Minutes* from the 1840s conventions in Bell, *passim*.

39. "Caleb," a writer to the *Weekly Anglo-African* in 1861, used these terms to describe black antislavery reformers and, as historian Donald Yacovone argues, they are "applicable to the entire black reform effort." Yacovone, 282 n.3.

40. Henry Highland Garnet, "An Address to the Slaves of the United States" (1843), in *Lift Every Voice: African American Oratory, 1787–1900*, ed. Philip Foner and Robert Branham (Tuscaloosa: University of Alabama Press, 1998), 201.

41. Glaude, 152.

42. Garnet, 204.

43. Ibid., 205.

44. Ibid., 199.

45. Ibid., 202.

46. Glaude, 158.

47. After Nat Turner's 1831 slave rebellion in Northampton, Virginia, for instance, cities and states across the nation enacted laws that restricted black assembly, demonstration, and movement in order to prevent black political and social organizing. For a good overview of the geopolitcal effect of the Turner uprising, see Louis P. Masur, "Nat Turner and Sectional Crisis," in Kenneth S. Greenburg, *Nat Turner: A Slave Rebellion in History and Memory* (Oxford: Oxford University Press, 2003), 148–61.

48. *1843 Minutes*, 18.

49. See Richards, 40–43, 92–93, 134–50.

50. *1843 Minutes*, 13.

51. Ibid.

52. Jill Lane, "Black/face Publics: The Social Bodies of *Fraternidad*," in Janelle Reinelt and Joseph Roach, eds., *Critical Theory and Performance* (Ann Arbor: University of Michigan Press, 2007), 144–47.

53. Frederick Douglass, *Autobiographies*, 96.

54. William Lloyd Garrison, "Preface," in ibid., 30.

55. Ibid., 31.

56. Crummell, 294.

57. Ibid., 296–97.

58. Maria Weston Chapman, "The Buffalo Convention of Men of Color," *The Liberator*, September 22, 1843.

59. Henry Highland Garnet, "A Letter to Mrs. Maria W. Chapman," November 17, 1843, reprinted in *The Liberator*, December 8, 1843. Later in the letter, Garnet writes that only two people read the address before its presentation at the Buffalo convention, "a colored brother, who did not give me a word of counsel," and Garnet's wife. See Glaude, *Exodus!*, 143–59, where he brilliantly outlines the significance of Garnet's speech to subsequent imaginings of black freedom and American democracy. He argues the speech helped reveal the "tragedy of African American politics"; that is, "the fact that we are constantly having to choose either to identify ourselves with this fragile democracy, struggling for its soul, or to define ourselves over and against it—and live with the consequences of such choices without yielding to despair" (ibid., 167).

60. William Lloyd Garrison, Maria Chapman, and Edmund Quincy, "To the Friends of Non-Resistance," March 1, 1839, reprint in *The Letters of William Lloyd Garrison*, ed. Walter McIntosh Merrill and Louis Ruchames (Cambridge: Harvard University Press, 1971–81), 435–38; Merle E. Curti, "Non-Resistance in New England," in *The New England Quarterly* 2 (1929): 41–57.

61. Garrison, in Douglass, 32.

62. Ibid., 32–33.

63. Douglass, *Autobiographies*, 65.

64. Ibid., 80–82.

65. *1843 Minutes*, 13.

66. Garnet, "Address," 202–4.

67. Of course there was always the possibility that Douglass inspired violent energies in some of his readers. What I am attempting to sketch, however, are the reasons why the Garrisonians endorsed the scenes of violence in the *Narrative*.

68. Peggy Phelan, "'Just Want to Say': Performance and Literature, Jackson and Poirier," *PMLA* 125 (2010): 946.

69. Crummell, 294.

70. Phelan, 946.

71. Maria Weston Chapman, "The Buffalo Convention of Men of Color," *The Liberator*, September 22, 1843.

72. Those who espoused moral suasion often spurned political agitation. Politics repelled the Garrisonians because they believed the Constitution was a slaveholding document and working within its structures only reified an inherently evil polity. Maria Weston Chapman, for instance, reserved a good deal of her censure of the 1843 Convention for the delegates' resolution to support the Liberty Party, a newly formed political party that broke with the American Anti-Slavery Society and, working under the belief that the Constitution was an antislavery document, dedicated itself to the abolition of slavery on legal grounds. She believed that the delegates' collective allegiance to the Liberty

Party was ideologically wrongheaded and, ironically, the work of white men who silently controlled the thinking and proceedings of the convention. Garnet fervently defended his decision to join the Liberty Party in his response to Chapman. See Maria Weston Chapman, "The Buffalo Convention of Men of Color"; and Henry Highland Garnet, "A Letter to Mrs. Maria W. Chapman," November 17, 1843, reprinted in *The Liberator*, December 8, 1843. On the rise of antislavery constitutionalism, see Hoang Gia Phan, *Bonds of Citizenship: Law and the Labors of Emancipation* (New York: New York University Press, 2013), 107-141.

73. *1848 Minutes*, in Bell, 18.

74. Wilson Jeremiah Moses, *The Golden Age of Black Nationalism, 1850–1925* (1978; reprint, Oxford: Oxford University Press, 1988), 41. Garnet's position would change in 1849, when he began to espouse black emigrationism.

75. Frederick Douglass, "Colored National Convention at Cleveland," *The North Star*, September 15, 1848.

76. Garnet, "A Letter to Mrs. Maria W. Chapman."

77. Orville Dewey, *A Discourse on Slavery and the Annexation of Texas* (New York: Charles S. Francis, 1844), 9–10.

78. Fredrickson, 101–2.

79. Ibid., 101.

80. F. R. Lees, *Text-Book of Temperance* (New York: Vose, 1869), 314.

81. Ibid.

82. Heather S. Nathans, *Slavery and Sentiment on the American Stage, 1787–1861: Lifting the Veil of Black* (Cambridge: Cambridge University Press, 2009), 227–34.

83. Harry Seymour, *Aunt Dinah's Pledge* (Boston: Dicks' Standard Plays, 1853). Seymour premiered the play in New York City in 1850.

84. "The Drama—Howard Street Athenaeum," *Boston Courier*, October 13, 1845.

85. Seymour, 4.

86. Seymour, "Dramatis Personae" to *Aunt Dinah's Pledge*.

87. Ibid., 4.

88. Tavia Nyong'o, *The Amalgamation Waltz: Race, Performance, and the Ruses of Memory* (Minneapolis: University of Minnesota Press, 2009), 118.

89. Nathans, 230.

90. Seymour's changes, it bears noting, were in line with the conventions of adaptations in the period.

91. "Zip Coon" (New York, 1834), in the *Harvard Theatre Collection, Houghton Library, Harvard University*.

92. Robert Toll, *Blacking Up: The Minstrel Show in Nineteenth Century America* (New York: Oxford University Press, 1974), 123.

93. Barbara Lewis, "Daddy Blue: The Evolution of the Dark Dandy," in *Inside the Minstrel Mask: Readings in Nineteenth-century Blackface Minstrelsy*, ed. Annemarie Bean, James Vernon Hatch, and Brooks McNamara (Hanover, NH: Wesleyan University Press, 1996), 267.

94. Eric Lott, *Love and Theft: Blackface Minstrelsy and the American Working Class* (New York: Oxford University Press, 1993), 134.

95. Toll, 69–76.

96. Charles White, *Charley White's Ethiopian Joke Book* (New York, 1855), 36–37.

97. The Hay Library at Brown University holds the largest and most extensive collection of antebellum joke books, sheet music, and songsters. For a representative selection of portable minstrelsy texts, see W. T. Lhamon, ed., *Jump Jim Crow: Lost Plays, Lyrics, and Street Prose of the First Atlantic Popular Culture* (Cambridge: Harvard University Press, 2003).

98. Robin Bernstein, *Racial Innocence: Performing American Childhood from Slavery to Civil Rights* (New York: New York University Press, 2011), 71.

99. Toll, 71.

100. Seymour, 10.

101. Yacovone, 286.

102. Ibid., 290. Yacovone finds that in the 1820s and early 1830s, some African American reformers separated temperance from abolitionist efforts; the influential William Whipper of Philadelphia, for instance, believed intemperance was a greater evil than chattel slavery. See ibid., 281–86.

103. *1848 Minutes*, 18.

104. Frederick Douglass, "To Samuel Hanson Cox, D.D.," in *Frederick Douglass: Selected Speeches and Writings*, ed. Philip Foner and Yuval Taylor (Chicago: Lawrence Hill Books, 1999), 40–48.

105. Holly Berkley Fletcher, *Gender and the American Temperance Movement of the Nineteenth Century* (New York: Routledge, 2008), 45.

106. Alexander Kinmont, *Twelve Lectures on the Natural History of Man, and the Rise and Progress of Philosophy* (Cincinnati: U. P. James, 1839), 191–92.

107. Fredrickson, 108–9.

108. See Mintz.

109. Seymour, 5.

110. Ibid., 5–7.

111. Ibid., 5. Seymour's stage direction suggests he intended the signing of the pledge to be a minstrelsy set piece. It reads: "*A good deal of comic spelling, and ad libitum business may be introduced whilst the above is being written.*"

112. Ibid., 6.

113. Ibid., 8.

114. Fletcher, 18.

115. Rev. Marcus E. Cross, *Mirror of Intemperance, and History of the Temperance Reform* (Philadelphia: Lange, 1849), 26 (original emphasis).

116. Seymour, 6.

117. Ibid., 14.

118. Ibid.

119. Ibid.,13.

CHAPTER 5

1. Lawrence W. Levine, *Highbrow/Lowbrow: The Emergence of Cultural Hierarchy in America* (Cambridge: Harvard University Press, 1988), 98–99.

2. Consider, for example, the family-oriented museum theatres that managers such as Moses Kimball and P. T. Barnum pioneered in Boston and New York City, respectively. Theirs were some of the most novel and influential of theatrical entertainments in the 1850s. See note 48 to the Introduction; see also Bruce A. McConachie, *Melodramatic Formations: American Theatre and Society, 1820–1870* (Iowa City: University of Iowa Press, 1992), 65–257.

3. Levine, 85–186.

4. Robert Toll, *Blacking Up: The Minstrel Show in Nineteenth-Century America* (London: Oxford University Press, 1974), 195–233.

5. Dwight A. McBride, *Impossible Witnesses: Truth, Abolitionism, and Slave Testimony* (New York: New York University Press, 2001), 4.

6. On the rise of black ambivalence toward performance, see my "Slavery, Performance, and the Design of African American Theatre," in Harvey Young, ed., *The Cambridge Companion to African American Theatre* (Cambridge: Cambridge University Press, 2012), 15–33.

7. See Toll, *Blacking Up*, 214–29, for a discussion of the admiration that nineteenth-century black minstrels garnered, particularly among black working-class audiences.

8. Daphne Brooks, *Bodies in Dissent: Spectacular Performances of Race and Freedom, 1850–1910* (Durham: Duke University Press, 2006), 11.

9. With the help of allies on both ends of his journey, Box Brown mailed himself from Richmond, Virginia, to Philadelphia in a "box, three feet long, and two feet six inches deep" and "for twenty-seven hours he was enclosed in this box." Henry Box Brown, *Narrative of the Life of Henry Box Brown: Written By Himself* (Manchester, England: Lee and Glynn, 1851), ii.

10. Brooks, 112–30.

11. Frederick Douglass, *Autobiographies* (New York: Library of America, 1994), 339.

12. Martin Delany, "Letter from M.R. Delany," *Frederick Douglass' Paper*, April 22, 1853. Delany also censured Greenfield because she fired her black managers in favor of a more connected white manager, a Colonel Wood. According to Delany, "a meaner, and more unprincipled hater of the black race [than Wood] does not live in this land of oppression." For more on Greenfield, see Alex W. Black, "Abolitionism's Resonant Bodies: The Realization of African American Performance," *American Quarterly* 63.3 (September 2011): 619–40.

13. Terry Eagleton, *Criticism and Ideology: A Study in Marxist Criticism* (1976; reprint, London: Verso Books, 2006), 74.

14. William Wells Brown, quoted in William Edward Farrison, *William Wells Brown: Author and Reformer* (Chicago: University of Chicago Press, 1969), 294. Literary critic Paul Gilmore argues Wells Brown "did not turn to the minstrel show simply because of its popularity, but because in the early 1850s minstrelsy provided perhaps the best forum through which to construct viable representative manhood." In my view, the latter factor greatly produced the former one. See Gilmore's fine article, "'De Genewine Artekil': William Wells Brown, Blackface Minstrelsy, and Abolitionism," *American Literature* 69.4 (December 1997): 743–80.

15. Saidiya Hartman, "The Time of Slavery," *The South Atlantic Quarterly* 101.4 (2002): 773–74.

16. Hortense Spillers, "Mama's Baby, Papa's Maybe: An American Grammar Book," *Diacritics* 17 (1987): 67. Spillers describes "pornotroping" as a representational practice in which personhood becomes flesh. In her discussion, she distinguishes body from flesh—the body earns and spends social value for the self, whereas the flesh only gives social value to others.

17. Houston A. Baker, Jr., "Autobiographical Acts and the Voice of the Southern Slave," in Charles T. Davis and Henry Louis Gates, eds., *The Slave's Narrative* (Oxford: Oxford University Press, 1985), 242–61; Frances Smith Foster, *Witnessing Slavery: The Development of Ante-bellum Slave Narratives* (Westport: Greenwood Press, 1979); Carla L. Peterson, *Doers of the Word: African-American Women Speakers and Writers in the North (1830–1880)* (New York: Oxford University Press, 1995), 24–55; Robert Stepto, "I Rose and Found My Voice: Narration, Authentication, and Authorial Control in Four Slave Narratives," in Davis and Gates, 225–41.

18. McBride, 5.

19. Stephen Best and Saidiya Hartman, "Fugitive Justice: The Appeal of the Slave," *Representations* 22 (2006): 9.

20. Christopher Castiglia, *Interior States: Institutional Consciousness and the Inner Life of Democracy in the Antebellum United States* (Durham: Duke University Press, 2008), 124.

21. Saidiya Hartman, *Scenes of Subjection: Terror, Slavery, and Self-making in Nineteenth-Century America* (New York: Oxford University Press, 1997), 20. The literature on the politics of sentiment in antebellum cultural production is vast. For the classic treatment, see Jane P. Tompkins, *Sensational Designs: The Cultural Work of American Fiction, 1790–1860* (New York: Oxford University Press, 1985).

22. Hartman, 19. Hartman's critique of empathy builds on Adam Smith's own proviso in his foundational theorization of the relation of empathy to modern economics, politics, and sociality, *The Theory of Moral Sentiments*. Smith writes, "After all this, however, the emotions of the spectator will still be very apt to fall short of the violence of what is felt by the sufferer. Mankind, though naturally sympathetic, never conceive, for what has befallen another, that degree of passion which naturally animates the person principally concerned. That imaginary change of situation, upon which their sympathy is founded, is but momentary. The thought of their own safety, the thought that they themselves are not really the sufferers, continually intrudes itself upon them; and though it does not hinder them from conceiving a passion somewhat analogous to what is felt by the sufferer, hinders them from conceiving any thing that approaches to the same degree of violence." Smith, *The Theory of Moral Sentiments* (1759; London, 1767), 26–27.

23. William Wells Brown, *Narrative of William W. Brown, an American Slave. Written by Himself* (Boston, 1847), in William L. Andrews and Henry Louis Gates, Jr., eds. *Slave Narratives* (New York: Library of America, 2000), 415 (emphasis added).

24. Ibid., 408–9.

25. See Jay Fliegelman, *Declaring Independence: Jefferson, Natural Language, and the Culture of Performance* (Stanford: Stanford University Press, 1993), 192–96.

26. Douglass, *Autobiographies*, 19.

27. Linda Williams, *Playing the Race Card: Melodramas of Black and White from Uncle Tom to O.J. Simpson* (Princeton: Princeton University Press, 2001), 23–24. See also Lauren Berlant, "The Subject of True Feeling: Pain, Privacy, and Politics," in *Cultural Studies and Political Theory*, ed. Jodi Dean (Ithaca: Cornell University Press, 2000), 42–62.

28. Peter Brooks, *The Melodramatic Imagination: Balzac, Henry James, and The Mode of Excess* (1976; reprint, New Haven: Yale University Press, 1995), 81. "Moral legibility" is Brooks' apt phrase.

29. Williams, xiv. I understand the melodramatic as a mode found in genres such as comedy or tragedy, and take melodrama as its own genre with its own aesthetics and poetics.

30. To give another example: when Wells Brown first mentions that he might try to escape to Canada, his sister responds, "'Brother, you have often declared that you would not end your days in slavery. I see no possible way in which we [sister and mother] can escape with us . . . I beseech you not to let us hinder you. If we cannot get our liberty, we do not wish to be the means of keeping you from a land of freedom.'" To this, Wells Brown writes: "I could restrain my feelings no longer, and an outburst of my own feelings, caused her to cease speaking upon that subject. I pledged myself not leave them in the hand of the oppressor. I took leave of them, and returned to the boat [on which he worked], and laid down in my bunk; but 'sleep departed from my eyes, and slumber from my eyelids." Wells Brown, *Narrative*, 386.

31. Ibid., 416. Douglass makes a similar claim in his *Narrative*: "The motto which I adopted when I started from slavery was this—'Trust no man!' I saw in every white man an enemy, and in almost every colored man cause for distrust." Douglass, *Autobiographies*, 90.

32. Ibid., 420–21.

33. Wells Brown, 371.

34. Ibid., 417.

35. Douglass, *Autobiographies*, 92-3.

36. See John Stauffer, *The Black Hearts of Men: Radical Abolitionists and the Transformation of Race* (Cambridge: Harvard University Press, 2002), *passim*.

37. Gilmore, 747.

38. Brooks, 35.

39. William Wells Brown, *Three Years in Europe: Or, Places I Have Seen and People I Have Met* (London: Charles Gilpin, 1852); *The American Fugitive in Europe. Sketches of Places and People Abroad* (Boston: John P. Jewett, 1855).

40. See Amy Hughes, *Spectacles of Reform: Theatre and Activism in the Nineteenth-Century America* (Ann Arbor: University of Michigan Press, 2012).

41. Hartman, *Scenes of Subjection*, 27.

42. *The Liberator*, August 1, 1856. The accounts of Wells Brown reading *Experience* in Vergennes that appeared in the *Liberator* were reprints from the *Vergennes Citizen* and *Burlington Press*.

43. Nehemiah Adams, *A South-Side View of Slavery; or, Three Months at the South* (Boston: T. R. Marvin and B. B. Mussey, 1854), 211.

44. Harriet Jacobs, *Incidents in the Life of Slave Girl* (1861; reprint, New York:

Norton, 2001), 62. Frederick Douglass explained how "the penalty of telling the truth" (e.g., whippings, separation from families, and/or sale) made "slaves, when inquired of as to their condition and the character of their masters, almost universally say they are contented, and their masters are kind." Douglass, *Autobiographies*, 27.

45. Brooks, 109.

46. Ibid.

47. Ibid., 108–9.

48. John Ernest, "Introduction" to William Wells Brown, *The Escape* (1858; Knoxville: University of Tennessee Press, 2001), xi.

49. Wells Brown, *The Escape*, 18.

50. Ibid., 23.

51. Ibid., 29.

52. Ibid.

53. William Wells Brown, *Clotel; or, The President's Daughter* (1853), especially the chapter "The Quadroon's Home." The fictional plights of Melinda and Clotel are based in part on the life of Cynthia, a fellow slave of Wells Brown who did not give in to the "vile proposals" of their master and, consequently, was sold down the river into "hopeless bondage." Wells Brown, *Narrative*, 392–93.

54. Wells Brown, *The Escape*, 30.

55. Ibid. In the next scene Dr. Gaines instructs Mr. Scragg, the overseer, to "take Glen out of the dungeon, take him into the tobacco house, fasten him down upon the stretcher, and give him five hundred lashes upon his bare back; and when you have whipped him, feel his pulse, and report to me how it stands, and if he can bear more, I'll have you give him an additional hundred or two, as the case may be." (Ibid., 32).

56. Ibid., 31.

57. Ibid., 11.

58. Ibid., 10.

59. Ibid., 11–12.

60. William Wells Brown, *Narrative of William W. Brown, an American Slave, Written by Himself* (London: Charles Gilpin, 1850), 134..

61. Douglass, *Autobiographies*, 337.

62. Wells Brown, *The Escape*, 32.

63. Ibid., 34 (emphasis added).

64. John Ernest, "The Reconstruction of Whiteness: William Wells Brown's *The Escape; or, A Leap for Freedom*," *PMLA* 113.5 (October 1998): 1112.

65. The most popular example from the period is the Native American hero vanquishing corrupt and depraved white villains, such as in John Augustus Stone's *Metamora; or, The Last of the Wampanoags* (1829) and in Dion Boucicault's *The Octoroon* (1859). See Laura L. Mielke, *Moving Encounters: Sympathy and the Indian Question in Antebellum Literature* (Amherst: University of Massachusetts Press, 2008), 170–92.

66. Williams Wells Brown, *Narrative of William W. Brown, A Fugitive Slave* (Boston: 1848; reprint, Reading, MA: Addison-Wesley, 1969), 55.

67. William Wells Brown, "St. Domingo: Its Revolutions and Its Patriots: A Lecture Delivered before the Metropolitan Athenaeum, London, May 16, and at St. Thomas' Church, Philadelphia, December 20, 1854" (Boston, 1854), 38.

68. Werner Sollors, *Neither Black Nor White Yet Both: Thematic Explorations of Interracial Literature* (New York: Oxford University Press, 1997), 241.

69. Daphne Brooks, *Bodies in Dissent: Spectacular Performances of Race and Freedom, 1850–1910* (Durham: Duke University Press, 2006), 32.

70. Wells Brown, *The Escape*, 24–25.

71. Ibid., 45.

72. Brooks, 1.

73. Ibid., 2.

74. Wells Brown in Williams and Gates, 386.

75. Ibid., 402.

76. Ibid., 408. The emphasis is Wells Brown's.

77. The trauma that slave families endured is one of the dominant themes throughout Wells Brown's antebellum work. See, for instance, his "A Lecture Delivered Before the Female Anti-Slavery Society of Salem" (1847), reprinted in Ezra Greenspan, ed., *William Wells Brown: A Reader* (Athens: University of Georgia Press, 2008), especially 110–12.

78. Wells Brown, *The Escape*, 45.

79. Hartman, *Scenes of Subjection*, 125–63.

80. Ibid.

81. Douglass, *Autobiographies*, 346.

82. Edlie L. Wong, *Neither Fugitive Nor Free: Atlantic Slavery, Freedom Suits, and the Legal Culture of Travel* (New York: New York University Press, 2009), 10.

83. Wells Brown in Greenspan, 110.

84. Wells Brown, *The Escape*, 12–18.

85. Ibid., 23.

86. Ibid., 30.

87. Dionne Brand, *A Map to the Door of No Return: Notes to Belonging* (Toronto: Doubleday Canada, 2001), 30–31.

88. Ernest, "Introduction," xi; Gilmore, 743–49.

89. The clearest example of this puppet possession act is Cato's involvement with Dr. Gaines' medical practice. The play opens with Dr. Gaines agreeing to treat the slaves of his neighbor, Mr. Campbell. While celebrating the "five hundred dollars more added to [his] income" that Mr. Campbell's new business will bring him, Dr. Gaines immediately thinks of Cato: "And I am glad to get all the negroes I can to doctor, for Cato is becoming very useful to me in the shop. He can bleed, pull teeth, and do almost anything that the blacks require. He can put up medicine as well as any one. A valuable boy, Cato!" The following scene begins with Cato, his first appearance in the play, concocting pills and ointments. Dr. Gaines instructs him to treat two of Mr. Campbell's slaves—"You see to them. Feel their pulse, look at their tongues, bleed them, and give them each a dose of calomel. Tell them to drink no cold water, and to take nothing but water gruel," he says—and then he leaves Cato who confides to the audience:

> I allers knowed I was a doctor, an' now de ole boss has put me at it, I muss change my coat. Ef any niggers comes in, I want to look suspectable. Dis jacket don't suit a doctor; I'll change it. (*exit* CATO—*immediately returning in a long coat*) Ah! now I looks like a doctor . . . Ah! yonder comes Mr. Campbell's Pete an' Ned; dems de ones massa sed was co-

min'. I'll see ef I looks right. (*goes to the looking-glass and views himself*) I
em some punkins, ain't I?

As this passage suggests, Cato can only imagine himself as a version of Dr.
Gaines.

90. Douglass, *Autobiographies*, 351–52.
91. Ibid, 351.
92. Brooks, *Bodies in Dissent*, 2.
93. Wells Brown, *The Escape*, 40.
94. Brooks, 2–3.
95. Wells Brown, *Narrative*, 417.
96. Wells Brown, *The Escape*, 40–41.
97. Brooks, *The Melodramatic Imagination*, 56.
98. Ibid., 54.
99. See my "Aesthetics, Ideology, and the Use of the Victim in Early American Melodrama," *Journal of American Drama and Theatre* (2010): 51–81.
100. Melodrama is most effective when it exploits and ultimately upholds
dominant social ideologies and norms. This formal conservatism leads to the
greatest release of collective emotionality, melodrama's aesthetic desire. For
this reason, melodrama insists on being understood as part and parcel of its
historical moment even if it strives toward ethical and moral transhistoricity.
101. William Whipper, "Letter to the Editor," in *Frederick Douglass' Paper*,
quoted in Samuel Otter, *Philadelphia Stories: America's Literature of Race and Freedom* (Oxford: Oxford University Press, 2010), 222.
102. See Wilson Jeremiah Moses, *The Golden Age of Black Nationalism, 1850–
1925* (1978; reprint, Oxford: Oxford University Press, 1988), 32–57.
103. Don E. Fehrenbacher, *The Slaveholding Republic: An Account of the United
States Government's Relation to Slavery* (New York: Oxford University Press,
2001), 231–32.
104. In a dazzling response delivered at the 1857 anniversary celebration of
the American Abolition Society, Douglass declared the Court's decision was
ultimately generative: "In one point of view, we, the abolitionists and colored
people, should meet this decision, unlooked for and monstrous as it appears, in
a cheerful spirit. This very attempt to blot out forever the hopes of an enslaved
people may be one necessary link in the chain of events preparatory to the
downfall and complete overthrow of the whole slave system." Frederick Douglass, "The Dred Scott Decision: Speech, Delivered, in part, at the Anniversary
of the American Abolition Society, Held in New York, May 14, 1857" (New
York, 1857).
105. William Wells Brown, *The Negro in the American Rebellion: His Heroism and
His Fidelity* (Boston: Lee and Shepard, 1867), 41.
106. Wells Brown, *The Escape*, 45.
107. Ibid., 41.
108. Glenda Carpio, *Laughing Fit to Kill: Black Humor in the Fictions of Slavery*
(Oxford: Oxford University Press, 2008), 38.

109. Wells Brown quoted in Farrison, 281.

110. Ibid., 281–82 (emphasis added).

111. Wells Brown, "Lecture to the Female Anti-Slavery Society in Salem," in Greenspan, 122.

112. William Wells Brown, *National Anti-Slavery Standard*, May 26, 1860 (emphasis added).

113. Otter, 223.


## EPILOGUE

1. William Wells Brown, "The Colored People of Canada," *The Pine and Palm* (Boston), November 30, 1861; William Edward Farrison, *William Wells Brown: Author and Reformer* (Chicago: University of Chicago Press, 1969), 341–51. The editor of *The Pine and Palm* was James Redpath, the Anglo-Scottish stalwart of the Boston abolitionist community, fiery defender of John Brown, and proponent of Haitian emigration. Redpath was so influential in the emigration movement that in 1860 the Haitian government appointed him to the highest office, General Agent, in their Haitian Bureau of Emigration. That same year, he edited one of the most important antebellum emigrationist texts, *A Guide to Hayti*, which is a compendium of geographical sketches that includes maps, government documents, and national history.

2. James Redpath, *The Pine and Palm*, May 18, 1861.

3. Farrison, 348–56.

4. Carla L. Peterson, *Doers of the Word: African-American Women Speakers and Writers in the North (1830–1880)* (1995; reprint, New Brunswick: Rutgers University Press, 1998), 117.

5. Colin Dayan, "A Few Stories about Haiti, or, Stigma Revisited," *Research in African Literatures* 35.2 (Summer 2004): 164–65.

6. Frederick Douglass, "A Trip to Hayti," *Douglass' Monthly*, May 1861.

7. Ibid.

8. Wells Brown lectured extensively on the promising future of the emancipated slave and recruited black soldiers for the Union in Massachusetts, New Jersey, New York, and Pennsylvania; Shadd Cary recruited in Connecticut and Indiana; and, beginning in 1863, Martin Delany, the most outspoken proponent of emigration, recruited in Connecticut, Illinois, Ohio, Rhode Island, and in seceded states. Delany also volunteered to serve as a surgeon to black troops, and in 1865 Lincoln commissioned him Major, making him at the time the highest-ranking African American in the history of the U.S. Army. Farrison, 357–98; Jane Rhodes, *Mary Ann Shadd Cary: The Black Press and Protest in the Nineteenth Century* (Bloomington: Indiana University Press, 1998), 135–62; Robert S. Levine, *Martin Delany, Frederick Douglass, and the Politics of Representative Identity* (Chapel Hill: University of North Carolina Press, 1997), 215–23.

9. Frederick Douglass, "The Present and Future of the Colored Race in America," *Douglass' Monthly*, June 1863.

10. Pauline Hopkins, *Peculiar Sam; Or, The Underground Railroad* (1879), in

Leo Hamalian and James V. Hatch, *The Roots of African American Drama: An Anthology of Early Plays, 1858–1938* (Detroit: Wayne State University Press, 1991), 103–5.

11. Daphne Brooks, *Bodies in Dissent: Spectacular Performances of Race and Freedom, 1850–1910* (Durham: Duke University Press, 2006), 12–13.

12. For example, both plays feature costumed, songful escapes to Canada and the transformation of a self-serving slave to a collective-minded free man; share the initiating circumstance of the sexually exploited "mulatta" ingénue; and re-appropriate blackface minstrelsy.

13. Brooks, 13.

14. Hopkins, 120.

15. Saidiya Hartman, *Scenes of Subjection: Terror, Slavery, and Self-making in Nineteenth-Century America* (New York: Oxford University Press, 1997), 7.

16. Micki McElya, *Clinging to Mammy: The Faithful Slave in Twentieth-century America* (Cambridge: Harvard University Press, 2007), 4.

17. Hopkins, 103.

18. Brooks, 282. See ibid., 281–342, for a fine discussion of how Hopkins and other contemporaneous female black artists within a "genealogy of postbellum black women's theatrical performances" crafted a body of "cultural work [that] fused racial uplift with revised black female subjectivity at the dawn of the new century" (287).

19. In the 1973 blaxploitation film, *Hell Up in Harlem* (dir. Larry Cohen), two mammy-like maids help the film's antihero, Tommy Gibbs, raid the gangster-owned mansion where they work. After murdering several of its guards, the maids and Gibbs force the captured bosses to eat a plate of soul food, triumphantly ridiculing the men as they reluctantly eat the pork-heavy meal. These characters, like Hopkins' Mammy, were subversions of the ongoing power of the normative mammy myth.

20. The Association of Black Women Historians called the representation of black domestics in *The Help* "a disappointing resurrection of Mammy," the "asexual, loyal, and contented caretaker of whites" that "allowed mainstream America to ignore the systemic racism that bound black women to back-breaking, low paying jobs where employers routinely exploited them." Association of Black Women Historians, "An Open Statement to the Fans of *The Help*," http://www.abwh.org/index.php?option=com_content&view=article&id=2%3Aopen-statement-the-help, accessed April 26, 2013.

21. Because of the harrowing legal setbacks and social conditions African Americans continued to face in the postbellum era and late nineteenth century, emigrationism resurfaced as a solution, picking up even more steam than it did in the antebellum period. Like earlier in the century, however, an extremely low percentage of African Americans actually emigrated from the U.S. See James T. Campbell, *Middle Passages: African American Journeys to Africa, 1787–2005* (New York: Penguin Press, 2006), 99–187.

# Index

abolitionist discourse, 167. *See also*
  Bobalition (broadsides); Doug-
  lass, Frederick; Garnet, Henry
  Highland; Garrison, William
  Lloyd; Jones, Absalom; McCune
  Smith, James; monkeyism; pa-
  rade culture; Purvis, Robert;
  Quakerism; Sidney, Joseph; Sip-
  kins, Thomas; Walker, David;
  Williams, Jr., Peter
    lecture circuit, 10, 110, 140
    oratorical style, 11
    Pennsylvania Abolition Society
      (PAS), 25
    and slave insurrection, 11
    staged, 18
    Washington, George, as symbolic
      figure, 78
    "white slavery" and, 59–60
Adams, John Quincy, 43–45
  *Lectures on Rhetoric and Oratory*, 44–
    45
  theories of oratory, 43–44, 45
Adams, Nehemiah, 147
  *South-Side View of Slavery; A, or,
    Three Months at the South*, 147–48
"Address before the Young Men's Ly-
  ceum of Springfield, Illinois"
  (Lincoln), 83
"Address to the Colored People of the
  United States, An" (Douglass), 1,
  10, 122–23, 131
"Address to the Slaves of the United
  States of America, An" (Garnet),
  79, 115–22
*Adventures of an Adventurer, The* (Bar-

num autobiographical novella),
  93–94
African Free Schools, 114
African Methodist Episcopal Church,
  57
African Methodist Episcopal Zion
  Church (AMEZ), 32
Aldridge, Ira, 114
Allen, Richard, 57
Amateur Theatre (New York City), 84
American Anti-Slavery Society, 35,
  110, 164
  New York City Anti-Slavery Soci-
    ety, regional precursor, 50
American Colonization Society
  (ACS), 5–6, 48, 165
Anderson, Benedict, 34
*Anti-Slavery Harp, The: A Collection of
  Songs for Anti-Slavery Meetings*
  (Wells Brown, ed.), 15
anti-slavery societies
  American Anti-Slavery Society, 35,
    50, 110, 164
  Female Anti-Slavery Society of Sa-
    lem, 163
  Massachusetts Anti-Slavery Soci-
    ety, 111, 119
  New York City Anti-Slavery Soci-
    ety, 50
  Pennsylvania Anti-Slavery Society, 75
*Appeal in Four Articles, Together with a
  Preamble to the Coloured Citizens
  of the World, but in Particular, and
  Very Expressly, to Those of the
  United States of America* (Walker),
  57, 62–63, 72, 82, 111

In *The Captive Stage*, Douglas A. Jones, Jr. argues that proslavery ideology remained the dominant mode of racial thought in the antebellum north, even though chattel slavery had virtually disappeared from the region by the turn of the nineteenth century—and that northerners cultivated their proslavery imagination most forcefully in their performance practices. Jones explores how multiple constituencies, ranging from early national artisans and Jacksonian wage laborers to patrician elites and bourgeois social reformers, used the stage to appropriate and refashion defenses of black bondage as means to affirm their varying and often conflicting economic, political, and social objectives. Joining performance studies with literary criticism and cultural theory, he uncovers the proslavery conceptions animating a wide array of performance texts and practices, such as the "Bobalition" series of broadsides, blackface minstrelsy, stagings of the American Revolution, reform melodrama, and abolitionist discourse. Taken together, he suggests, these works did not amount to a call for the re-enslavement of African Americans but, rather, justifications for everyday and state-sanctioned racial inequities in their post-slavery society. Throughout, *The Captive Stage* elucidates how the proslavery imagination of the free north emerged in direct opposition to the inclusionary claims black publics enacted in their own performance cultures. In doing so, the book offers fresh contexts and readings of several forms of black cultural production, including early black nationalist parades, slave dance, the historiography of the revolutionary era, the oratory of radical abolitionists and the black convention movement, and the autobiographical and dramatic work of ex-slave William Wells Brown.

Printed and bound by CPI Group (UK) Ltd, Croydon, CR0 4YY

09/06/2025

14686143-0003